Wise Latinas

WISE LATINAS

Writers on Higher Education

Edited and with an introduction

by Jennifer De Leon

University of Nebraska Press
Lincoln and London

Library of Congress Cataloging-in-Publication Data
Wise Latinas: writers on higher education / edited and
with an introduction by Jennifer De Leon.
pages cm
Includes bibliographical references.
ISBN 978-0-8032-4593-8 (pbk.: alk. paper) 1. Hispanic American
women college students. 2. Hispanic American women—
Education (Higher) 3. Hispanic American women—Ethnic identity.
I. De Leon, Jennifer, 1979–
LC2670.6.W57 2014
378.198268—dc23   2013034450

Set in ScalaOT by Laura Wellington.
Designed by Ashley Muehlbauer.

For all my students and all my teachers

I will tell you something about stories.
They aren't just entertainment.
Don't be fooled.
They are all we have, you see,
All we have to fight off
Illness and death.

You don't have anything
if you don't have the stories.

LESLIE MARMON SILKO, *CEREMONY*

Contents

III. Inside These Academic Walls

IV. In Tribute, In Time

Acknowledgments

Many, many people helped to build this anthology, piece by piece, stage by stage. In 2004, over a meal of chicken parm in a West Roxbury apartment, my friends Patricia Sánchez-Connally and Wanda Montañez encouraged the idea. It wasn't until five years later that I took a class called Finding Your Book at Grub Street in Boston taught by Executive Director Eve Bridburg. Until then I had no idea how much went into the foundation of a book. I had been fixated on curtains when the building had no floor. That summer a friend from the Voices of Our Nations Arts Foundation (VONA), Yalitza Ferreras, put me in touch with another VONA member, Erika Martínez. Erika and I spoke on the phone while she was living and doing research in the Dominican Republic. We talked for an hour. When I returned to my computer, I saw that she had e-mailed me a proposal for an anthology she was putting together as well. We had never even met. In the following months and years, the spirit of generosity surrounding this project was nothing short of magical. Women trusted me with their stories. I sent out a call for submissions, mostly to Latinas I'd met at writing conferences over the years, including VONA, the Macondo Writers' Workshop that Sandra Cisneros founded in San Antonio, and the Bread Loaf Writers' Conference in Vermont, and to authors I'd admired for years. Soon the word spread. I was thrilled and humbled when I received interest from a New York publisher. I woke at dawn, took the bus from Boston to New York City, swapped my sneakers for brown suede boots at the last minute, and rode the elevator up a dozen floors to meet with two editors. The meeting went very well. I'd never felt so alive. A few months later, however, the press dropped the project. *Why Latinas?* they wondered. Then I remembered something a writer friend told me once. He gave himself only twenty-four hours to feel down about a rejection. That was it. After that, it was back to work. So, a day later, I got back to work. I called Charles Rice-Gonzalez. I contacted Daisy Hernández. Then, serendipitously, Joy Castro e-mailed me that morning and asked how the anthology was going. I was so embarrassed. What would I tell all these talented writers who had already shared their stories with me? I told Joy the truth. She suggested I reach out to the University of Nebraska Press. I owe tremendous thanks to you, Joy.

For their friendship, feedback, and support—I would like to thank the following: all the women who courageously share their stories in this anthology; my editor at the University of Nebraska Press, Kristen Elias Rowley, for encouraging the project from the first e-mail; all my dedicated teachers and mentors (too many to name here); my family (*way* too many to list here); Stuart Bernstein and Susan Bergholz, for all your help; Connecticut College; the MFA program at the University of Massachusetts–Boston; Grub Street; the Bread Loaf Writers' Conference; Voices of Our Nation Arts Foundation; the Macondo Writers' Workshop; my sisters Karen and Caroline and my parents, Luis and Dora De Leon, two of the hardest working and most gracious people walking in the world; and lastly my son, Mateo, and my husband, Adam Stumacher, for our life and our words together.

Source Acknowledgments

The following essays have been previously published:

"Rapunzel's Ladder" in Kathleen Skubikowski, Catharine Wright, and Roman Graf, eds., *Social Justice Education: Inviting Faculty to Transform Their Institutions* (Kumarian Press, 2010). © 2010 by Julia Alvarez. Reprinted by permission of Susan Bergholz Literary Services, New York, New York, and Lamy, New Mexico. All rights reserved.

"On Becoming Educated" in *Scholar and Feminist Online* 8, no. 3 (Summer 2010). © 2010 by Joy Castro.

"La Silla" in Ruth Behar, *Traveling Heavy: A Memoir In Between Journeys* (Duke University Press, 2013). © 2013 by Ruth Behar. Reprinted by permission of Duke University Press, www.dukeupress.edu. All rights reserved.

"How to Leave Hialeah" in Jennine Capó Crucet, *How to Leave Hialeah* (University of Iowa Press, 2009). © 2009 by Jennine Capó Crucet.

"Only Daughter" in *Glamour*, November 1990. © 1990 by Sandra Cisneros. Reprinted by permission of Susan Bergholz Literary Services, New York, New York, and Lamy, New Mexico. All rights reserved.

Introduction

JENNIFER DE LEON

Spring of my senior year in college I needed to buy a dress for graduation. Not just any dress, of course. *Vaya*, my mother, had said. So we drove to the mall, our special mother-daughter terrain. We were experts at tracking discounts. Tuesdays were retail markdown days. The salespeople at Macy's gave out coupons. And twice a year, if you purchased full-price panties at Victoria's Secret, you got a free lip-gloss. That day, weeks before I would be the second in my entire extended family (next to my older sister) to graduate from college, my mother and I had a clear goal: find the dress.

Then, suddenly, there it was underneath the shade of soft lighting bulbs inside Ann Taylor. Magenta, magical. My mother and I gazed at the silk fabric through the storefront window. A headless mannequin showed off the exquisite A-line cut. Sleeveless, sophisticated. Nothing but a pane of fingerprint-proof glass parked between us. We stepped inside the store and were greeted by the sweet smell of leather and cashmere-blend tops as the aura of credit card transactions hovered around us like a mist.

"How much?" my mother asked.

I massaged the crisp white price tag between my thumb and forefinger. "How much do you think?"

We left the mall that day, defeated. The dress cost one hundred dollars, well over what we could afford. I was a scholarship student at Connecticut College, a private liberal arts school that resembled a country club. My mother worked as a housekeeper. I made six dollars an hour babysitting for families near campus. I would need to buy a suit for upcoming job interviews, not to mention outfit an apartment in Boston where I planned to live with two friends from college come September. My mother and I, expert shoppers, knew storefront items wouldn't be marked down for weeks, maybe months. Graduation was in seventeen days.

"I'll find a dress at the mall near school," I assured her, my voice rinsed of confidence as I pictured the crowded racks inside the mall in New London. She pursed her lips, lowered her lashes.

My college graduation dress was as important to her as a wedding gown. Ever since my mother was a schoolgirl in Guatemala, where she had often carried the flag in the annual school parade (an honor for the students with the highest marks in each grade), she dreamed of going to college. Education was like a religion in our household. She preached the importance of straight As. She snuck in *consejos* like mashed-up vitamins in our morning *mosh*. If you study hard you can get a good job and then you can do whatever you want, she'd say. Or, Books are your friends. When she was driving my sisters and me to gymnastics or Girl Scouts or church, and we couldn't escape, she'd tell us about a family whose house she cleaned, how the son went to Duke (the name made me think of a prison), and how he got a scholarship (the word sounded like a disease).

Thanks to my mother's persistence I eventually learned the meaning of a scholarship when I earned one to attend Connecticut College. One semester she spoke to my Women & World Studies class. Seated at the far end of a rectangular wooden table in the snug classroom of an ivy-covered campus building, my mother crossed her arms and described her experience moving from Guatemala to the United States at the age of eighteen, and we discussed the ways in which globalization played a role in our family's economic, political, and cultural trials. I got an A. Then she visited me at the offices of *Ms.* magazine in New York City where I interned one summer. I'll never forget the moment that Gloria Steinem's long-fingered, delicate hand knotted with my mother's coarse, nail polish–chipped hand—just for an instant. How lovely to meet you, Ms. Steinem said. You too, my mother replied. The next fall, when I studied abroad in Paris, my mother came to visit. She insisted on taking pictures of the small cars she said looked like sneakers and then asked me to take photos of her posed in front of them. In between visits to the Louvre and the Sorbonne, where I was taking a feminist philosophy class and attending lectures by Hélène Cixous, my mother bought miniature replicas of the Eiffel Tower for relatives in Boston. Throughout the years she held tight the picture in her mind of each of her daughters on that all-important day: graduation.

Dress or no dress, I still needed to prepare for Class of 2001 senior week, a to-do list that, after failed attempts to find a dress at the local mall, included raiding my friend's closet for graduation day. While I was fixated on campus matters, the country was still celebrating turn-of-the-century events, unaware of the events on September 11th that would occur just a few months later. Around the time of my graduation, across the country, the University of California–Berkeley hosted a conference on Hispanic judges. One of the speakers at the conference was Justice Sonia Sotomayor. In a speech that is now famous, Sotomayor said, in response to a discussion of an appellate court with multiple judges, "I would hope that a wise Latina woman, with the richness of her experiences, would more often than not reach a better conclusion than a white male who hasn't lived that life." Years later, when she was nominated as a Supreme Court justice, this comment inspired furious backlash from conservative commentators. On the cover of the *National Review*, cartoonists portrayed Sotomayor as a Buddha with Asian features. Rush Limbaugh and others labeled her a "racist." Yet in her 2001 speech Sotomayor was using the term in a specific context that addressed the group dynamics on a U.S. Supreme Court of nine justices who converse publicly during oral arguments and privately during conferences over cases. In these settings a justice's identity undoubtedly affects his or her thinking about cases. By 2050 Hispanics will make up 30 percent of the U.S. population, yet of 111 Supreme Court justices, all but 4 have been white men. Sotomayor's controversial comment was nothing more than common sense: shouldn't our judicial system better represent our population?

For me, when I hear the words *wise Latina*, I immediately think of my mother. She came to the United States at a young age, alone, speaking no English. Four years passed before she returned to Guatemala with platform shoes, a new hairstyle of pressed waves, and a black-and-white television as a gift for the family. Then, she left again for Los Angeles and eventually Boston, where she married and had three daughters. All her life my mother wanted more. She learned English, became a U.S. citizen, and bought a house. [Education, she believed, provided a set of master keys that unlocked multiple doors—career, money, travel, health, relationships, even love.]

Through her daughters, she would live the lives she had imagined for herself, and every one of these included a college education. A Latina housekeeper who drives her caravan full of daughters to admissions tours at Brown, Alfred, TCU (yes, we drove to Fort Worth, Texas) may not be Rush Limbaugh's picture of a wise Latina. Then again, Limbaugh doesn't exactly embody my ideal of wisdom, either. To such myopic commentators, the phrase *wise Latina* was controversial because they considered the term an oxymoron. The dominant media narrative does not include Latinas in medicine, the arts, or politics. We are encouraged to laugh at Latina housekeepers on sitcoms, to ignore the invisible Latina workers in public restrooms. The term *wise Latina* continues to unfold preconceptions and stereotypes of what it is to be wise and what it is to be Latina. In the same way, through this anthology, I hope to dispel myths about the Latina college experience. *Wise Latina* had to be in the title.

Higher education is a complex experience for many Latinas, who are traditionally expected to leave home when they get married. When I was in college, I yearned for a book of stories by different Latinas that could help me feel, for once, like I had company. Of course there were books and authors that grounded me and inspired me, but I longed for a book that made me feel less alone. A chorus of voices, an anthology. In building this book I was always brought back to poet and cultural theorist Gloria Anzaldúa, whose famous work *Borderlands/La Frontera: The New Mestiza* shaped so much of my consciousness as a Latina, as a writer, and as an educator. It gave voice to the questions, emotions, and realizations I grappled with as a young woman struggling to find my way in the world. Of anthologies in particular, Anzaldúa believed: "Making anthologies is also activism. In the process of creating the composition, the work of art, you're creating the culture. You're rewriting the culture, which is very much an activist kind of thing."[1]

In many ways this anthology stands as a form of activism. It seeks to unveil the truth about our educational experiences and to challenge the stereotypes. With mainstream media and those in power in charge of the writing of history—herstory—as a means of controlling what is considered true, the need for authentic stories—by women of color in particular—is critical. Each of the women who share their stories in these pages is in her own way a wise Latina. These women are dispelling myths about the roles of Latinas who come from immigrant families. They are exploring the higher education experience within the context of being a woman of Latin American descent in a predominantly white system. Not one story repeats here, and the common denominators are sometimes unexpected. Some of us were expected to marry and have babies shortly after high school. Others of us were expected to go to law school or become *doctoras*. Some of us earned scholarships. Others lived at home and commuted to save money. We lost our virginity, came out of the closet, gave birth, earned Fulbrights, studied abroad in places our parents never dreamed of visiting. We wrote research papers while home on spring break, cousins buzzing in our ears. Our families filled three entire rows at graduation. As Latinas, as writers, as college graduates, we each have something unique to say—to ourselves, to our ancestors, to those middle-school selves in all of us.

Individually and collectively, these women's stories inform the larger discussion of Latinas and higher education. In these pages we hear from the community college student and the PhD candidate, the adult student and the first-generation student, the commuter and the globe-trotter. We read about the college experiences of Latinas from diverse backgrounds and in different parts of the United States, at small private schools and big public institutions, and from different generations. These authors reflect on different issues—sexuality, body image, academic preparation, alienation, race, class, parent weekends, spring break, work-study, financial aid, dorm life, drugs, drinking, and identity. Others write about postgraduate adventures and their paths as professors. For some, college was a place where we experienced culture clash. For most of us, it was a space where we grew, where we shaped our independence and struggled to make sense of our surroundings. In her essay "Only Daughter," Sandra Cisneros writes, "After four years in college and two more in graduate school, and still no husband, my father shakes his head even now and says I wasted all that education." It is also the first time, for some Latinas, that they are immersed in American culture outside of their home—and where the values of two cultures often clash. Jennine

Capó Crucet's "How to Leave Hialeah," a work of fiction, so accurately describes this experience that I felt it needed to be included in the anthology despite its genre classification. Crucet reflects on the process of writing a "true" story inside the container of short fiction in "How to Leave 'How to Leave Hialeah': A Real-Life Epilogue." Others in this anthology use unique structures to tell their stories. Yalitza Ferreras explores the topic of education through the lens of her family's television sets. Celeste Mendoza depicts her experience through monologue, while Erika Martínez tells hers through a letter to her younger self. While there is no one Latina college experience, each of the writers here contributes her individual thread to this shared textile.

My goal is for these stories to be in conversation with statistics of matriculation and retention rates for Latinas in order to paint a more cohesive picture of what might be done to create change. Forty-one percent of Hispanic female students do not complete high school with a standard diploma; part of this figure can be attributed to Latinas having the highest teen pregnancy rate of any racial or ethnic group.[2] A July 23, 2010, article in the *New York Times*, "The Latino College Lag," reveals that only 13 percent of Hispanic adults have received at least a bachelor's degree, compared with 31 percent of non-Hispanic whites, 18 percent of blacks, and 50 percent of Asians, according to U.S. Census studies. The proportion of sixteen- to nineteen-year-old Latinos who have dropped out of high school—9 percent—is more than twice as high as that for whites, four times as high as Asians, and higher than the rate for blacks, which is 7 percent, according to an analysis of 2008 census data by the Pew Hispanic Center. And only 28 percent of college-aged Latinos are enrolled in universities, compared with 45 percent of whites, 64 percent of Asians, and 34 percent of blacks. Formal studies are valuable. Narrative is too. These pages, these stories, these *testimonios* by Latina writers, are the nourishment and validation I sought as a first-generation college student right up until the moment I needed the "perfect" graduation dress.

The final weekend before college graduation, my mother came to visit me on campus. She had packed a weekend bag and drove the two hours down to campus. By now she knew where to park and how to type in the seven-digit code required for entering the dorm. There, inside my room she relaxed on the purple comforter (the one that she had sewn herself) and talked to my grandmother on the phone while I wore headphones and worked on a final paper. That night we ate dinner in Mystic, a quaint seaport town fifteen minutes away. We sat upstairs in a restaurant overlooking the bridge, where we ordered piña coladas and split an entrée of stuffed scallops. Afterward, back on campus, we drank frothy beers from plastic red cups and met up with my friends. By then they knew and loved her. The following morning, my mother and I ate brunch in the dining hall and then took a long walk in the school arboretum. Before she returned home, she handed me a department store bag full of hair gel, toothpaste, shampoo, and raspberry-flavored Fig Newtons. I stood on the dorm entrance concrete steps and watched her drive away, the car a little lighter, both of our hearts a bit heavier. I could tell she was already mourning her visits to Connecticut College. Monday passed. Tuesday. Finally, on Wednesday morning of my last week of classes, I dug in my closet for a shirt to wear to my final presentation in women's studies. There, tucked between a sparkly tank top and a white button-down, I felt the crinkle of a cream-colored plastic garment bag. I pulled it out gently and immediately recognized the magenta fabric peeking out the bottom. I didn't have to look because I already knew what was inside.

NOTES

1. Andrea A. Lunsford, "Toward a Mestiza Rhetoric: Gloria Anzaldua on Composition and Postcoloniality," *JAC: A Journal of Composition Theory* 18, no. 1 (1998): 1–27.

2. The findings are the result of a joint study by the National Women's Law Center and the Mexican American Legal Defense and Educational Fund (MALDEF).

I.
Worlds Apart

Going the Distance

BLANCA TORRES

People often ask me how I ended up earning my bachelor's degree at Vanderbilt University, a school 2,500 miles from my hometown in Eastern Washington. The inquiries have a tone of disbelief, just like asking someone how they won the lottery or managed to climb Mt. Everest, as if going to Vanderbilt was something peculiar and nearly impossible—for a Latina reared in the Pacific Northwest.

Even though I've been asked that question probably hundreds of times, it still catches me off guard. I don't have a solid, ready answer. I usually mumble something vague, like, "One of my teachers recommended it," or, "They offered me a big scholarship." Sometimes I tell the truth: the decision was a whim. That sounds ironic since I began preparing for college around the time I started preschool, when my parents explained to me that eventually I would go to college. When we drove past the community college on the outskirts of my hometown, my parents often pointed to the campus with its sky-blue sculpture of a hawk and said, "That's a school where people go after high school."

As a young child, it all seemed simple enough.

For most of my childhood, my parents, two immigrants from a rural town in Mexico, worked at a local potato processing plant. They earned enough for us to have basic necessities—a house, food, transportation, vacations to Mexico. None of it was fancy, but it was stable. My father had grown up in a small dusty rancho, where he left school after sixth grade to work on his grandparents' farm and later came to the United States as a laborer. My mother's parents encouraged her to become educated and sent her to a boarding school run by nuns from the time she was ten until she turned fifteen. Later, she earned a degree from the teachers' university of Jalisco. Before teaching full-time, she spent a few years working in the city hall of her hometown and had aspirations of running for mayor one day. She had no intention of ever moving to America.

Years later, after my parents were married and my father brought my mother to live in Washington, she hung her framed certificate in our living room even though her degree was basically worthless in this country. As a child, I remember looking at the sand-colored paper with ornate script and an oval shaped portrait of her. I didn't know what a *titulo* was when I was a child, but I knew it looked official and that my mother was very proud of it. I also knew that to my parents, education was the most important aspect of our lives. Everything revolved around earning good grades and impressing our teachers.

Luckily for my siblings and me, we were fairly accomplished students and took to academics well. I discovered a love of books when I was in second grade and have devoured them with *gusto* since. My brother flourished at math and science. My sister could handle words and numbers and thrived in accounting and finance classes. I felt giddy when a teacher announced that I had scored the highest grade on a test or complimented the skillful writing of my essays. I loved the thrill of showing my report card to my parents lined mostly with As and the occasional B. I loved books and wore glasses—I was a quintessential nerd, but I always had the satisfaction of knowing the hard work would pay off one day.

My parents told me I could choose any career I wanted as long as I was good at it. I started out dreaming of becoming a ballerina and later dropped that in favor of other options such as novelist, Catholic nun, psychologist, and eventually journalist. Whatever I wanted to do, I knew I could pursue it at a university and that having a college degree would ensure me a secured entry not only into a professional job but a world of education and esteemed people. I never wanted anyone to doubt I was intelligent.

When I was seventeen and poring over acceptance letters from three schools, Vanderbilt—the one I never took seriously—rose to the top. I had added it to my list of colleges after my AP English teacher mentioned it briefly as a school I should consider. I had received hundreds of viewbooks and applications for schools all over the country after taking a standardized test and Vanderbilt was one of the schools that had sent me materials. I mailed them back with little concern about whether I'd get in because I had my heart set on my first choice, a school outside of Chicago with a well-known journalism program. It was the only school I visited and one I spoke about obsessively most of my senior year.

The day the yearbook staff took club photos, I happened to wear a shirt with the school's name emblazoned across my chest. Since I was involved in lots of organizations, pictures of me wearing that shirt are featured numerous times in my senior yearbook—enduring proof of my doomed aspiration. The day I received the notorious thin envelope, I cried in the passenger seat of my mother's car on the way to run an errand. "Stop crying, you're ruining your make up," she told me. "It's going to be okay. You are still going to go to college." I was an emotional wreck, but the logical part of my brain that was still working realized she was probably right.

Weeks earlier, I had received a thick, express-mailed package from Vanderbilt offering me congratulations, options for housing, and a financial aid form with a very generous sum on the bottom line. I had, however, put all the forms and documents back in the envelope and buried them under a pile on my desk. I also had been accepted to two Catholic universities in California, which seemed like obvious choices after my years of Catholic education in elementary and middle school and my somewhat dormant desire to become a Catholic nun. I figured being on a Catholic campus would provide easy access to a convent, should I decide to enter religious life at any moment.

Before the painful first-choice rejection, going to Vanderbilt didn't even seem plausible. It was in Tennessee, a place I had never been and, frankly, had no desire to visit. Still, it fit some key parameters I had come up with: private, midsize, in a city, not a college town, and it was reputable. After receiving my acceptance letters, I looked up a copy of *U.S. News and World Report* at the public library and discovered Vanderbilt ranked twentieth among national universities. When I saw the ranking, it was a blissful surprise, like discovering you have more money in your wallet than you previously thought. At one point my older sister, who had attended Gonzaga University—the closest thing to an elite college

Washington has to offer—told me Vanderbilt had name recognition, something that would pretty much always be an asset.

My sister was a lone voice in advocating for Vanderbilt. Many of my friends had said, "What? Tennessee? That's too far!" My mother told me the decision was mine to make, but she would prefer if I stayed closer to home—like the community college with its sky-blue mascot. My high school guidance counselor also tried to dissuade me. The counselor I had for my first three years, Ms. Ferrari, who wore stylish skirt suits everyday and encouraged me to be open-minded about colleges, retired just before I began my senior year. Her replacement, a mid-forties Latina divorcée, used our one-on-one meetings to tell me about how lonely she was after her two children left home for a state college only a few hours away. She had met my mother through a parental outreach program and learned that my father had died. She also knew my brother and I would be shipping off to college at the same time. "You don't really want to leave your mother all alone, do you?" she asked. I told her I wanted options and mentally brushed off her comments. My mother wore black clothing for an entire year after my father died and often had crying spells at random times of the day. After I made a college visit trip to Chicago, I returned to find my mother anguished because my return flight had been delayed. She told me she couldn't handle me being far away. I didn't apply to any schools in state, and after a while I began to think: If I'm not within driving distance of home, does it matter how far I go? California, Tennessee, what's the difference?

Finally, after weeks of debating mostly between the two Catholic universities and one day before my postmarked response was due at my prospective schools, I filled in Vanderbilt's forms and mailed them in. I felt like a game show contestant who has to choose the right button to win the grand prize—you may try to employ logic, but in the end it is a split-second decision that affects the rest of your life.

I was following an impulse. I was born and raised in the same place, where I felt established and comfortable. I had lifelong friends, attended the same Catholic Church where I was baptized, knew all the major roads and freeways. Even my part-time job as a news clerk at the local paper was somewhat of a sure bet—my editors doted on me as their future star reporter once I finished college and came back to work for them. I could have easily stayed in Eastern Washington for the rest of my life.

Instead of fueling any desire to stay close to home, my father's death was the kindling I needed to leave. My father had died of heart attack on a spring day toward the end of my sophomore year. It was unexpected and devastating, but I knew I had to carry on and continue my education—as my father would have wanted—despite my grief. For some people the death of a loved one often results in the proverbial realization of not knowing what you have until it's gone. That wasn't the case for me. I enjoyed a loving and close relationship with my father and appreciated him when he was alive. For me, losing my father forced me to realize that I had to make the most of my life, forgo the conventional paths, and seek new challenges. My father grew up in poverty and could have stayed that way were it not for his willingness to move north, work hard, find opportunities, and succeed in an unfamiliar terrain. As is the case for many immigrants, my father's experience in America was met with struggles, racism, and obstacles, but he managed to establish himself and raise a family here. How could I not challenge myself to achieve more than the expected?

My first encounter with Vanderbilt happened on a muggy July day when I traveled to Nashville for a three-day orientation program. I took a cab from the airport and realized when we arrived on campus that I didn't have cash to pay the driver. He told me not to worry, turned off the meter, took me to a nearby ATM, and waited patiently until I had cash. It was my first taste of what I took to be southern hospitality. Other than what I read about the Civil War and slavery in my history classes, I knew very little about the South when I arrived. I assumed most of those historical issues were long gone. Surely, racial tensions and feelings of southern superiority were as buried as Abraham Lincoln's corpse. I compared the South to what was then my idealized perception of Washington, a place once ruled by Native Americans who now lived peaceably on reservations and were celebrated for their powwows and dream catchers. Perhaps I fell into a classic dynamic of youth: I possessed equal parts bravado and naïveté. My curiosity about college—something I felt like I had been working toward since preschool—was enough to distract me from the dramatic shift on which I was embarking—and all the comfort and familiarity I was leaving behind.

I attended several presentations and took placement tests in large auditoriums. During a session on registering for classes I scanned a list of other orientation attendees; I noticed lots of hometowns in the Midwest, Northeast, and Southeast—almost none from the West Coast besides my own. I didn't panic right away because I was still under the spell of thinking of Nashville as just like home but with a different zip code, climate, cuisine, and people. Many of the fellow freshmen-to-be came with their parents or a family member in tow. No one in my family could take time off work so I came alone. I began to notice subtle differences from what I was used to back home. The mothers reminded me of the characters on *Designing Women*, like Delta Burke with big hair, perfect makeup, and a singsong accent. They, and their daughters, carried designer bags with names like Gucci and Prada. I began to feel rather ordinary in my khaki shorts and polo shirt.

One evening during the orientation, I went on a group tour led by an upperclassman. At the end, we sat down in a student lounge to ask questions. One girl inquired about the "Vandygirl" stereotype—something I never heard of. Our guide explained that yes, there were women who liked to dress up for class and football games, but not every female student was like that, nor was there an expectation to look nice all the time, so there was no need worry. This struck me as odd. I couldn't see why being more dressed up, or "high-maintenance" as I liked to called it back then, could be seen as stereotypical or something to worry about.

I learned later.

Before I came to Vanderbilt, my vision of college was shaped by the visits I made to my sister on her campus and a hodgepodge of Hollywood images. I thought everyone dressed down—pajama pants to class, hair pulled back in a bun, little or no makeup, droopy eyes from sleep deprivation. That may have been okay on some campuses, but not at Vanderbilt. Each morning I saw hordes of girls looking like they were on their way to a date or job interview. "Why not dress up that short skirt with stiletto heels?" seemed to be a common mantra. Oh, and the tube tops! Did any girl wear sleeves anymore? In high school I considered myself somewhat of a stylish dresser. During senior year I did most of my shopping in Seattle, where my older sister had moved, and discovered brands the local mall stores didn't carry. Friends and classmates were impressed by my various T-shirts bearing an unfamiliar brand's logo. Once I arrived at Vanderbilt, I realized that not only was the brand not cool enough, T-shirts were not cool. The Vandygirls' attire was all about tight, short, and skin baring—not the comfort-over-style look I was expecting. I didn't want to look like a bum by any means, but I also couldn't afford designer tops to wear to class, or a Louis Vuitton tote for my books.

It was not as if I had never been exposed to wealthy people before, but at Vanderbilt the majority of students were not just rich; they were elites—kids whose families were multimillionaires, who took luxury for granted, whose grandfathers had campus buildings named after them. These were people who came to Vanderbilt to keep up their status quo—not to make the socioeconomic leap I hoped to achieve. They needed Vanderbilt to keep up appearances; I needed Vanderbilt to help me attain a different place in the world.

When I talk about my first year at Vanderbilt, I often sum it by saying, "I was pretty much miserable." Not only did my fashion choices feel wrong, but I felt like a foreigner in almost every possible way. I was the only person I knew who described herself as a Mexican American from Eastern Washington. Back home, most of my close friends fit that category. Until Vanderbilt I had never had to tell people what I was. About half the population of my hometown was Mexican or of Mexican descent, and having a medium-brown complexion, dark hair, and dark eyes was not unusual. No one had ever stared at me and asked in an overly courteous voice, "So, where are you from?" or, "Do you speak English?" which happened on a regular basis on and off campus. Sometimes I told people I was Mexican, and they assumed I was an international student, not an American. Others quickly asked what part of Texas or California I was from, because few people conceived that Mexican Americans could come from Washington.

I sought out groups like the Hispanic students association and encountered Latinos of various backgrounds. My initial observations were that the Nuyoricans loved *salsa* and *merengue*, varieties I had not grown up with. The Tejanos drove big trucks and discussed football a lot, and the Cubans from Miami thought they were way too cool.

Besides my feeling like an outcast, my freshman year was my first experience away from home and from my family. My brother had opted for the University of Washington in Seattle. He moved in with our older sister, who was still living in the area, and could make the drive home to Pasco in three and a half hours. Going home for me meant six to eight hours on a plane and tiresome connections. As with my father's death, I realized that nothing could have prepared me for adapting to life away from my mother and siblings. I longed for the feeling of being surrounded by people who knew me and cared about me. And people whom I don't feel the need to impress.

Eventually my college friends filled in the gap, but that took a few semesters. Organizations became an outlet. Most of my close friendships stemmed from the Hispanic students association. At the start of my sophomore year I joined a group of women interested in starting a Latina sorority. By the end of the year seven of us succeeded in founding a chapter of Lambda Theta Alpha Latin Sorority Inc. I remain close to many of those women today. I also spent many late nights writing articles and editing pages for the campus newspaper, the aptly named *Vanderbilt Hustler*. I traveled to Lima, Peru, during spring break of my freshman year for a community service project among the city's poor. My group for the trip consisted of the same kind of blond, entitled kids with whom I didn't feel like I could associate when I first arrived on campus. Like focusing the lens of a camera, I began to see other students beyond the stereotypes I had of them and began to feel like I contributed to my environment—I wasn't just a specimen that got lost along the way.

The years that followed my freshman year were less and less miserable. I started taking courses to major in English during my second semester, and pretty soon I had become enamored with the department. Other than medieval literature, I loved every class I took for my major. I picked up a minor in Latin American studies and took classes about Mexican culture, history, and art. While I loved most of the classes I took, the academic standards were much more rigorous than my high school. It was an adjustment, but it taught me to push myself harder than I ever had before.

By senior year I loved Vanderbilt for all the experiences and opportunities I had there. Although my freshman year often felt like a disaster, I never regretted my decision. I managed to maintain that stirring but seemingly foolish belief that the journey would be challenging, but it would all work out in the end. On the day of my graduation I walked across the stage and accepted the diploma folder from the university's chancellor, about whom I had written a profile for the school paper.

He shook my hand, then leaned in for a hug and said, "We're going to miss you."

Earlier, during his keynote address for the ceremony, he made a simple yet poignant statement, "You are not the same person today as you were when you first arrived." It was perhaps a cliché repeated many times in graduation speeches. But at the time, I felt as if I had not heard truer words. I thought of my father and looked out at the stands where my family was sitting and wondered if they knew it, too.

Scrambled Channels

YALITZA FERRERAS

SAMSUNG SERIES 4 LCD 19"

I called my brother at his job as a security guard at a mental hospital in Queens to tell him the big news: "I bought a TV."

My decision to buy a television was driven by political fervor. On several occasions my shaky Internet connection in Ann Arbor, Michigan where I was two months into a creative writing MFA, had kept me from following the 2008 presidential campaign, and I didn't want to feel out of touch with the world. History was being made, and I was missing it. Besides, I was a sucker for the various news channels' use of colorful and interactive 3D maps predicting electoral votes across the nation.

"Finally! I don't know how you can live without one. How long has it been? Four, five months?"

"I'm trying to be a serious writer. Serious writers don't watch TV."

I had not hauled my old television with me when I moved from California to Michigan to attend a fully funded graduate writing program. The fellowship was the only way I could afford school, and leaving behind my work as a graphic designer and pursuing a master's degree in writing was a way to commit to my writing.

"Whatever. I told you not to talk to me about writing and books. It's flat, right?"

My brother didn't want any reminders that I thought he should read a book once in a while. I bought him books anyway, and when I visited New York I would see piles of them gathering dust on top of the refrigerator or under shoes in his closet.

"Yeah, it's flat and nineteen inches." And I don't mention that its sexy, thin slickness is obscured by the two columns of books flanking its sides. My studio apartment is too small for a bookcase so I have stacks of books against any available wall space or surface such as under my desk, which means I can never fully stretch out my legs when I write, and on the kitchen counter next to my toaster, which is probably a fire hazard.

"Nineteen inches! Can you see anything on it?"

"Of course I can! I thought about going the next size up to twenty-one, but it seemed too big for my apartment."

"What do you mean too big? I don't understand this too big."

"I'm putting a nice scarf over it so that I don't feel like I'm looking at it all the time."

"What's wrong with looking at it all the time? That's why it's there."

"I live in a tiny studio. I don't want my whole space to be about the TV. Besides I'm not going to watch it very often. I just want to be able to turn it on and watch the news."

"You are so weird."

I wasn't as weird as he thought. Buying the television was sending a message to my writing. As winter was approaching I had already started a threesome with Ben and Jerry, enjoying their Chocolate Fudge Brownie during *Law and Order* or *Family Guy*, while procrastinating and numbing the loneliness I felt being away from my family in New York and my friends in California. Most of all, the learning and writing support I was receiving gave me performance anxiety—I had a community of peers and professors waiting to read what I wrote. Though grateful, I had never been in that position and wasn't sure I could deliver.

Growing up, I did homework, read books, listened to music, and talked to friends on the phone, sometimes watching shows with them as if we were in the same room, all while achieving stellar grades. I am convinced that this multitasking ability made me smarter and enhanced my brain's processing capacity—a scholastic superhero—if you factor in my amazing juggling act.

At some point I got the brilliant idea to use television for research. After all, television had informed some of my aesthetics and thematic preoccupations, which had ranged from Looney Tunes cartoons to PBS documentaries.

Many of my stories featured natural disasters, often with characters lashing out at each other, while nature lashed out against everything. I was interested in the idea of displacement and people's behavior when their way of being is disrupted by outside forces. While I was writing a story that featured a hurricane as backdrop to a conflict between a mother and son, I watched a marathon of weather shows, featuring houses and trees flying around in hurricanes and tornadoes. As the storm chasers struggled to capture their footage, I struggled with the distraction, the hours slipping away.

Experiencing the world and everything it had to offer through television spurred my interest in experiencing people, countries, and education firsthand. Years earlier, during a show about volcanoes on the Discovery Channel, I told my brother about how I almost stepped into Kilauea's lava flow because I got closer than every sign and every person there advised, and he said, "Of course you did. You always have to get too close, and you always have to figure things out, don't you?" His reactions to my inquisitiveness always made me feel brave and adventurous. I used to seek out thrills, but now the biggest risk I was taking was not using my time wisely, and I knew my brother would be disappointed in me.

OLEVIA LT42HVI 42"

"Hold on. Let me turn down the TV."

In order to relieve the boredom of sitting at the security desk for long periods of time, my brother kept a TV on the desk. I always told him that if I couldn't get a job after graduate school, I would hit him up for one. I thought of the hours I could spend at work reading and writing.

"Prices went down. We're getting the biggest one we can get."

"Can you afford it? I mean they're still expensive."

"We're going to charge it."

My brother and his girlfriend couldn't afford one, but they felt that they couldn't afford not to—it's the first thing they turned on when they walked into their apartment.

"What are you going to do with the old TV? It still works, right?"

"We're putting it in the bedroom for Christopher so he can have a bigger screen and getting rid of the other one."

Christopher, my two-year-old nephew, walks to the television every time he is handed a bottle of milk. He watches *Wonder Pets* or Sponge-Bob SquarePants DVDs. He drags his pillow—and plops himself on the floor in front of the traditional tube television in their bedroom, which they all share until they can afford to move to a bigger place. I worried about the health of my nephew's beautiful, tiny eyes.

"But then you'll have three TVs."

"We'll probably put the other one in the kitchen."

"Isn't it too big for the kitchen? Why do you need so many TVs?"

"We want an HD, and springing for the higher resolution 1080p is pointless if you're getting a screen that's forty inches or less."

"Oh, I see you've been reading up on it."

SONY BRAVIA V-SERIES KDL-42V4100 42"

I called my mother to tell her I was overwhelmed with school responsibilities, and I would be home for Christmas instead of Thanksgiving.

"The new TV will be here by then."

"Don't tell me you're buying one, too."

"How's yours doing?"

"It's fine. Mami, you can't afford a new one. How are you going to buy it?"

"We're doing layaway."

"You still can't afford it."

They are on Social Security and live in Section 8 housing in Queens. Going to graduate school was a luxury in many ways, but mostly because I was supposed to be helping my parents. The more I thought about my own needs the less I could take care of theirs. I had struggled with the decision to apply for years.

"The TV is acting funny. Your father probably messed it up. You know how he's always trying to fix things. Christopher probably did something to it, too."

The last time I was home I had witnessed my two-year-old nephew pushing macaroni into the vents in the television.

"The flat screen will save room."

There is no room to save. They don't throw anything out, so they keep things as long as possible, even if they are broken. Their closets are full of objects my mother buys at flea markets, like closeout sheet sets in every size even though they only have one queen-size bed. My mother's rationale is that one must always be prepared for everything.

"I'm worried about you and Papi."

"Why are you worried? Besides, they're adding more channels to the Dominican cable channel package. We'll have more to watch."

I am astounded that there is a Dominican cable channel package showing programs filmed in the Dominican Republic catering to the talk, game, and variety show needs of Dominicans all over the world. Living in San Francisco for about ten years, I felt out of touch with my culture because there weren't many Dominicans, and I was surrounded by Mexicans or South Americans, much like the TV world I experienced growing up, which was mostly made up of Mexican variety shows, or Venezuelan *telenovelas*. I haven't watched the Dominican cable channel and wondered if they have managed to create something approaching the comedic brilliance of the Mexican series *El Chavo del Ocho*, my favorite show when I was a kid. I was always hiding in small spaces and wanted to spend all my time crammed into a barrel just like El Chavo.

"That's not what I'm talking about."

"Your aunt Carolina is getting an even bigger one. You know that Felito has always been a man that cares about progress."

My mother has complained that my father doesn't care about progress for all of my thirty-eight years. She says he is the one that never wanted to send money back to the Dominican Republic to build a house. My aunt Carolina's husband is considered the only sensible person in my family. He has a good job, never buys anything on credit, and will buy my aunt the biggest television he can afford.

"Mami, you know I would help you if I could, right? Why don't you wait until the summer, until I can work? I'll buy you a new TV."

"No, just do your writing thing or whatever it is that you're doing over there. You'll make more money when you're done with school, right?"

"Umm, yes."

I haven't had the heart to tell my family that writers don't make any money.

SAMSUNG PN50C430 50"

When I arrive at my parents' apartment I admire the new television that is clearly too big for the living room. It is on top of an old, ornate, dark wood cabinet that a rich tenant had given my father when he worked as a janitor at a fancy building in Manhattan, one of the many free objects given to him, which he often presented as offerings to my mother. The cabinet is solid wood and will probably outlast the television, but it is too deep, its style too clunky, made for a time when televisions were large heavy boxes that required the heft of a serious piece of furniture. I laugh at the television's placement on the cabinet, set back touching the wall, no doubt my mother's attempt at keeping the television safe from toppling over. I knew my mother would never get rid of the cabinet, and that their new television would never be wall mounted.

After taking a nap for a few hours I visit Aunt Carolina and Uncle Felito, who live two blocks away. On the way there I have to be careful that I don't step on the vast amounts of dog shit mixed in with the snow. Ever since moving away, I am always amazed at the amount of garbage and filth in my family's neighborhood. Ann Arbor is comfortable, adorable, and clean. I had never lived in such a small city, especially one filled with mostly young people who wore leggings and flip-flops even in the winter. I can't imagine walking in flip-flops through this slushy, dirty snow.

Uncle Felito greets me at the door with a long, lingering hug.

"You are so smart. I am so proud of you. The first to graduate from college, and now graduate school. Are you going to keep going after that? A doctorate maybe?"

"I don't know about that. I'm pretty tired already."

"Oh, don't talk like that. You can do it." He unfurls his arms toward the inside of the apartment as if he is showing off a prize on a game show. "Then you will be able to buy yourself one of these."

That's when I see it. Their television is bigger than my parents' television. The Christmas tree is right next to it.

"Wow, that's really big. Congratulations."

OLEVIA 252TFHD 52"

We stop by my cousin Luz's apartment on the way to the big family Christmas party at her brother José's house. I hear her television before I see it because the apartment has been rigged with surround sound speakers that I can hear from the first floor before I make it to her apartment on the second. Luz gives me a big hug.

"I didn't know you were coming home for Christmas."

"I'm on break from school."

"Oh, that's right. What are you doing over there? Writing or something, right? Where are you again? Mississippi? I don't know how you get up and move all by yourself without knowing anybody there like that. You're like a man. You look cute though. Did you lose weight?"

LG ELECTRONICS 60PG60 60"

I hadn't been to my cousin José's new house yet. He is the only one of my local relatives that doesn't live in an apartment. We walk the ten blocks from my parents' apartment and stop in front of what looks like the last scene in the movie *Poltergeist* before the ground swallows up the house. Blue flashes of light are radiating out from the windows, as if lightning is exploding inside of it. I hear rumbling noises, and I know it is my imagination, but the whole structure seems to be shaking. One of the last scenes of the movie is of the father putting the television out in the motel hallway because the television had been the portal to an evil spirit world.

My cousin José greets me at the door.

"Hey! I didn't know you were coming home for Christmas."

I can barely hear him over the television.

I yell, "Yup, I'm just here for a few days. I'm on break from school."

He laughs and says, "Oh, that's right. I heard you were in school again. Come see the TV!"

I can't not see the television. Taking a few steps into the house reveals the biggest television I have seen in my entire life. I didn't know regular, non–movie theater screens had gotten that big. I feel like when you see a picture of a painting your whole life, and then you see it in person at a museum. It seems unfathomable that the painting is actually over twenty feet wide and takes up a whole room, like when I saw Picasso's *Guernica* at the Museo Reina Sofia in Madrid.

"Wow. How big is that thing?"

"Sixty inches. Isn't that crazy?"

"Yes."

I am five feet one. His television is as wide as I am tall.

Calvin, José's ten-year-old son, runs up to me and says, "I play my video games on it. It's like being in heaven."

The room swirls with children. My younger cousins dance in front of the television, which is tuned to the Dominican channel, showing close-ups of scantily clad women dancing in front of a merengue band.

There is lots of hugging, talking, and screaming—essentially chaos, but I sometimes miss the craziness of my family. My life in Michigan seems so staid.

As usual, the men are in the living room, the women in the kitchen. In my usual defiance I purposely don't join the women—I never do whenever I am home. I stay in the living room, where José is explaining the many features of his giant television. The men start to make jokes about the merits and drawbacks of watching giant porn in high definition.

That's when I get up and go into the kitchen.

My aunts become jittery when I enter the kitchen. My mother tells me to wash vegetables. I feel I should be more helpful and say, "I can chop or make a salad."

"You don't know how to cook," says my cousin Marisol, who is younger than I am but has already moved into the ranks of cook at family dinners, a job usually reserved for the aunts.

"Of course I do." This is not a lie, but I don't know how to cook Dominican food, because when I was growing up I thought being in the kitchen would keep me in the kitchen. This is one of my biggest regrets, and I miss my mother's cooking every day.

"Do you cook for yourself?"

I don't cook very often, instead eating microwave rice flour pasta mac and cheese, because I think it's lower in carbs than the regular flour pasta version. My body had been rounding, so that I now look more like my mother and my aunts. I look just like them, but feel so different among them, out of place.

"No, I starve every day."

Back in the living room, the men are trying to tune to a particular channel, but it isn't coming in.

José says, "I think there is something wrong with the way the cable channels are programmed. Who has the manual?"

My brother said, "Let Yali look at it. She always figures stuff like this out."

The thought of controlling one of these televisions and the cable interface seems akin to trying to land a space ship. "I don't know how to deal with these TVs. This is beyond my knowledge."

Everyone stops to look at me, for the first time focusing on something other than the television.

Uncle Felito says, "What's the matter? The college genius doesn't know how to fix the TV?"

I don't know everything. If I was smarter I would quit school, stop being a student and a writer, and I would get a job where I could make enough money to be able to afford a giant television.

I want to go home to my own television. Not my parents' or my brother's apartment, where I have been staying on this trip, watching *To Catch a Predator* with my brother and his girlfriend. You can watch a man jump from behind a fake plant to entrap a child molester only so many times.

I want to watch *The Lord of the Rings* marathon. Yes! All three movies back to back, and ignore my writing, my life, and everything I am supposed to be achieving.

But, I know I will work hard again and get back to what has always felt most comfortable; the home that has always made the most sense—my mind and my writing. Whether I send a man adrift on a raft, or a girl seeks shelter in a closet as a storm rages on the other side of the door, the narratives I envision, no matter what time and place in which they are set, are mine. I will get back to that place where I create my own worlds, and reconnect with my power.

WhiteGirlColorlessAfriPana

GAIL M. DOTTIN

Hey Gail,
They told you that you could tell them anything—"No matter what it is you can always come to us." That's what they said. Did they mean this? They didn't come from Panama for this. Part of the first generation of the family born in this country to go to college here, right? They didn't send you to school for this.

Dear Inside,
Everything is cool. I'm cool. I'm safe. I have this school. This campus. Pretty English Tudor buildings. Big lawn. Half an hour from Greenwich Village. My friends. Her. People know I can rock a party with the joints they've never heard, the jams I dance to at house parties in Queens, something more bumping than all that Depeche Mode the other DJs play. I have them doing their free-form hippie-type dances to LL and Kurtis Blow and the Jungle Brothers. I do sound and lights at the theater department. I always have someone to sit with for lunch and dinner at Bates. Valentine's Day is next month, and my birthday is the day before that. I have her to celebrate with. Things are good. Everything is good.

Hey Gail,
You cannot stay here forever. Graduation is in four months and then what? They want you to be normal. They want you to have babies. You can't really do that if you're a freak.

Dear Inside,

I'm not a freak! I'm not. It's okay here. People see me kissing Lindsey all over campus, grinding on her at dances.[1] She smells real good when we're sweaty. And Rachel's boyfriend complains when he comes from the city and stays with her down the hall on the weekends. Complains about how loud we are when we're fucking. "Can't help it!" I tell him. "What am I supposed to do when it hits, man? Can't really hold that shit in." Rachel just nods and laughs like she knows, "Right!"

I know I can't bring Lindsey home. Not for real, but it's all right. I mean, we tried that one time when the machines at school were busy, and I figured that the forty-five-minute drive to bring my laundry from Bronxville to Queens would be cheaper and easier than waiting for just one machine to be free at school. Lindsey had laundry, too. Told Mom she was my friend. She is. I wanted her to see where I live. I love her. I've been to her house with her parents in Vermont. I'm her friend, too. Mikey caught us in my bed holding each other in the morning. "Younger brothers in sneakers," Lindsey cursed when we didn't hear him coming up the hall. No one knocks in my house.

And so what, the black girls on campus don't talk to me, look at me like I'm some traitor. Shit they say gets back to me, and it's usually some combo meal of my regular offenses: 1) I'm not black enough because I hang with a lot of white people; 2) I sit out on the lawn like they think only crunchy white people do; 3) I like girls, and my girl is white, and some of the people I hang with are girls who like girls and boys who like boys, and they're all white. But I'm used to that. Didn't I hear that crap from the kids at Windsor? Middle-class black kids going to a private high school in New York telling me, "You act like a white girl!" because I had good grades, because I was always talking about Springsteen. (I also had Run-DMC and DeBarge tapes in my backpack, but they didn't ask me about that, did they?) Because I wasn't walking around in Lees and suede Pumas and doorknocker earrings. Because my style wasn't like theirs, and I dressed sorta preppy some days or comfortably in corduroy jeans and long-sleeve T-shirts and my sneakers weren't pristine, scrubbed with a toothbrush like they all did. Miguel and Valentina looked at me that way, and they're my cousins. Blood was never thicker with them, always imitating how I talk, tried to beat me up a couple times. They didn't even speak English when they first came here from Panama as little kids. The kids at church saw me with those eyes, judged me with them. They'd say stuff about me being "a stuck-up white girl" because Mom had told their moms or the Sunday school teachers that I made honor roll again. And then there was that time when the church had that class about teens and sex. After I answered a question, said that "sex should be about adding to the relationship and shouldn't be about conquest," Troy Baxton asked me real loud, "Why can't you just speak regular English?" Everyone laughed hard when he said it. My parents and teachers liked that I had a big vocabulary and didn't use a lot of slang. Maybe he was trying to prove something; he speaks like I do. I'm tired, but this is my life. Just how it is. I wanted it to be different at college, but it's not.

Hey Gail,

Oh my God, you suck! Fix it. Fix you. How long have you been waiting for this, to be free of the kids in high school and your neighborhood and your family who all look like you, trying to tell you that you're not doing black right? And here you are, going to this expensive school in the suburbs with black kids just as smart as you, had the same kind of grades as you, did the same extracurriculars as you. They are you. But still you are hated. You are such a problem. Now on top of everything you like girls? Ab-fucking-normal. So now you really know you can't be black. You can't be black if you're gay. And why is it that whenever anyone around here is talking about anything related to homo-ness, you gotta be in the conversation? So terrified of what you are you're trying to out-gay everyone. You're the only person you've seen with your brownness claiming that label, and you're actually proud of it! In those lesbian lit journals you read, all the poems and stories are about white women. There aren't even any Spanish people. Remember what happened the one time you got up the guts go to a Harambee meeting? Those girls acted like you were diseased. Eyes clawing you as you entered and then across the table. Sitting in their sanctum, which is really just one of the classrooms in Westlands, but on Thursday nights it's where they talk about black student revolution issues and whatever. (What revolution? There are only 30 black students on a campus of 850 undergrads.) Like a knucklehead you raised your hand when they asked if anyone had any announcements, and you had the nerve to show them the fliers you brought from the Gay Community Center in the Village. Told them about the gay gospel choir you heard was performing in the city. You don't even like gospel music! Their eyes melted the color right out of you. Melted the black out of you for good.

Remember that convo you had with your mom freshman year? She wanted you to take the commuter railroad and the bus to Queens with your friends since she couldn't pick you all up and bring you to the house for your birthday weekend. You were sitting in the phone booth in your dorm and the minute she told you to take the train home you saw Jamaica Ave. You saw South Road, the liquor stores and the trashy buildings, the ghetto that you have to ride the bus through before you get to your Cosby Show block. You saw your friends Mona, Lana, Celeste seeing all that and seeing you. So you told your mom, "I can't bring three white girls on the Q40."

"Why would you go to school and pick only white friends?" she asked, acting like you chose this. She was super impressed with the black girl who gave the tour when you visited. But school tour guides are supposed to be nice, and anyway, she graduated.

"Black people don't like me, you know that! It's always been that way."

"What? You have to try."

"They don't like me, and it doesn't matter anyway. I'm not black."

"What!"

"I'm not black anymore, Mom! I'm not black! I'm colorless!"

She was hurt, said, "I can't tell your father about this conversation."

But you had the right idea. Quit. Be colorless. Done. Solved. Fixed.

And don't go home anymore. We have established that this is unwise. When your mom calls and wonders why she hasn't seen you in a while, tell her you're busy. So what you have a car now? So what you go home and she's making you arroz con pollo and fried platanos or sloppy joes or ordering shrimp egg fu young from the really good Chinese spot or getting you whatever you want? Still. We have a solution. They sent you here to be busy with school, right? They're always talking about Panama and how much easier you have it than they did. About how going to school there in the 1940s was rough for both of them because they're Panamanians, but with dark-skin, West Indian blood mixed in. About how hard your dad studied. He said something about how his high school was segregated because they didn't want white kids on the Zone going to the same schools as the black Panamanian kids. And your mom, her school in the city only had one classroom for the kids like her and the rest of the building was for the "real" Panamanians though she was born there. How many times have you heard about some word, chombo*? It sounds like it was sorta like "nigger," and the other kids used to call her that—"Chombita, Chombita, Chombita." Then she'll go on with how poor she was: "I had a dollar, and I'd have to get my deodorant and soap and buy something to cook for dinner, a piece of pork, some* gandules *(think those are beans), and rice for my brother and sister and your grandmother because she was working." Always telling you this stuff even though they must know it annoys you. But they came to America so that they could have kids and so those kids would be busy with getting educated in America. That's why they sent you to private schools, right? To go to college and be busy. So stay with your girl. She'll be back in Vermont after graduation. They don't have to know who you're busy with. They don't have to know anything.*

Dear Inside,

So fucking confused. Why are they here if they're that pissed off? Those Harambee women are causing trouble. Protesting. They want the administration to add more classes and services for black students. But they don't have to go to school here. You don't see any of the Latin kids doing this. Gotta be about thirty of them, too. If these women are that upset they could save their parents a pile of cash on tuition and go to Spellman or Howard. I mean, I've been reading about gay rights and all the stuff we have to fight for, and I saw *Eyes on the Prize*, but I don't know. They make me feel weird, like when I'd flip channels on Sunday afternoons, and that show *Like It Is* was coming on with those pictures of Africans with giant nose rings and the tribal drums in the opening. I'd flip past real fast but see my parents watching it in the other room. Either they were going on about Panama, and Mom was talking to my aunts in Spanish I don't understand, or they were talking about how unfair white people are to black people. I don't get it. And why do they even produce shows like that anyway, talking about prejudice and "black issues"? It's 1989. Except for some random KKK dude doing craziness on the news, racism is not really a problem anymore. I get more crap from black people, really. White people like me. I mean, sometimes they ask me questions about what happens to my hair when it gets wet and if I tan in the summer, and I feel kinda awkward, like I'm too different from them. Still, I don't understand the protests like I didn't understand why my parents felt like they had to watch that stuff.

Should I be angry, too? No. I can't. I'm colorless. It's not my fight.

Hey Gail,
Do you have a mirror?

Dear Inside,

I heard you. I heard you when Lindsey said what she said: "If they're that upset why don't they go to a black school." We were in bed this morning, talking like we always do, like I love that we do, and I heard you, and then I was just going off on her: "They pay the same tuition!" "You're always talking about how important it is to be a feminist. How would you feel if you were the only woman in a school that's supposed to be for everyone?" "What kind of real school in this century doesn't have an African American studies department?" I felt my body become hot and my brain kind of erupt, and then I was throwing on my clothes and walking across campus. Which is how I ended up here, in my funky hat with the multicolored fish, sitting on the banister at Westlands, all dark wood and burgundy carpeting, watching and listening to Camille and Nicole from Harambee as the they stand on the wide landing of the stairway leading up to the deans' offices. They're telling everyone what the demands are, standing there like it's their stage, flanked with the other women from the group like they're daring some dean to try to pass them. They've taken over the building. Lots of white kids are here, too, looks to be about one hundred students altogether. Blankets are on the floor like those sleepovers I used to have as a kid. But these people are serious, slept here last night. Spring break is six days away, and some kids are saying that this is the week that the school makes the affirmative action acceptances. I've heard that the Harambee women and their crew don't want another black kid admitted until the deans make changes.

I find myself here. I don't know why. I saw the surprise in Lindsey's flushed face. She looked as confused as I feel, and I heard the shock when she realized how upset I was. "Why is this bothering you so much? You're not one of those people I thought this would be an issue for. You don't really talk about being black like that." And, actually, I don't know why what she said is bothering me so much. Why is this hurting? And why can't I leave? I'm sure I've got work to do, a paper to write. I can't believe I'm here with them. *With Them.*

Hey Gail,
    You are black.

Dear Inside,
    Yes, I am. And I'm angry about it.

Hey Gail,
    I know you're angry.

Dear Inside,
    I am an African American. I am.

Hey Gail,
    Well, not really.

Dear Inside,
    Concerned Students of Color. That's what those women and their supporters are calling themselves now. Thought all this hectic tension would chill out after spring break. But it's April, and we're back, and they've organized. Every conversation is the same around school. Bates, the Pub, classes—same talk: race. Sit-in. Protests. Friendships being shredded. It's spring and the weather is warmer, but things feel heavy. And I'm saying I'm African American. Me. Finally. Feels good. I mean it's not totally comfortable, but it's just new. The black women are being a little nicer to me. A little. Not as many dirty looks. Unless I'm walking with Lindsey. I am an African American. I am.

Hey Gail,
    African American? Really, now? Where are your parents from again?

Dear Inside,
    Why? Both of my parents are from Panama, born there. They're also Caribbean, from Barbados and Jamaica, I think. I don't know how

they're both. Maybe they got that from their parents. Whenever they start talking about Panama and my dad growing up on the Canal Zone, and Mom starts talking about whatever neighborhood she grew up in in Panama City and about my family that's still there in Rio Abajo or my great uncle's tailor shop in Chorillo, I stop listening. They want me to understand "my culture." That shit makes me feel weird, too. How can Panama be my culture if I only went there once when I was five? When I don't even speak Spanish and they never tried to teach me? What's your point anyway? I've dealt with enough. I've dealt with you. Besides, I was born here. Doesn't that make me African American?

Hey Gail,
    If a cat has kittens in an oven, does it make them biscuits?

Dear Inside,
    You are making my head hurt.

Hey Gail,
    You are so scared your family will call you a freak, slap that on you like a "Hi, My Name Is" sticker, then push you away. You're so scared about what will happen if they really know about Lindsey. But you want them to know. You do. You want to be real. Gotta start by being real with you. About everything.
    So where are your parents from?
    Their stories. Look at those stories they've been trying to tell you. Sit with them. Let them marinate.

Dear Inside,
    Seriously, come on! I can't do this anymore. I graduate at the end of this month. I'm losing my safe place, and my girlfriend is going back to Vermont. I finally owned that I'm black. Isn't that enough . . .

And my parents are West Indian and Panamanian.

My family is Panamanian.
    I am of my family.
    Okay.

Okay.
I'm sitting with that.

Hey Gail,
  Happy graduation!

NOTE

1. Names have been changed.

Nomadic

INGRID ROJAS CONTRERAS

My parents and I traveled from Bogotá, the city of eternal spring, to Chicago, the city of winds, to get me settled into my college dormitory. I had never before experienced winter, and even though we arrived in Chicago in late August, I thought with dread toward the months ahead.

I had never seen snow. The cold I knew ranged from forty degrees Fahrenheit to sixty degrees. That was the weather of Bogotá—a city on top of a plateau twenty-six hundred meters from sea level, or as Bogotanos like to say, twenty-six hundred meters closer to the stars. The cold I knew increased with the altitude and had nothing to do with seasons. The seasons explained the Northern Hemisphere's allegory of death to winter—so my poetry teacher had once said in Colombia as we studied the poems of Emily Dickinson and Robert Frost. She pointed out that to Pablo Neruda death was a broom, licking the floor for the deceased, and that to Álvaro Mutis death was an increment of time, in which eventually death and dreams become confused. Meanwhile, to Gerard Manley Hopkins, death was a tree losing its leaves with the coming of winter.

My first night in Chicago, sharing a hotel room with my parents, as the city turned cold with teeth, I hoped I would gain the allegorical understanding of death. My family, a typical South American family, was mainly Catholic, but we also believed in the divination of dreams, the reading of the tarot spread, the reading of tealeaves, protections and amulets, the evil eye. But I was tired of superstition, and moving to the United States, I yearned for clean-cut logic.

I looked out of the fifteenth-floor window of the Hilton Hotel and wrapped myself in the taupe curtains, gazing into the bed of lights of the city down the Magnificent Mile and into the mercurial black of Lake Michigan. My thoughts went back and forth between death and winter and the verge of my new life. I worried about my dorm roommates. If we didn't get along, I would take myself to the ballet. I would see operas, sneak into piano bars, wander in the city library, go to the Colombian restaurants, and make friends.

My parents would never allow me to transfer to another school. I, too, was afraid that my student visa would be revoked. I imagined repeating the interminable interviews in Colombia at the American Embassy, shut up again in the breathless white room with the red light of a recording camera blinking high in the corner, and the immigration official writing on his notepad like a psychologist.

Studying in Colombia was also out of the question. I had promised my father I would study overseas after the guerrillas kidnapped two of my uncles. I wanted to be a journalist, but my father worried because in Colombia journalists were regularly kidnapped and disappeared. So it was decided that I would study in the States. Of all the places I could have gone, I chose Chicago because of its size. Size was all that mattered to me. In the perfect-sized city, excitement was plentiful and manageable, and I liked to feel in control.

In the morning my parents and I decided to search for the nearest bank to open my account. Papi said it was the first thing you did when arriving to live in a new place. My family had grown up moving from country to country (from Colombia to Venezuela to Colombia to Argentina) because of my father's job in the oil industry. In the international schools I spoke English because that was the language everyone had in common. My friends hailed from Lebanon, Cuba, Brazil, Argentina, China, the United States. The teachers were mostly from the United States, and that's how I came to know about the culture. In Bogotá, for example, first impressions are everything, and it was unthinkable for my father not to wear a tie and my mother a dress suit when going to a bank to open an account. What, do you want them to think we came off the streets? Mami said. I knew this was not the way things worked in North America, but I dressed up, too.

"Good afternoon, my friend!" Papi said to the hotel doorman. The English Papi knew was transliterated from the Spanish that old gentlemen spoke in Bogotá. They were all sticklers for the politeness from the gilded age and tipped their hats to every woman of any age they saw, made reverences, called them My Lady (*Buenas tardes, Mi Señora*), and performed any chivalrous deed that was needed.

The doorman tipped his hat. "Daughter," Papi said, "ask the gentleman to point the way to the closest bank."

"Is there a bank nearby?" I said in English.

"Yes," he said. But his directions were confusing. Mami and I hooked onto each of Papi's arms. We were a family going to an important business meeting, my mother and I in heels and my father in suit and tie—except we were stranded in the middle of the gritty streets of Chicago's South Loop. A man with missing teeth sat on cardboard glaring at us, and beyond, a woman was holding onto a gate as she finished up a fifth of vodka.

"Look, the train!" I said, trying to avert my parents' attention from the questionable characters of Chicago. The El train rode high above us, at second-story height. "We should get some coffee and ride it. It'll be nice!"

As we rounded the corner, we finally came upon a bank. I exhaled audibly and smiled. I was beginning to think I would have to admit I didn't know where I was taking us.

"There it is," I said. "Right where he said it'd be." Actually, I had stopped paying attention to the doorman's directions after he said, "Take the first right . . ."

The sign read, Chicago Community Bank.

"It looks official," Mami said.

"Shall we?" Papi said.

We entered ceremoniously through the double doors, but the bank appeared empty. Then past the sofas and table lamps, peeking over the wood of the counter, green eyes and glasses flashed at us.

"How can I help you?" the woman said in English, rising.

"I want to open a bank account," I said.

"Is she saying she can't see us?" Mami whispered in Spanish. "Tell her we're here from out of the country, tell her we're under a deadline." Mami was used to the inefficient businesses of Bogotá, where you only got good treatment by a mixture of charm, sob stories, and bribes. I knew that in North America nobody accepted bribes nor heard sob stories, so I ignored my mother and smiled at the woman, raising my eyebrows.

"If you step over this way," the woman said, "my manager, Roy, can set you up with an account."

In the small office Roy talked me through the paperwork as Mami and Papi sat next to me in plush seats smiling at him, their cheeks tight with effort. They were trying to use all their charm. Papi knew a little bit of English, but he could only understand when it was spoken slowly. He bided his time until there was an opening in the conversation and then he said, "Sir, please." He smiled apologetically as if he were interrupting, even though no one was talking.

"Sir," he began, "This is my only daughter." Papi put his heavy hand on my back. I looked up nervously because I did have an older sister, which meant Papi was about to launch on a sob story.

"She knows nobody in Chicago. Nobody," he said. While factually true, my cousin lived in a suburb an hour away. "She's very important. Ingrid is our treasure. We are very far away. We worry. So, sir, if you please, treat her as if she were your daughter. Please, sir? Yes?"

I burned with embarrassment. I knew boundaries were important in North America, and nobody talked to their banker that way. I held my breath.

The banker chuckled. "Sure," he said. "I will watch out for her." Roy turned to me and said, "Tell me, Ingrid, do you have a winter coat?"

"*Qué dice el señor?*" Mami said.

I was tired of translating, so I didn't turn to look at my mother, and I shook my head at Roy.

"You'll need a coat in Chicago."

"Okay," I said. I didn't believe I would really need a coat. It wasn't that I took winter lightly—I was terrified—but I also harbored the irrational belief that when the moment came, my mestizo genes would take over, and my skin would reveal itself to be impervious to cold weather. I was confident it would be so.

"*Que dice?*" Mami pulled on my sleeve.

"He says that I'll need a coat," I told her in Spanish.

"Ah," she said. She turned to the banker and reached across the table and held his hand. "God bless you," she said in English.

At the door to Roy's office, Mami and Papi one-upped each other's cordiality. Papi shook hands, so Mami hugged Roy, and then Papi thanked God for Roy aloud, so Mami kissed Roy, and, finally, Papi invited Roy out for dinner.

"We should really get going," I said as Mami hugged Roy. "We have so many errands to run," I said as Papi was thanking God for Roy. Meanwhile, Roy was turning from Papi and Mami beaming. "Really, we should leave Roy to his work," I said, but Mami brushed me off. When Papi invited Roy out to dinner, the moment before Roy answered seemed interminable. Papi was lifting his black eyebrows amiably, Mami was nodding her head in agreement with Papi, and Roy seemed stunned. I looked back and forth at all their faces. Finally, Roy laughed and said perhaps another time; he was working late that day.

Unfazed, my parents insisted on looking for a winter coat after we left the bank. I went along with them, but it wasn't the season. On our way back to the Hilton, my father scrutinized the sidewalks while my mother, hooked to his arm, filed her nails.

"Look how clean," Papi said. "Of course you realize, here they have garbage bins. Such a thing would never happen in Bogotá. They tried it once, but people stole them."

I nodded, not knowing if it was true. There was certainly a lot of litter on the streets of Bogotá. Driving on the highways emerald grass gleamed with orange and purple plastic and red aluminum.

"*Ahí esta pintado el Colombiano,*" Mami sighed. It was typical, I thought—that brilliant Colombian capacity of salesmanship—stealing city garbage bins and turning a profit. It was a common business, after all, to sell river-bottled water at traffic jams, oral summaries of breaking news, and entertainment at traffic lights—swallowing swords, spitting fire, juggling balls, telling jokes.

"Do you also see how the mail is put into little tin boxes that anyone can open? That's a lot of trust!" I said.

Mami agreed. "Remind me to get a little lock for you."

My parents left for Colombia after helping me settle into the college dormitory. I was two days early and played Colombian music and attempted a few Colombian dishes. After dinner, I danced and twirled myself on the brown carpet of the living room.

When my roommates arrived to our dormitory, I realized we were different because they were not up to date on the world's current events and didn't know where Colombia was—my two favorite subjects. I envied their privileged lifestyle. They wore heavy eyeliner, played music loudly, cursed left and right, and only worried about having a good time.

I wanted to fit in, so I wore converse shoes and jeans. I shopped with my roommates and copied their style: hoodies, jeans, ironic T-shirts. But once it got out that I had seen war, everyone wanted to know about it. I always changed the subject but then the subject was brought up again, reminding me I wasn't carefree.

There were five of us in our apartment dormitory—the two Maggies and the two Kates. I longed for another Ingrid I could hook my arm to every night. "There go the Ingrids," people would say. Instead it was always, "There go the Maggies and Ingrid." The Kates had extricated themselves pretty early on from our little group. Kate S. set up permanent camp at the telephone booth to call her long-distance boyfriend, and Kate B, a professional mud wrestler, disappeared into her room. Kate B. emerged days later, wheezing and coughing at the doorway, pale and scratching a rash on her arms, smoking weed, in heels and naked underneath see-through black lace. Hills of candy wrappers piled on the floor behind her. That was one of Kate B.'s common states. In the other state she was ravishing—her skin glowed, her eyes were smoldering and exuberant. Kate B. scared me. She was like Dr. Jekyll and Mr. Hyde, and you didn't know whom to expect when you saw her.

All the Maggies and I ever did was play euchre and drink vodka at night before going to someone's house party. At the parties people huddled around each other. In Bogotá, when you went out you only had one or two drinks and then you danced under the fluorescent green laser lights, the thump of the music in your chest. At Chicago house parties there were always beer kegs, but I hated beer. The Maggies and I drank tequila, sharpie lines on our forearms to indicate how many shots we'd had. We drank until our words slurred. I always expected people to dance, but nobody ever did. The temperature began to drop.

It was early November when the Maggies hung Christmas lights in the kitchen as I, wrapped in blankets, sipped coffee.

"It's not going to get much colder than this, is it?" I said. I had forgotten about winter in the excitement of meeting new people, but now the worry returned: that I would not be able to survive paired with the egotist belief that my mestizo genes would save me.

The Maggies looked at each other.

"It'll get much, much colder," Maggie N. said. "This is just the beginning. It'll drop another twenty, thirty degrees."

Degrees meant nothing to me, but their stories terrified me. Maggie S. said it was common for people in Michigan to get snowed in. She said hills of snow pressed on the windows and door, and if you were snowed in, you waited and hoped for the snow to melt. She said you could go crazy looking at windows of fuzzy white, your thoughts quieting down until they were replaced by a kind of radio static. I bought canned food and stocked my cupboard. It wasn't out of the question, I imagined, that snow would fall in an avalanche from the sky. I imagined storms, white flashes of snow burying each floor of the dormitory.

In Bogotá the grandfathers and grandmothers told mythic stories of how in the 1800s hail fell from the sky and covered the city regularly. In the old days there were horses, fur coats, and thick-soled boots. The Kogi tribe lives in the Sierra Nevada of Santa Marta, which is one of the only places in Colombia where there is snow. Every once in a while, the Kogi descend to the bottom of the mountain (from thirty degrees Fahrenheit into eighty degrees) to protect their sanctuaries. They come in a line, chewing coca leaves, but they do not linger. They prefer to be with the snow, the dwelling of the ancestral souls, where their prayers are heard clearly. The Kogi say they learn everything they need to know from listening to the snow.

Once when I was thirteen, my family drove through Suba, which is a town ten degrees colder than Bogotá. There was hail falling from the sky. "This is snow," Papi said, leaning over the steering wheel, and my mother, my sister, and I cooed and urged him to pull over so we could collect the snow in our plastic cups. We put on sweaters and by the side of the road, my sister and I frolicked and put our heads back, opening our mouths to taste the snow. We ate the snow with spoons on our way to Melgar, a vacationing sunny, poolside spot. Papi realized it was hail once we stopped, but he never corrected his statement.

In Chicago I went to the Harold Washington Public Library to research winter. I wanted to be ready for whatever was coming, and I also wanted to know how the Native Americans survived winter. Native Americans and my type of genes, I told myself, weren't that far apart. If they could do it, so could I. I sat at a long table on the fourth floor. To my right, high windows looked out onto State Street, and people underneath were walking around with light jackets and scarves. I opened my laptop and took out the coffee I had hidden in my bag and placed it on the table. The girl sitting on the opposite end of the long table lifted her eyes from her notepad and open books and whispered hotly, "You can't drink coffee in here."

I looked around. It was just the two of us, hemmed in by a tall shelf and the window.

I was confused. "Do you work here?"

"No," she said, "but you can't drink beverages in the library."

I shrugged and sipped my coffee. I didn't understand why North Americans were so uptight about rules. All the cars stopped at the stop signs, nobody tried to pay anyone off, and the lines (at banks, the cafeteria, at the stores) were respected as if they were sacred. The girl exhaled disapprovingly. I smiled at her and continued to sip and type with one hand, October, November, December, January, into the weather backlogs of the previous Chicago winters. The numbers had no meaning: fifty degrees Fahrenheit, thirty degrees, zero degrees, minus nineteen. Even when I translated the numbers into degrees Centigrade, the numbers remained abstract.

To me, zero degrees Fahrenheit seemed the official temperature in which people should die. I imagined it was similar to being in zero gravity—all bets were off; if you were not tied down to anything, you could float off into the infinite until you starved or were quartered by a black hole.

My Native American search led me to an oversized book of photographs of Indians in the early twentieth century taken by Edward S. Curtis. In the book an Apsaroke man on a horse gazed far off into the distance, while a fog of luminous snow hazed the background. It's a beautiful photograph. The horse is powdered in white and looks straight at the camera, his hoofs disappearing into the snow, like a magical thing. The man hugs a wool blanket to his chest, and his feet, I noted, were dressed in deerskin boots. Everything is hazy like a dream.

All I needed was a blanket and deerskin boots.

I returned the book and went back to my dorm feeling better. The Apsaroke man wasn't even wearing a hat. So I got myself a wool coat and light brown leather boots. I went to class like that until the temperature lowered to forty degrees. Then the Michigan Avenue wind hit me and blew burning cold through the wool to my skin. I ran as fast as I could back to the dorm three blocks away, my feet and hands numb. With my coat still on I jumped in bed under the blankets. I thawed, warmth burning into my limbs. I cried in anger and disappointment. My genes, it seemed, would not come to my rescue.

I skipped class the next day and ran shivering to the department store, wearing two layers of socks, my pajamas under my jeans, and four sweaters one on top of the other.

I ran my hand over the racks of coats: soft rabbit fur, balmy leather, rayon and wool, sheepskin fur, sherpa, windbreakers filled with fluff. I fitted my hand into each material for thirty seconds, trying to determine which material was warmest. I bought a thigh-length hooded fleece. Sheep, it seemed, were warm creatures. I walked home against the biting gusts of icy wind. I felt warm for a week. Then, the temperature dropped to thirty.

Inside my apartment, my roommates insisted the temperature remain at sixty degrees when I turned the thermostat dial up. "But aren't you freezing?" I pleaded. "It's so cold in here!" I had a blanket around my shoulders and was wearing gloves and a hat.

"You'll get used to it," the Maggies said.

I decided to take matters into my own hands. I waited until the apartment was empty and I turned the knob to ninety. In the empty apartment I settled in the couch, looking out into the cold city, waiting for it to get warmer. With the heat, my muscles relaxed, and the blankets slipped from my shoulders. My teeth stopped chattering, and I dropped back into the backrest of the couch. I closed my eyes and felt the warm air tingle my ears and neck. I imagined palm trees, blonde sand, the warm ocean beating on the shore. I sat there smiling until the door opened and the Maggies rushed to the thermostat exclaiming, "Oh, my God! It's so hot in here! What the hell are you doing, Ingrid?"

Soon, I was spending all my money on coats. No coat was ever good enough. Fur was itchy, and the chill of the wind still got through. Leather was constricting and though it blocked the wind, it was never warm. Sherpa and wool were not warm enough on their own. I took to wearing my coats inside the apartment, rotating them to match them with my socks and shoes. My hands were cold and rheumatic. I drank whisky to warm myself.

"When is this going to stop?" I said. We were playing euchre at the dining table, the Maggie's in hoodies, jeans, and flip-flops. "When does summer come back?" I said. I twirled my hair and rubbed my tiger-patterned slippers on the carpet. Outside the window the sky was a gray slate.

"In August," Maggie S. said. "But listen, once it snows, we'll go out and have a snow ball fight. You'll like it."

It would be nine months until August. I felt depressed and claustrophobic.

Mami called from Venezuela, where she and Papi were now living. Her voice echoed, bouncing in telephone distances: "How are you holding up?" repeating itself down a long hall of doors.

"Oh my god, it's miserable," I said. "I'm cold all the time."

Papi hummed in the background. They were driving, on their way to Puerto La Cruz, Port of the Cross, a city of beaches and fancy boats, sand soft like flour on your feet, the sea and sky merging in a royal blue at the edge of the earth. I ached to be with my parents.

"I don't know how you do it," Mami said. Her voice was loud, fighting off what sounded like wind. I grew angry, thinking about the sun and the beach and my parents driving with their windows down. I imagined them smiling, Papi wearing one of his light nice shirts, and Mami holding down her black straw hat on her head against the warm wind.

"You guys should come for Christmas," I said, pinching my lower lip between my fingers, staring off at the carpet in my apartment.

"When it's snowing?" Mami said. "Are you out of your mind?" Then to Papi who was driving, "Do you want to say hello?" There was some mumbling, the radio was turned up; then, "Your father can't talk; he's driving. Maybe we'll see you in May; is that when you said it would be warmer?"

The first snow fell that year in early December—the white burial of the city. The snowflakes fell at a slant, buoyed by wind, eliminating entire cars. The streetlights wore white caps, and the snow covered the pavement, the doorsteps, and the parked cars in a white aura that insinuated their shapes. I put three pairs of socks on and then my rain boots. I put on my zip-up fleece underneath a sherpa coat and went out. I stood outside for about five minutes, my limit of resistance time to winter. I balled up a handful of snow and threw it as high in the air as I could. It rose amid the falling snowflakes. I held my breath, rapt, watching the beautiful snowfall. The moment was everything I imagined it would be. It was exactly as being in a snow globe, and everything seemed as magical and austere as in the photograph of the Apsaroke man.

The next day I was over the snow. It was no longer white, but gray and slushy. I went out to buy different gear. I bought sherpa-lined leather boots and a flannel-lined nylon jacket. If only I could find the right combination. I bought another fifth of whisky.

"Do all Colombians drink as much as you do?" Maggie N. said.

"I have to drink something if I'm going out of the apartment."

It was half an hour before class. I sipped whisky from a brandy glass and rubbed my hands together. In order to go out into the city, other than sipping whisky, I had a list of places I could stop in if I felt like I wouldn't make it. The Harold Washington Library had great heating. If I was going to English, poetry, or journalism class on Congress, I stopped at the Starbucks on the corner of Plymouth and Harrison. I stopped at the Starbucks so often, the server stopped charging me for my soy latte. "How you doing?" he'd say. "Oh my god, I am dying!" I'd tell him. "This is the coldest day ever." I said that every week, and I meant it every time. The server smiled at me and handed me my drink.

If I was going to philosophy or fiction class on Michigan Avenue, I walked a block, then cut through an indoor parking lot, walked another block, and then sneaked into the Hilton lobby. There still remained a brutal half-block walk on Michigan Avenue. Every day, I rounded the corner, and the glacial chill coming off Lake Michigan hit me with force. The wind lashed my face and penetrated through all my layers. I ended up again trembling through class.

When it dropped to zero degrees, I refused to go out. I stayed in bed and read *Anna Karenina*. I got sick in regular cycles. It felt good to have a fever, to sweat through the sheets. I imagined the fever was the heat from the sun. In between sleep and the lull of the medication, I imagined myself asleep at the beach, the hot sun warming my stomach, the water foaming at my feet. I didn't want to get better.

"Can I get you anything?"

It was Maggie N. peeking around the door.

"I just want to go home," I told her.

"I'll make you soup. You'll feel better, you'll see."

On Christmas Eve I flew to see my sister in Minnesota, where she was going to college. I tried on my sister's coats. Francis is two years older than I am, and she had already been in the United States for a year. She had leather boots and only wore a sweater inside the cold house. I stared at her, and within an hour I was dizzy and descended, lengthily and comatose, down, down into my first flu. I was lost in the pillowy comfort of her warm bed, only rising to throw up in the bathroom and open presents on Christmas Day. I was sick for my whole visit, Francis's face foggy and her words echoing, coddling me to eat something or take some medicine.

No one in our family had gotten the flu before. My parents called from Venezuela, insisting my sister take me to the emergency room and make me a tea infusion of garlic, lemon, and ginger and give me rice to eat.

"No, she shouldn't eat anything," my sister's boyfriend, Geoff, explained. "She'll just throw it up. That's what the flu is."

My parents didn't understand. Francis decided to listen to Geoff. My parents called back every hour to see if I had stopped throwing up and asked my sister to take my temperature to see how bad the cold was.

"It's not a cold," Geoff said, but it was no use.

I apologized profusely every time I awoke from the nonsensical, fevered dreams, calling to her through the fog of sickness, into the dark room where she was watching a movie with her boyfriend or was having dinner by candlelight. "I'm so sorry," I said. "I'll try to get better," I promised. There were Christmas lights in the corner and blue snow glowing in the window.

Back in Chicago, going to fiction class became harder and harder. I used an umbrella as a shield against the snow, but as I rounded the corner of Michigan Avenue, the wind always raged and crashed against me in front and in back, blasting open my coat and then flipping the umbrella inside out. I battled to take the ten steps left to the safety of the building, my eyes watering from the wind, and the tears freezing on my eyelashes. It all seemed very inhuman. I ran shivering to the bathroom, tidied my hair, straightened my clothes, and stood under the hand drier warming myself.

One day, as I stood inside the building bracing myself to go out, I met Jeremiah, now my husband, who was locking his bike to a post in that weather.

"Biking? Are you out of your mind?" I said as he entered the building.

"It's fun!" he said, taking his helmet off. Snow in clumps fell from it onto the carpet. "Even if you fall, you hit a mountain of snow, and it's like landing on cotton."

I was impressed. I was also impressed with Jeremiah's odd timing. He showed up at my doorstep at two in the morning to see if I would go grocery shopping with him and five in the afternoon to see if I would go drink coffee with him at a diner. We got intensely excited about cooking dinners, hip-hop and art, readings, Hemingway. We fell in love reading Hemingway. The heartbroken words floated back and forth between us. They felt palpable, resting on the surface of things, even after we closed the book and lay in silence on his bed. We went to the Velvet Lounge, an underground bar where some of the city's best jazz musicians played to a crowd of ten. Our friend Nick took us there the first time. The tables were old and falling apart, and behind the small stage paint chipped from the wall in volcanic patterns. We sat there every other week in a trance, listening to the music, Nick writing poetic tidbits in a napkin, and my friend Adam tapping his feet to the drums. For the first time since arriving, I felt fulfilled. The cold wind I had to bear in order to get to the Velvet Lounge seemed a small sacrifice, a part of a kind of pilgrimage.

The Maggies reproached me for not hanging out with them. "Come with me," I told them. "You'll love the Velvet Lounge. The music is incredible." But the Maggies were going to another house party. It was March when we finally went out to dinner. Amid the deep red curtains, the noise of tinkling cutlery and glass, Maggie D. said, "We never really see you. Where have you been?" I realized I didn't know anything about them, and they didn't know anything about me. I started looking for one-bedroom apartments.

I watched all the classic American movies. The Hollywood stars wore fur muffs and mink coats, making winter look as if a sensible affair. I bought a thigh-length goose-down parka, the perfect combination at last. "I love geese!" I went around saying. "They're the best birds in the country!" I was elated. For the first time I felt that I could be outside for longer than five minutes without drinking.

I researched where and when goose feathers were collected. It was important information in case the city froze over. I loved the salt on the street, those magical crystals that could make snow disappear, even though they ruined the leather of my boots. I began to like how puddles of water froze on top on the street. When you stepped over them, they cracked deliciously, and the unfrozen water underneath sloshed about.

I moved out that May into my own apartment in Lincoln Park. The building used to be a hotel in the early 1900s, and two things of interest had happened there. In the 1940s a couple living in the building was charged for running a call-girl ring, and in the 1950s a pilot who lived on the sixth floor died a hero when he crash-landed his plane away from the crowds. Other than that, there was the exciting preexistence of maid service, fireplaces, and four grand pianos. It was a dilapidated place, chipping paint, but with those great old elevators with wire cages. I think I moved into that place for the elevators and the view of Lake Michigan from the bathtub.

The weather was beginning to warm up, and I was so excited that in the mornings I sat drinking coffee in the bathtub and meekly opened the window as I looked out to the water. The wind was cool, but the sun was warm. I was ecstatic to see things growing again, trees sprouting green boughs, the birdsongs becoming boisterous, and Chicagoans finally shedding their layers. As the weather warmed, I experienced what I had only read about: the feeling of rebirth, the emergence of life after the oppression of winter. It was with spring that the winter allegory to death resonated with me.

"It was not death, for I stood up / And all the dead lie down," Emily Dickinson wrote. I stared at the line. That was spring.

A week later my parents came to visit me. I was cheery and had prepared a Colombian dinner: *ajiaco* soup with arepas, avocadoes, capers, yellow potatoes, *pico de gallo*, fried plantains, caramelized onions, and white rice. I always kept the temperature dial at seventy, but as we sat down to dinner, both my parents began to shiver.

"It's cold!" Papi said.

"Can you make it hotter?" Mami said.

"But it's seventy. And this is spring! It's not winter!"

"Turn it up. It's cold."

I turned up the thermostat to eighty, but soon my parents got me to turn the dial a few degrees higher until it was ninety.

"Ah!" Papi said. "Now it's comfortable. We are not cold-blooded like the snakes, you realize." He unraveled my pink wool scarf from his neck and took off my blue hat with pompoms. "Now this is more civilized."

"Yes, I agree," my mother said. She took her arms out from the sleeves of the fur coat and let it sag at her waist.

"But now it's too hot!" I said. "When we go out we are going to be shocked with how cold it is! You can't live like this!"

Papi put his soupspoon down. "Daughter, don't tell your own father how to live."

I nodded. I brought out wine. I poured a glass for my father and a glass of lemonade for my mother. I filled my glass with ice cubes and brought out a pitcher of water. My nostrils dried out, and I went out to buy a humidifier. I wore summer clothes inside the house. My father got allergies that first night, but he emphasized it was a cold because of winter. I reminded him it was spring, but it didn't matter. He began to walk around my apartment dressed in my winter gear, until we went out and bought him a winter coat.

When all of us went out of the house, my dad wore his coat and my mother borrowed one of mine. Wool hats, gloves, boots, layers of sweaters and socks: I avoided being outside with them as often as it was possible. When my parents met Jeremiah, the first thing I explained was my parents' bizarre attire: "They come from South America. They're not used to the cold," I said. "It's probably hard for you to imagine."

Mami said, "I suppose you're telling him we've descended from the monkeys."

"I'm saying you're not used to the cold," I told her in Spanish.

"Oh, cold," Mami said in English to Jeremiah, her face brightening. She shivered excessively and flashed the whites of her eyes. "Too cold," she said.

"Sometime hot," she continued, blowing on an imaginary cup of a hot beverage, "but, wind, rain," she said, shivering again, putting out her tongue, and dropping her arms to her sides, lifeless. "Hard," she said. She was serious, but then the next second she broke into a laugh, which was free and loose.

I realized then how far I had come. Watching her do her charades, communicating this primal fear of too cold, too hot. I rubbed her back.

"You just grow a thick skin," I told her in Spanish. "That is all you have to do."

When winter returned, I told myself I would face the cold. After the first snow, I dressed in my goose-down parka, hat, and gloves, and walked along Fullerton Avenue past North Pond Park and the Nature Museum. I went under Lake Shore Drive and down the steps to the very shore of Lake Michigan. I had expected for it to be completely frozen over, but what I saw was even more beautiful. Beneath the silver sky, in the cerulean lake floated small white glaciers. Even more impressive was the sound: the low nonhuman roar as the ice cleaved and came together as it traveled over the water—clean, white, nomadic ice. I sat down on the rocks, staring at that winter moonscape, hearing the ice groan. I closed my eyes, and imagined my Kogi ancestors, as the ice roared and I listened.

Leaving Miami

CHANTEL ACEVEDO

It's my senior year in high school. My friends and I are smart kids. Honor students, good scores on APs, the whole package. But either our parents think that only sluts leave the home before marriage, or we are terrified of leaving them behind. One friend applies to Florida State, which is in Tallahassee and seven hours away from Miami by car. She dreams of being a lawyer. She tells me this the same day she tells me about coming to Miami from Cuba during the Mariel boatlift when she was only five years old, recalling with surprising accuracy the feel of rocking waves and the hairy marine who lifted her off the boat. My friend has no trouble getting into Florida State. But when her father finds out that she's sent in her acceptance forms, he yanks the telephone line out of her room and lashes her with it.

I think: if she'd made it out, seen snow for the first time, observed how Christmas trees actually grew out of the ground, noted the difference between a Gulf breeze and that great shaft of wind that comes blowing between the skyscrapers in New York City, then we might have all had a chance. We could have said to our *mamis* and *papis*: look, she's survived. She's not pregnant or anything. Let us go, too. The thought that I might *never* see snow, or suspension bridges, chills me, makes my chest ache like when I think of being dead.

I throw out all of the college catalogs that come in the mail, except for the one from Mt. Holyoke. I'd read somewhere that Emily Dickinson went there (though I must have missed the part where it's revealed how much she hated it), and I am entirely seduced by the images of white, freckle-faced girls on the cover going on study-abroad trips or happily lugging their books across a picturesque, fall-tinged campus. I keep it until I get married, and even then, it hurts to throw the book away.

When I do get married, my husband and I settle into a townhouse in Hialeah, Florida, a city so Cuban it makes Havana seem like a melting pot. I take a job teaching high school language arts less than a mile from my house. I'm a rookie teacher, fresh out of school with my MFA in creative writing from the University of Miami. I know why Chekhov is important. I use words like *particularize* and ask my students to do as Henry James urged, to be the kinds of learners "on whom nothing is lost." I am very brave before them. Though I have thrown out my Mt. Holyoke book, I can picture the images still, and I feel like one of those girls on the cover. The world is fresh and conquerable.

One morning, I stand with arms crossed as one of the assistant principals searches all the book bags in my homeroom. He is looking for contraband goods—eggs to throw, cans of spray paint, drugs, permanent markers. Mine are the gifted students, and they bear this intrusion into their privacy with all of the intellectual adolescent rancor they can muster. I can see the arguments piling up in their heads. They are recalling their rights, their records as good students, planning the articles they'll draft on this injustice for the school paper, writing the speeches they'll read at graduation, scathing remarks about the "administration" and "oppression." They're smart kids, and I love them.

They also happen to be Cuban kids. They are all Cuban. Their names are Yoslani and Marisleysis, Usmail and Antonio and Elisabét.[1] After the assistant principal is done, having confiscated a tiny, tiny robin's egg from the purse of Yamilet Cruz (she says she found it on the ground and that she is going to hollow it out like the Chinese do, and gild it), he clears his throat and introduces a certain Ms. Ross, who has been standing in the doorway of my classroom so silently that I've missed her.

Eileen Ross is a very tall woman. The top of her blond, frizzy hairdo scrapes the tips of the mobiles I've hung up on the ceiling—paper cutouts of swordfish to set the mood for our reading of *The Old Man and the Sea*. Ross is the new college counselor, and she's holding a stack of financial aid forms, rubbing her palm over them, and I imagine that they are still warm from the copier.

She addresses my students without a word to me, saying, "Ladies and gentlemen, my number one job is to get you out of Florida. There are good schools out there, and as honors students, you are honor bound to represent your community outside of this bubble." Ross says more, but I'm not listening. Neither are my students. The girls, especially, look as if someone has just murdered a puppy before their eyes. After Ross leaves, my female students crowd my desk. Some are crying. "I can't leave my *abuela!*" "What'll I do without Mami?" "My brother's still in Cuba!" "I can't abandon my parents!" "I'll die!"

I tell the girls they don't have to go anywhere. But I don't mean it. I, too, want them to take their tropical lives deep into the icy corners of Chicago, Pittsburgh, Boston, New York. Even Georgia will do, for God's sake. I want them to be brave. I want them to be like those Mt. Holyoke girls, to choose the path I did not take. But I pat their heads and hug them, hand them tissues to wipe the smudged eyeliner from their cheeks, and promise that yes, yes, I'll write your letters of recommendation to Florida International University and the University of Miami, and even Barry College. Yes, I'll write them all so that you can stay home.

At the end of the school year it becomes clear that my husband (also Cuban) wants to pursue a PhD in chemistry, and that to do so requires a move out of state. It surprises me how quickly my courage falls apart. In Pittsburgh I see snow for the first time at the age of twenty-four. I slip on ice and fall on my ass. I discover hills, rivers, and, for the first time, televisions that can't be turned to Univision or Telemundo.

There's more. When we move away, my mother becomes depressed. She calls every night, and every night the conversation ends with her in tears, and my throat aching from trying not to cry. I want her to be brave for me, because I am not brave after all. I think of my baby cousins, how I won't be at their birthday parties, or of having to eat Thanksgiving dinner without *arroz* and *congris* and *platanitos*. I am like my students. So much like them. Everything feels wrong.

I have another story to tell. It's the story of my grandmother's farewell to her mother, and I swear I could recite it by the time I could talk. It was 1959, just before Fidel Castro and the rebels came down from the Sierras to claim the country in the name of revolution. A *santera*, a prac-

must rove, the message from our families is that do so, to leave places like Miami after all the effort it took to get whole as a family, is unspeakable.

I have a few Cuban friends in academia. Very few. Precious few. Our mothers all took to their beds upon our leaving home. The guilt of parting hangs around our necks as securely as those academic hoods drape over us during graduation ceremonies. Once we left, we were past remedy. We know that, too. We've seen snow, we've tried Ethiopian food, we've dreamed of places far from the goldfish bowl where our children might go to college, we've been to Mt. Holyoke, and *coño*, it's a neat place. We were right about that.

Here's another story. The tenure-track job search has led us to Alabama, and I settle down in a southern college town with my husband and six-month-old daughter. Her ears are pierced, and I dab *agua de violetas* onto her neck; she thrusts plump arms into the air and can already say, "*Upa*, Mami." My mother is missing all of this, and the knowledge of it is bitter, like plantains not yet ripe. Her birth exacerbates the guilt I feel about leaving Miami, even though the actual leaving took place long ago.

Alabama is hotter than Miami. I never thought a place could get so hot. But the breezes don't reach this far inland, and the live oaks are stunted, little things, bare without their furry, dripping mosses, so different from the ones in Savannah or even North Florida. I have a hard time understanding the accent, the "y'alls" and "might coulds," and people keep telling me I speak too fast. I also make lots of usage mistakes, a big no-no for a new assistant professor in an English department. I say *floor* when I should say *ground*. I say I feel *repugnant* when what I mean is *repugnada*, or so full from the delicious new faculty orientation lunch that I'm about to burst. My bilingualism is a curse.

A colleague asks where I earned my degrees. I tell him I got them both at the University of Miami. The eyebrows arch. "So you stayed for graduate work at your undergraduate institution?" he asks, but I'm not about to go into all that noise about being Cuban and leaving Miami, because to do so would include a long story about how my grandfather filled our backyard with guavas and *mamoncillo* and *fruta bomba* and other plants native to Cuba, as if through their woody roots he would rebuild his island in Miami, and through that native fruit we might all retain our Cubanness in our bodies. I know this is lunacy. Just as I know that when

58   *Acevedo*

titioner of that syncretic Cuban religion that blends Catholicism with Yoruban ritual, was invited to the house. The woman took one look at my grandmother, who was only thirty years old or so at the time, and said, "A small band of water will separate you from those you love. You will be parted forever." And so it came to pass. My grandparents left Cuba with my aunt and mother on the eve of the revolution and never saw their own parents or many of their siblings again.

I share this story because it was part of the fabric of my life, the thread of narrative that shaped me. And because I think that for Cuban Americans in academia, this narrative also entangles us, keeps us from straying too far. The Cuban exile trauma has embedded the fear of leaving home into our very cores. The academic life is nothing if not nomadic. So what is a Cuban American academic to do? Our parents and grandparents fled the Cuban Revolution, abandoning home, family, language, and whatever value their own educational degrees had to come to the States. Even photographs were left behind. I don't mean to play the victim. As much as my family and my friends' families discouraged us from leaving Miami, we, too, felt as if we couldn't bring ourselves to go. It would be too much of a betrayal to the efforts of our parents and grandparents, who took years sometimes to bring everyone back together in exile—visa applications, exorbitant fees, long waits, and some even took to the sea to join us—to up and leave for *college* or *jobs* of all things, when there were perfectly good colleges and jobs in South Florida.

It turns out that the Cuban definition of "perfectly good college" is not the academic definition. When I applied to the MFA program at the University of Miami, the director told me that my chances weren't great, not because my work was not good, but because universities, in general, did not like to channel their own undergraduates into the graduate program. I did get accepted, earned a fellowship, won a fiction prize, and to this day keep getting asked to come back and visit. Nevertheless, the message that one must embrace the wandering spirit of academia in order to be successful was received, loudly and clearly. And that wandering spirit is the very thing the children of Cuban exiles have been taught to suppress in their lives. A thin band of water still separates countless Cuban families. The ninety miles between Key West and Havana might as well be a million. To add to those miles, to splinter these splintered families into even smaller pieces, feels like a sin. If the message from the academy is that one

I call my grandmother, she will ask me when I'm coming home for good, as if buying a house and getting a job in another state is a flight of fancy.

Later, another colleague asks to see one of my short stories. After she reads it, she says, smiling, that she's sick of Cuba, to tell the truth, and that folks should just get over it. And I want to say that I'm sick of it, too. But what can I do? I can't *not* be the daughter of Cuban exiles. I can't douse that small flame that runs under my skin because I can't even reach it without damaging myself. No, this can't be explained.

That night, I dream of that old Mt. Holyoke catalog. In the dream my grandmother holds it, and I, looking upon her, feel anger, a sort of smoldering heat about what might have been. When I wake up, the guilt about even thinking it smolders, too.

NOTE

1. These are not their names. They had names very much like this, however. Theirs were artful names that mashed up Spanish and Russian from the old Soviets-in-Cuba days. Some names were taken from unlikely places. The term *U.S. Mail*, certainly seen on remittance packages sent to Cuba from Miami, in the hands of a new Cuban parent became the melodic Usmail—uss-mah-eel.

II.
Rooms of Our Own

Las Otras

CELESTE GUZMAN MENDOZA

Mira, when I decided to go to Barnard College, my parents didn't talk to me for days. *Nombre*, neither of them were happy that their *unica hija* and *la mas joven* of their two children was leaving San Anto for New York City. And neither of them knew what to expect for me or for them *como mis padres*. I was the first woman *en toda la familia, y hablo de generaciones*, to go to college and *la primera persona* to leave San Anto to pursue an education. *Ay*, no, they had no idea what awaited me. *Pero bueno*, I filled out the forms *qué sí*, and I was on my way.

Before I left for New York, I received a letter from Barnard that told me my roommate was Chinese. They gave me her name and address and told me to write her a letter to introduce myself and to talk about me and my culture. She was asked to do the same.

I remember in the letter I was fairly forthright about how proud I was of my Tejana heritage; I saw myself as a Mexican American, a Chicana, and a Latina.

I broke it down *así*. I was a Tejana through and through because not only was I born in Texas, *pero* my family had been in San Antonio since the late 1700s; eight generations had been born and raised on a homestead near downtown. And two relatives fought at the Battle of the Alamo and at San Jacinto *against*, not *for*, Mexico. *Además* I grew up speaking *puro* Tex Mex, which is not Spanglish, and I know the words to every Selena song—*más* Tejana. American because I was born in the United States, knew "My Country 'tis of Thee" by heart, and could quote Emerson, Plath, Shakespeare, and Madonna. Mexicana because I eat chili, enchiladas, fajitas, and crispy tacos, *and* I know how to make all of them from scratch (*pero* not tortillas—I'm not *that* Mexican). Finally, Latina because I saw myself *como parte de la comunidad* of brown *gente* in this country who all have been looked at as less-than merely because of the color of our skin, our *apellido*, or a light *sabor de azucar* in our walk and talk.

Pero I also said that I saw myself *como una mujer*, which meant I was bred and raised to cook, clean, and heal. My mother worked the night shift when I was young, so I learned how to cook dinner by the time I was seven or eight. As the only girl I helped my mother with all the housework, which included laundry, dusting, sweeping, and mopping. Plus, my grandmother was a *curandera* who taught me how to clean wounds and set bones.

However, all this caring and tending didn't mean that we were docile ladies in waiting. *Ay* no, no, no. *Las mujeres* in my family were *espinas* plucked from the cactus—sharp and prickly. But we knew how to laugh— loudly—and knew how to drink—heartily.

All of these characteristics formed my *cultura, mi identidad*. I was sure that these characteristics weren't shared by anyone else. I had never come in contact *con gente ajena de otras culturas o origenes* so my sense of self was informed *más o menos* by not only what I knew but also what I didn't know.

Pobresita de mi roommate, no? I can just imagine her face as she read my letter. She must have thought that she had met a crazy woman from Texas. She probably hoped I wasn't armed.

In her *carta*, which was one page in comparison to my three-page saga, she mentioned that she was born and raised in China until she was eight; then she immigrated with her family to Anchorage, Alaska. She included *álgunas detallítas así como qué* she played the violin, and she worked at her parents' Chinese restaurant, but she didn't say *ni nada más* about her *cultura* or how she defined herself. *Entonces* I assumed she was shy like most of the Chinese people I had encountered at the grocery store or at the mall.

Dejame decirte, after two weeks of sharing that little *cuartito* with her at Barnard I was *segura* that she must have some Latina blood in her. No, no, no, no. First, she ate chiles. She was from the part of China where they grew *más chiles que la fregada*. And she ate them like crazy. Then, she was bilingual and spoke Chinese *con su Mamá* over the phone, and a *un volúmen, para qué te cuento.* I thought my mom and me were loud. No, we were quiet as little mice compared to her and her *mamacita*.

Además no era shy *para nada.* She would tell you what for and then more and more. She could cook and clean, was a matriarch-in-training (like me), and got over 1,000 on her SAT. We both liked dirty jokes, whiskey, tequila, oranges, and to eat (she loved Mexican food). I thought, "I met the Chinese version of me." The only thing we didn't share was religion; I was Catholic, while she didn't practice any religious faith, though she believed in God.

I began to rethink why I called myself all those names—Tejana, Chicana, Mexican American, Latina—what did they mean to me, *pero de deveras*? Were they that *importante*? Did they really define me?

Forget it. Then I met the other *chicas* who would become for me my family away from *la familia*.

Había, my roommate's closest friend from Alaska, was *una mujer* who was born and raised in Korea but who had lived in Califas and Alaska with her family since she was in elementary school. Then there were *las otras mujeres* who lived on our floor: a self-proclaimed "ABC"— American Born Chinese—girl who had lived her whole life in Queens excepting the annual trips to her mother's hometown of Hong Kong; a New York Muslim who was originally born in Lebanon to parents of Egyptian heritage; and a Queens girl whose parents of Indian descent were from Guyana in South America. *Lo que teníamos en común* was that all of our parents spoke English as well as they spoke *cualquier otro lenguaje* that was native to their country of origin or heritage—Korean; Chinese, both Cantonese and Mandarin; Arabic; and Guyanese. *Cuando salíamos juntas*, which was at least two to three times a week, we looked like a United Colors of Benetton commercial. *En serio.*

We became the best of friends. We studied together, ate together, stayed up late together. *Nos platicamos de todo.* From school work to work work, to all the work it took to keep in touch with our *familias* back home or across the Brooklyn Bridge. We talked about why we came to Barnard, why we left home, and *como a veces* we felt *uno poco* at odds with our decision to leave. *Era tan difícil para cada quien de nosotras* to be the good daughter while being *fuera de la casa*, not able to help with chores and other familial *que haceres* and responsibilities. We had all been raised for marriage, not for higher education.

I cooked for my family when my *madre* worked the night shift. My roommate helped manage her parent's restaurant. *Y eso no era nada mas ser la mesera* or hostess; *nombre,* she paid the bills and did the taxes every year. *Para la de* Korea there was the helping her mother raise her six-year-old brother from regular babysitting to making his meals, dropping him off at school, and meeting with his teachers when her mother could not. *Para la amiga que era* Muslim *pos* she had to work at her father's mosque; he was an elder and leader *pero como era mujer* she wasn't allowed to read from the Quran in public. *A la misma vez* Ms. Self-proclaimed "ABC" and the friend from Queens were their mothers' "go-to" girls in their home who helped keep the family drama in check.

En el primer semestre I realized that these *mujeres* shared so many *caracteristicas conmigo, algunas que pensé que eran solamente* specific to Latinos—a strong work ethic, family-centered culture, bilingualism, and the straddling of our American and our ethnic identities.

Pero más que nada lo que sí compartimos was the development of ourselves as women, women living outside the home and educating ourselves at an Ivy League school where we were all looked at as "Other," and not just from our fellow Barnard Anglo or Jewish women but from our own *familias.*

At Barnard we were minorities. *Ay, dios!* Some of our Anglo-American and Jewish classmates would ask us some hilarious *preguntas, y sin verguenza, eh, nos preguntaron cosas,* such as, "Does your mother wear traditional dress at home?" "Do you only eat 'rice and beans' or 'kim chi' or 'dahhl'" or whatever other typical food was associated with our cultures. *Pero* our all-time *favorita* was, "Do you have a green card to live in this country?" We would laugh so much when we traded these stories. *Pero a la misma vez* we were aghast that we were all having to endure this kind of *tratamiento en la mera mera* Big Apple, the cultural melting pot *de los estados unidos,* and at an Ivy League institution—if our classmates could score so high on their SATs why were they so culturally *tonto.*

In our families we were *raras.* Traveling so far and spending so much (or taking out so much in loans) *y para qué?* Not even to find a husband. Spending so much time in front of books and not enough at the salon or at church. Speaking too much, too loud. Who did we think we were?

And we didn't always know, which we talked about, too.

My first year *cuando conoci a mis comadres* my sense of identity and self

underwent *una tranformación* fundamental. I still felt Tejana/Chicana/
Mexican-American/Latina, nothing could change my past—my history,
my brown skin, my bilingual upbringing—but I realized that I couldn't
claim any human characteristic any more so as Latino as Chinese or
Muslim or Korean or Guyanese. *Como mujer* I was growing with five
other women, trying to hold one or more jobs to help cover our college
costs, working to get at least B's in all of our classes, and trying to stay
close to our families, but more than anything trying to find our way
into the future we hoped to have, the future that *todas nuestras familias*
had worked so hard to have us lead, the future they left behind in their
paises de orígen so we could be in that dorm room together and become
what we left behind—family.

Pancakes at 2 a.m.

STEPHANIE ELIZONDO GRIEST

I had anticipated this moment my whole entire life, but now that it was here, I didn't know what to do. Mom and Dad were driving home to Corpus Christi without me, after our soggy good-bye in the parking lot, and I was perched atop the purple comforter we had just bought at Target, staring around the 13x17-foot dorm room I was about to share with a stranger.

This was it. College life had officially begun.

Should I cry? Laugh? Jump up and down on my pull-out bed?

Instead I called Daniel, a guy I had met that summer. "They're gone!" I wailed, seeking sympathy.

"Awesome," he said. "I'll be there in a sec."

And he was, in his sleek black Explorer, blaring Jane's Addiction. He slowed down just enough for me to hop in and then tore off to Sixth Street, Austin's music lane. We stormed a dive bar called the Black Cat, where a band called Soul Hat seized the stage. And suddenly I was dancing at my first live show. Drinking my first illicit beer. Celebrating my first night of freedom.

A long-locked girl soon joined me on the dance floor, her jeans slung low beneath her belly. A tattoo of a phoenix splayed across her back; silver rings festooned her nostrils. She looked cultured and artistic, like she read Nietzsche in coffeehouses all day, snuffing her cigarettes in empty espresso cups. I glanced down at my Gap jeans, Gap shirt, Gap socks, and gleaming white Keds. I had so much sophisticating to do.

But not that night! Daniel and I closed down the Black Cat and then roared up Congress Avenue toward the Texas State Capitol, all flood-lit and glorious. Daniel asked if I wanted to go out for pancakes.

"But it's 2 a.m.," I protested. I had never eaten at that hour in my life. He leaned over and patted my shoulder. "That's what you *do* in college."

So we did. Daniel didn't deposit me on my dormitory doorstep until 3:30, hours later than I'd ever returned before. Guilt churned in my belly: what would my new roommate think? I envisioned her standing in the middle of the room with a watch in her hand, wearing my mother's expression. Cautiously I turned the key and inched open our door. There was a T-shirt. Then jeans. A sock. A shoe. The trail of clothing led all the way to my roommate's bed, where she lay spread-eagle across her own Target comforter, clad only in underwear. This must be something else you *do* in college, I thought as I stripped off my clothes and did the same.

Lots of people from my high school moved to Austin that year to study at the University of Texas. Some even lived in my dorm. They roomed together, ate together, took classes together, drove back to Corpus Christi on weekends to visit their boyfriends together. One of them was my best friend—or, at least she was in high school. We spotted each other in the cafeteria one night, and she invited me to join them for dinner. Grateful to see familiar faces, I shared my recent adventures on Sixth Street. Had they heard of Soul Hat? They were my new favorite band! Had they tried Shiner Bock? It was my new favorite beer! Did they know Kerbey Lane served pancakes at 2 a.m.? Gingerbread, blueberry, buttermilk, and apple wheat! Was this city great, or what?

They listened politely until I had finished and then started gossiping about who took who and wore what and partied where at our senior prom, four months before. Ugh. That was not a night I cared to rehash. Nor, frankly, were any of my high school nights. I had never carved a niche or formed a tribe there. College, however, held great promise. For starters, there were nearly fifty thousand of us. We had eight hundred different student organizations to choose from, ranging from the Anarchists to the Log Cabin Republicans. Our two-hundred-page course catalogue offered classes on everything from astrophysics to harp, Marxist theory to Swahili.

Something crystallized as I looked around the dinner table that night. I had known these people since junior high school—elementary school, even. As long as I was with them, I would always be the teacher's pet who never let anyone copy her homework. The preppy who worked part-time at the Gap. The prude who broke up with a football player sophomore year and never got asked out again. The gringa-looking Mexican who spoke lousy Spanish.

Why stay the same boring person when I could completely reinvent myself?

In the months that followed, I rejected everything I had previously known—my high school friends, my hometown, my beloved breakfast *taquitos*—and explored only what was new. I ripped holes in my Gap jeans, tied flannel shirts around my waist, and stamped around in a clunky pair of Doc Martens. (I know, I know. But it was the mid-1990s!) Swore off *barbacoa* and moved into a militant vegetarian co-op. Enrolled in the journalism department and wrote profiles of drag queens. Studied the language of the farthest country I could fathom—Russian—and signed up for a semester abroad. Befriended people from the Ukraine, Ethiopia, Pakistan, Japan. Took up fencing. Rock climbing. Belly dancing.

And then something surprising happened. Despite the majesty of the Central Texas hill country, its wildflowers and its lakes, I started aching for the vast swaths of South Texas desert. However much I adored gingerbread pancakes at 2 a.m., I hungered for Abuelita's hand-rolled tortillas, warmed on the stove and slathered with honey and butter. Although I grew up thinking Corpus was the lamest place on the planet, my foreign exchange student friends made me realize it was just as exotic as their own faraway lands. "Your uncles are *cowboys*?" they would ask. "You grew up near *Mexico*?"

While I loved spinning stories about South Texas, I always cringed at the inevitable follow-up question: Why don't you speak Spanish, then? That was a complicated matter. Mom's (brown) side of the family had faced so much ridicule for their Spanish accents growing up, they decided not to pass it on. Spanish, for me, was the language of hushed whispers followed by laughter, of jokes I didn't get, of *quinceañeras* and rosaries and weddings and funerals, of *tios* in cowboy boots calling me *mija* and Abuelita in an apron feeding me beans. I couldn't say much more than *hola* and gravitated toward Dad's (white) side of the family because of it.

Yet Mom's was the heritage that won me a slot at UT. My "Hispanic Achievement" scholarship not only included funding but also a faculty adviser, a student mentor, and invitations to clubs and mixers. Although I enjoyed meeting the other scholarship recipients, I was intimidated by the hardships they had endured. Some were the children of migrant farm workers. A few had spent summers picking grapefruit themselves. They told lonely stories of walking into classrooms and realizing they were the only person of color there. Of being asked to speak on behalf of "their people" during group discussions. Of dirty looks and derogatory remarks. Because of my light complexion, I had experienced none of this, which plagued me with guilt. Did I deserve to be here?

"*Hell yes!*" Mom snapped when I called her up to ask. Maybe *I* hadn't faced overt discrimination, but my family sure had. My scholarship was ancestral payback time.

Well then. If I was destined to be a multi-culti karma girl, the least I could do was act like one. My sophomore year, I vowed to become the Hispanic "H" emblazoned on my transcript. I decorated my walls with images of Frida Kahlo and the Virgen de Guadalupe. Enrolled in Chicano politics classes. Devoured Latino literature. Got a job at the Admissions Office and fought to increase minority enrollment. Switched from Shiner Bock to margaritas. Dated a Colombian. Changed my white-bread middle name (Ann) to my mother's maiden name (Elizondo) and made everyone use it.

What truly solidified my connection to Mexicanidad, however, was leaving it entirely. During the spring semester of my junior year I studied abroad in Russia, and let me tell you: nothing makes you appreciate where you came from like ordering chips and salsa at a Tex-Mex restaurant in Moscow and being served Doritos and ketchup instead. That summer I traveled throughout the former Soviet Union and encountered scores of people who had risked their lives to uphold their native culture during the decades of government tyranny. Like the woman in Riga whose sister got shot for laying flowers at the feet of Milda, the lovely statue symbolizing Latvian independence that for years faced down a statue of Lenin. Or the elderly Lithuanian in Vilnius who spent his twenties in prison because he refused to denounce Judaism.

I finally started asking myself the hard questions: How did I lose such a fundamental part of who I am? And why had I never invested serious energy recovering it?

As soon as I returned to Texas that fall, I signed up for an intensive

Spanish language class that met from 10 to 5 every Saturday and spent my weekends conjugating verbs. That Christmas Mom and I traveled to Mexico City together, my first trip to the interior. There, I met cousins I had never known. Climbed a two-thousand-year-old pyramid. Danced in the Zocalo to the pounding of drums and shaking of dried bones. Developed a taste for *mole*. Bought a *rebozo*. Meditated history.

This, to me, is the true gift of college. Not only did it show me the world, but it also deepened my understanding of myself. At UT, I laid the foundation for the person I have since become: an author who has published two memoirs about cultural identity; a journalist who investigates social justice issues in the borderlands; a travel writer who has explored forty countries but who favors Mexico. Along the way I've discovered that life is a series of concentric circles. No matter how far I venture from Corpus Christi, it remains my gravitational center. And the older I get, the more my roots pull me home. It has become where I most want to be.

Now if you had told me any of this that first night in my college dorm, as I perched upon my Target comforter, I would have called you *loca*. Travel the whole world just to find my way home? Pancakes at 2 a.m. were hard enough to fathom!

But college, *mis hermanas*, is full of surprises. Grab it, seize it, make it your own. Throw away the Gap gear and get a little feral. Surround yourself with people who share your crazy dreams. Reinvent yourself any way you please. Your true self will eventually find you and guide you back home. But it's amazing to see who else you might become along the way.

Independence

IRIS GOMEZ

Independiente wasn't a nice word in the Spanish I learned at home. A villain, Independence arrived like darkness, a dangerous figure in the tales of lost innocence, *niñas* lured into committing *un disparate*, that ultimate disgrace otherwise known as teen pregnancy. Even adult women succumbed to his influence, only to end up on the streets of infamy. A woman alone, vulnerable in solitude, saved solely by her family: that was my childhood lesson on feminine independence.

But my own father had been MIA because of health problems most of my life, and I'd been left with my mother, a woman alone. Afraid, perhaps, of her own independence. So when I embarked upon my youthful career path, I knew there had to be more than those useless childhood lessons.

The college dormitory assigned to me was a red brick building that stood among maples and oaks rustling with pencil-yellow leaves beneath September blue skies. A *Highlights* magazine child's-eye view of college, many cultural miles from my little pink house in Miami.

I'd never slept in any home but that of my family. Never attended a "camp" or any "sleepaways" like my American girlfriends at school. That was the stuff of a foreign language my traditional Colombian *mami* had never quite mastered, even after a decade of living in the United States. Imagine her dismay when I declared my eighteen-year-old independence by accepting myself into a four-year sleepaway with scholarships and financial aid won by completing the many bewildering forms she had dutifully signed.

I'd been proud of my courage then, but now as my cabbie, huffing and puffing, heaved my enormous suitcase out of the trunk and dumped it onto the curb near Justin Morrill Hall, and then drove off in the direction from which I'd come, I vaguely wished I were still back there, a girl on the precipice of freedom and self-determination rather than here with nothing but her independence. Maybe it was easier to confront an adversary on familiar turf. Or maybe it was easier to confront the adversary you knew, like your own *mami*, than to stand up in the world with the wind blowing your hair and sweater about and a dark, atavistic feeling growing within you—that a dangerous adversary might be out there whom you just couldn't see.

I shivered, glanced down at my gigantic suitcase, then up at the distant dorm entrance, and back at my *maleta*. It was an immigrant's suitcase, the type only hard-working migrants dragged determinedly through airport terminals on leather belts—in order to bring back the treasures of the modern age to loved ones in the Third World. With a sigh, I bent down to lift up my treasure chest of worldly goods, but the New World proved too much too soon, and my knees buckled. Awkwardly, I twisted around and plopped myself, butt down, on the spine of the suitcase. I considered ladylike options for shoving or kicking the suitcase up to the distant building entrance while I surveyed the people who bustled around me. Mothers and fathers and the little brothers and sisters of *americanas* were zipping gaily between the station wagons and dorm with rolled-up rugs, bulletin boards, cozy lamps, and a potpourri of Puff the Magic Dragon fancifulness. From my perch on the suitcase, I affected a distanced demeanor and watched while pretending not to feel scared or alone. After a while, a grizzled father came along, kindly offering to help me—a temporary rescue from my status *sin familia*, this new "independence."

I'd always known that where I slept didn't really matter, of course, despite the traditional upbringing. Even whom I slept with turned out to be a very peripheral part of my college education. The hardest lesson of independence was changing my relationship with my mother. I missed her, first of all, because of those things she did for me that I suspected, deep down, no one in the world would ever do for me again. Silly things, like patiently pulling out every last clump of disgusting hair from my ancient hairbrush or emergency hand-washing some essential garment at the last minute for an event I suddenly *had* to attend.

But much more than simply missing my mother and her acts of devotion, I felt horribly guilty for leaving her. So I tried my best to replicate as much of our precollege interaction as possible during school vacations and on our required-at-least-once-a-week telephone calls—calls in which we attempted a long-distance process of me solving as many home problems as possible, as if I still lived there. Later she'd mail me the packages of official correspondence from the government, bill collectors, and so on, that I promptly answered for the family and then explained back to her in plain Spanish. As much as these unusual burdens amused or perplexed my American friends at school and often weighed upon my student shoulders, I wanted to remain my mother's trusty eldest *confidente* and adviser on everything from my younger siblings' struggles with the public school system to the mysteries of debt collection to the infinite array of American policies or customs that continued to distress and confuse her. I shared bits of my college experience with her too, focusing on the parts likely to comfort her and reassure her that I was exactly the same girl I'd always been—attending church, doing good deeds, earning high marks. The telephone wire simulated an emotional umbilical cord that had never been cut.

A consequence of my liking school so well was that I swiftly recognized that I would be going on beyond an undergraduate education. The first time I floated that idea during an early trip home, though, Mami promptly flushed it down the toilet as *pura faltedad*—some silly nonsense she wouldn't hear talk of again. So I kept my nonsense private, resumed the simulated phone life with zeal, and tried to send extra money home from my paltry part-time earnings and loan proceeds—convinced that if I contributed to solving more of the family's problems, my mother might not need me so much down the road when I'd have to move on.

But problems at home didn't seem to end. New ones replaced those that got resolved. When my uncle died my junior year and my father's fragile health deteriorated, I took a Greyhound bus home, a thirty-six-hour bus ride, to help out my mother. But things had settled by the time I arrived, and there wasn't much left for me to do; surprisingly, the family had rallied without me. I was more taken aback when I witnessed my mother, not a smoker, puffing on a cigarette in the back of the funeral parlor all by herself. Of course, the usual guilt kept me from reporting on my LSAT results.

As graduation approached, and along with it the necessity of confronting my mother with the news that I'd decided to go to law school—*in Massachusetts*—I began to rue how poorly I'd prepared her for my intended career plans. Instead of slowly laying the groundwork, as marriage-track girlfriends had done when acclimating their mothers to gradual and greater exposure to The Beloved, I'd offered precious little to account for why my future should now take me another great distance from home. How could I tell her that the temporary sleepaway had morphed into a life-away? Could noble Odysseus betray the faithful Penelope waiting at home all those years?

These epic difficulties kept me procrastinating for months, but of course the cliché of reckoning comes eternal. One Sunday night I squared my shoulders, took a deep breath, and picked up the phone. Immediately, before I could chicken out, I launched into the dreaded subject. This wasn't a regular conversation at first, though, since I played the part of the lawyerette, fast-talking and pumping my mother with impressive details about rankings and professors' recommendations and useless admissions data in the most primitive form of argumentation children the world over know—denying your opponent a chance to get a word in edgewise.

When eventually I *had* to catch my breath, Mami's response seemed slow in coming—or perhaps deceptively mild. In a quiet voice she wondered, weren't there any law schools in Miami, *mijita*? As I braced myself for the fight ahead, the tail end of her question faded a little, as if she didn't really expect me to answer—so I certainly didn't try to. Instead, I resumed a spirited defense of that great bastion of legal education, Boston, Massachusetts. Mami listened peacefully for a good while, and when I nervously gave her another chance to speak, she offered only an *Ah sí*, if she were actually taking in all my gibberish. For some reason, she didn't seize the chance to fight back with her own rhetorical arsenal, the well-kept inventory of biblical teachings the Apostles invented to keep us compliant—nor did she fight back with any tears. She didn't say much at all. Perplexing me further, she started to explain some problem she was having with a neighbor that required her to *repicar el mango*, as if she'd moved on to the more pressing issue of cutting back the mango tree she'd worked so hard to nurture. A picture flashed in front of me then of Mami, standing in our kitchen in her *chancletas* while gazing out the window at her old tree. A small yearning passed through me, but I shook it off as the sentimental vestige of the younger girl who used to stand beside her at the window. We began to drift into our customary exchange of problems-and-solutions until that river ran its course and left us in the simple bedrock of our *cuídate muchos*.

After we hung up, I didn't get up from the couch right away. Confused by my mother's strangely benign acceptance of my *noticias*, I stared at the beige telephone—the solid anchor for so many conversations. Not only had my months of anxiety proved completely unnecessary, but the telephone truths I'd been telling myself for the past four years had dissolved, a childish lie. While Mami had been off quietly practicing life without me, I'd been the one who'd forgotten to practice the *I* in *independence*.

Stories She Told Us

DAISY HERNÁNDEZ

My mother is a short woman with a familiar face. As a child, I see her in my social studies textbook, in the pictures of women and men and children arriving at Ellis Island. The women in the photographs are stoic with the obligatory bleak faces and thick eyebrows, their lips as thin as Mami's. The caption next to their pictures begins: "They came . . ."

What comes next varies. They came looking, they came searching, they came hoping. The verbs are always more lively and ambitious than the women in the pictures whose faces suggest another refrain: "What the hell are you looking at?"

The year I turned twenty-six, a women's publishing house e-mailed to ask if I'd be interested in editing a book of personal essays about feminism by young women of color. The idea was that while many women's studies departments were, by 2000, actively teaching the books of Audre Lorde, Gloria Anzaldúa, and Barbara Smith, young feminists of color were, as a group, absent from most syllabi. How were young Chicanas and Arab and African American women—that is, women who came of age in the 1980s and 1990s—thinking of feminism?

I agreed to the project, and a few months later the manila folders began arriving from around the country. My coeditor and I sifted through the essays, carefully choosing pieces, calling contributors, supplying them with copious line edits. Within the year, we were ready to arrange the chapters into sections.

This was when we noticed a small curiosity: many of the essays could be filed in the section she and I had plainly labeled: "MOTHER."

This shouldn't have been surprising. After sex, mothers are arguably the second favored topic of public conversation. American cinema and literature and viral YouTube videos brim with cruel mothers, smothering mothers, martyr mothers, controlling mothers, gossiping mothers, and shopaholic mothers. For the most part, we read, we watch, we hit replay, and we feel that that's our mom.

But I was only twenty-six. I thought it was novel that we were young Dominican and Indian and African American women, women from New York and Kansas and Texas, and we had all turned instinctively to writing about our mothers. We described what they had suffered (generally they suffered), retold their stories, which we hadn't seen in books, and enumerated how much they had given us.

I had already done my part in this. Writing for *Ms.* magazine, I had recounted how I had tried to woo my mother to feminism:

> At the end of my lecture in Spanish to my mother on the economic oppression of immigrant women and how she and the other mujeres need to organize at the factory and demand their back pay, she nods and asks, "¿Qué es eso—feminis?"
>
> "Good question!" I answer in Spanish. "What is a feminist..."
>
> I pause. I don't know what to say, or rather I don't know what to say in Spanish, my mother's language. I don't even know how to say the word feminist. Feminista? Una feminist?
>
> It strikes me that I have gone to college, read feminist theory, learned about women's rights and now I have no way of bringing it home to my working-class community where women call their children in from the street at night in every language except English.

I wanted my mother to know about feminism because I had no doubt that once she understood the ideas, she would be liberated. And liberated she must be—from factory work, from minimum wage, from xenophobia, from my father's alcoholism, from my father himself. Saved, actually. If I'm being honest, the verb would be *saved*.

The white board stands on a tripod and is magnetized, which makes it into a sheet of paper that has come alive. I place upon that alabaster landscape the plastic magnets in the shape of letters: *a b c d e*. The letters are bursts of blue and red and orange, and to me at the age of nine they feel precious. They are not letters, not even *letras*, which in Spanish sounds so dignified. They are what makes the day possible. They are the tiny springs and steady hands of a watch. They are reliable.

My mother, I have decided, needs to have them—in English.

I stand at the white board on the second floor of our little house. My mother sits before me and the precious letters.

"Repeat after me," I instruct in Spanish and then switch to English. "*A, b, c.*"

My mother grins. She's not at this moment like the women reaching Ellis Island, glaring at the flash of cameras. She's not bracing herself for a new world of sounds and terrors. She's soft and round like a spool of thread. Her hair is the dark red of a setting sun, the result of dying it with Clairol. Her pale face is tired and satisfied. She spends weekdays steeped in fabric and thread and women's voices at the factory. On weekends, she cleans the house, washes our school uniforms, takes in extra sewing work, bundles us up in coats for trips to Bergenline Avenue.

She repeats after me in English—*a, b, c*—but then something grabs her attention. The sound of my younger sister's voice in the other room. The clock signaling the hour for the *telenovela*.

I scowl, glare, and whine. "*Pon atención*," I demand, my jaw as tense as that of my own teacher.

My mother feigns the guilty face of the chastised and tries again. But then something bigger happens (something is always happening). The phone rings. My sister wants more soda. An auntie arrives. And my mother is off with that vicious promise of "*siguimos más tarde*," as if learning English were a game that could be interrupted, paused, and resumed at leisure.

My memory argues with me now. It wasn't a magnetized white board. It was a notebook or a child-sized blackboard. I wasn't nine. I must have been ten or eleven.

The uncontested ground, the one thing my memory and I don't bicker about, is the letters—the luring curves of the *a* and *b* and *c*—and the absolute and aching need I had that my mother learn them, that she have them in her mouth, in her bones and fingernails, my complete assurance that these sounds would save her, which is to say that they would make her happy, would give her what she needed to argue with the forelady at the factory who failed to pay on time.

I thought language was all a woman needed.

My mother tells the same stories every night.

In her stories she is the heroine, the *innocente* who scares easily and whom everyone knows to be gentle and kind. She is not ambitious. In fact, she wants nothing more than to marry a good man with blond hair and blue eyes and have children who look like him. This is what she tells my sister and me when the lights are turned off. She rubs our backs and whispers stories into our dark hair.

At fifteen she arrives at a factory to work. It is the 1960s; the violence is in the jungles, and Mami is in the capital. She wears clean, sturdy shoes and a navy knee-length skirt. Her dark hair frames a plump face. She has never been in a factory, but the nuns taught her to sew, and her mother's family had the connection.

The factories.

The only women she has known are her mother, her sisters, her aunties, and the nuns, all of them decent women, God-fearing women. But the factory in Bogotá teems with a different sort of woman, the kind who talks from her sewing machine about abstract subjects Mami has only heard allusions to: men, sex, pleasure, jealousy.

The factory women spit curse words. They do not go to church with their mothers. They do not say hello each morning. They do not pretend to be friendly.

But it is good work. Sewing. It is also solitary work. It is much like writing. Spools, thread, and needles. Mami takes yards of cotton and polyester, cuts, assembles, and sews; at the end she has a piece done, *un sweter*.

She's good at it, and she can do it anywhere. It is a profession *sin idioma*. It is respectable work despite the factory women who have those dreadful words creaking out of them. "I'd never heard anything like it," my mother whispers.

My mother's story is Victoria Ruffo's story. Not the real Victoria, but the *telenovela* star, the dark-haired heroine of classic soap operas like *Simplemente María, Triunfo del Amor*, and, of course, *Victoria*.

The plot line varies, but not the fictional Victoria. She is the pious Mexican mother who lives for her children and her husband, who oversees the kitchen and balances the family and business checkbooks, who is patient and polite even as she suffers. They have the same face, my mother and Victoria: endless curves, bushy eyebrows, small lips.

It would be inaccurate to say that Victoria is rescued at the end of each *telenovela*. She is rewarded with a lover, that's all, like the women arriving at Ellis Island to be bestowed with a better life.

But first, before any thought of a prize can be considered, Victoria must bear the trials and tribulations of being a good woman.

She has doubts.

The plane ticket is tucked in her pocketbook, and my mother, she has doubts, the kind she has to keep to herself.

It had felt innocent at first, akin to a new love. The invitation from a friend to visit New Jersey, her sister's encouragement and money. The promises of how easy it would be over there, the daydreams of dollar bills like sheets of satin in her hand.

She would earn real money, that's what everyone said, and in *dolares*, more than she could make at the factory in Bogotá. She is twenty-eight and unmarried. She has no reason to not go. *Y ademas*, the men over there have hair the color of the sun and eyes clear like the ocean at San Andres, which she has never seen but that isn't the point. She is lucky to be asked to go, and so, yes, she has said she will go for a month, set eyes on that famous country where mountains are made of steel and glass, and she will work to earn the money to pay back her sister and then some.

But now it is true what they say: the time of leaving is the time of reckoning. It's December 8, 1970. It's a Tuesday morning in Bogotá, and my mother is dressed in a dark pantsuit. The newspapers are chatty. There's the war in Vietnam and in the mountains of Colombia and also a new development: a socialist president in Chile. Salvador Allende has been in office a month. The world is a series of explosions, of maybe this will happen or that, but my mother is quiet. She is busy thinking about what the Jewish forelady at the factory told her.

The woman has been to the United States, and she says it runs like a beast. It is a hungry, ill-tempered, unforgiving place. And my mother, who has never left her mother's home, the poverty and wide *abrazos* of these streets, the choking embrace of a dozen brothers and sisters, nephews and nieces, she nurses doubts and keeps mute. The ticket has been paid for, after all. It cost her sister a lot of money. It's nothing that can be changed.

I imagine her picking up her one suitcase and giving her bed a long look. Then seeing she has no place to hide her doubt, she swallows it whole and shuts the door.

It's hard to tell from reading about 1970 if Americans wanted to save anyone at that point. There's a weariness to the reporting in the gringo daily newspapers from December of that year, most of it due, of course, to Vietnam. Seymour Hersh has informed the world that American soldiers murdered hundreds of unarmed Vietnamese women and children in My Lai. The women drew their babies to their bellies as the bullets made their deadly descent. Protestors in South Vietnam are shouting "Yankee, go home!" and the rest of the world, Americans included, are beginning to share the sentiment.

Vietnam catches my attention as a child because we never get to it. Year after year my social studies class begins with the Pilgrims, lingers on the American Revolution, details the Constitution, prances through the Civil War and women's right to vote, dances around the start of the Cold War, but by the end of the school year, it is slightly miraculous if we've arrived at Rosa Parks sitting on the bus. It is 1985, 1986, 1987, 1989, and I am ten, then eleven, and so on, and each year as May approaches, I am expecting that this time—surely this time—we'll finally reach the chapter on Vietnam. But we don't.

The war in Vietnam came to have many meanings. I'm struck by the idea that it was a pause, however brief, from the notion that Americans could or should save anyone. When people shudder "another Vietnam," I don't believe they mean the endlessness of that war but the pause in the narrative of American grandiosity.

The pause, unfortunately, didn't last. Forty years later, American celebrities are saving Africa, American college students are saving sweatshop workers, and Glenn Beck is saving America.

While I refuse to believe that Glenn and I have anything in common beyond inhabiting Planet Earth, I can't ignore the history we share. It's a *cultura* of empire, a zealot anthem of "We know best," an impulse that when we see a picture of women and men and children arriving at Ellis Island, we write: they came in hope of a better life. We don't note that they came because the wars in Italy and Germany clawed at people's dreams, because the American government was desperate for white Protestants to fill out the corners of a brown country, because people make mistakes.

The stories my mother tells at bedtime are crowded with monsters.

There are the factory women who curse, the woman who invites her to come to the States, the woman who uses her as a distraction while she shoplifts. Sometimes, the monster is a sister, the one who lent her the cash to leave Colombia.

In the States Mami expected to find dollars plastered to sidewalks like fallen autumn leaves. "That's what they used to say," she whispers. "That it grew on trees."

But nothing is what it was supposed to be.

The week she arrives, a lieutenant—one, single white man—is charged with the massacre at My Lai. Thirteen members of the Black Panthers are accused in Manhattan of planning to blow up department stores. Twenty miles south of Jersey City, where my mother has found work at a factory, men and women are recovering from explosions at an oil refinery. The bombs were reportedly to protest the imprisonment of Angela Davis and Bobby Seale.

My mother finds herself working three jobs, desperate to pay off the debt to her sister. Once the debt is gone, it is another sister who wants come to the States. And then another who needs medical treatment.

At twenty-eight, she lies in bed in New Jersey *solita*, and she cries and wonders, "What did I do?"

My bold question more than thirty years later: "What did you think of doing?"

"What could I do?" she answers, her face now wrinkled at the corner of her eyes, the corner of her lips, the cheeks still soft, still circular.

"You could have gone back to Colombia, you could have—"

"I owed your *tía* the money."

It's something about the way she says this—"I owed your *tía* the money," a snapping in her voice, a trace of bitterness—that makes me pause.

The year I start college, I know so much more than my mother did when she left for the States. I know at least three curse words in Spanish and twice as many in English. I know that girls can be atheists. I know women can live alone. Granted, I haven't met these women, the ones who live without aunties, but I've read about them in *Glamour* magazine and watched them on *90210*.

Like my mother, I am expecting to become Victoria Ruffo: beautiful, *casada*, tragic. But I'm also expecting to be unstoppable like the bionic woman and divorced and perfectly happy like Kate and Allie. I am still singing along to Salt-n-Pepa, who are commanding men to push it (though push what I'm not exactly sure at that age). I write a brief essay in grammar school about what I would do if I were elected not vice president of the United States but *presidente*. My political platform consists of universal child care as well as government-sponsored manicures. By executive order men would have to buy the women in their lives diamond rings.

The men themselves are a lost cause—not just my father with his alcoholism or my boyfriend, Julio, with his janitor job, but Ronald Reagan as well. The president insists he has no memories of secretly financing a war in Central America. Fidel Castro isn't doing any better, either. The Soviet Union has collapsed, and by 1993, there's less of everything—*pesos*, potatoes, *huevos*. The country is entering into what the communists will call a "special period." Special because it's not supposed to last. In California propositions are voted on to strip immigrants of public services, of bilingual education, of that elusive thread called dignity.

For all my pride about how much I know, I don't know about the social justice movements of the 1970s. I don't know the word *feminism*. I don't know why white people are leaving town, buying homes further north, or why there are elderly Latinos working at McDonald's. I don't understand why there are never enough doctors and dentists at the clinic at Englewood Hospital. I can't grasp why the waiting rooms are filled by women and children, brown mostly, Latinas for the most part.

My mother doesn't understand how the woman can love her child.

She's seven or eight at the time, not in Bogotá yet. She's still in Ramiriquí, a dot of a town a few hours outside of the capital. She attends mass with her mother, stands next to her in the pews, bows her head, and catches sight of the woman. The woman is there with her own child. He's an ugly boy; he has dark skin.

My mother is incredulous. She turns to her mother and asks in a whisper: "How can she love that child? He's *feo*."

Her mother smiles or scowls or shakes her head. That's not the important part. What matters is what she says: "No matter how ugly, a child is always beautiful to his mother."

This information shocks my mother. She can't imagine that it's true, that love could ask nothing of its beloved.

The only reason I take a women's studies class in college is that it's required.

The professor has short hair and a curvaceous, overweight body, much like my mother. Unlike my mother, the professor suggests this: "Consider the way you are you sitting right now."

I have my legs crossed and my arms on the desk. It is the way I've always sat in class. The professor wonders aloud: "Why are you sitting this way?" Then she adds that oftentimes we are taught to sit in certain ways on account of being girls or boys. Crossing your legs isn't natural; it's what we're expected to do as *mujeres*.

I consider the idea and uncross my legs. It feels strange. My knees are as far apart as a boy's and that is almost as uncomfortable as realizing that it's never occurred to me before to do this.

The professor suggests that maybe we don't have to cross our legs. Maybe a woman can have her knees as far away from each other as my boyfriend does when he is watching *fútbol*. Maybe we don't have to do anything else that we have been told we must do as young women. Maybe we don't have to wear underwire bras, blue eye shadow, high heels. Maybe these social customs are part of the larger reasons why women aren't paid as much as men and why we do the brunt of the housework while husbands take buses to Bergenline for cigars. Maybe it is hard to know if we cross our legs or go on diets because it's what we want for ourselves or because it's what we see in music videos and commercials.

The professor's words feel mysterious and intriguing, as if I have stumbled across a new religion, a world with an entirely different set of *costumbres*.

My curiosity is piqued.

I start sitting on the subway with my legs not just uncrossed but apart like a boy's. I am wearing pants and I'm not sure what I expect will happen but I hold my breath and keep my eyes on the floor littered with gum wrappers and scraps of newspaper. I feel terrified. I am violating a rule of some kind. I glance around once and then twice and find that no one is staring at my uncrossed legs.

I take my experiment to the buses. There I begin to notice that men generally claim the armrests. Women, by and large, silently and as if by collective agreement, treat the armrest on the bus as a *frontera*, a border between you and me, between my pocketbook and yours, my shoulders and yours.

But not men. They spread their legs. They lay not just their elbows but the entire length of their arms on the armrest. They cross the border, over and over again.

This isn't true of all men but of many, and I begin to wonder what would happen if I wanted to share the armrest. My silent war begins.

I start taking a seat on the bus and placing my elbow on whatever small portion of the armrest is not claimed. Sometimes, the man moves his elbow to give me room, and sometimes he surrenders the entire armrest. Other times, he pushes back, the bulk of his forearm pressing against the pointy bone of my elbow. In this scenario I find that the key is to not give up even a fraction of my territory (yes, the Palestinian people come to mind). I keep my boney elbow in place and pretend to read the book in my hands. I keep my eyes on the same line while the enemy pushes. Sometimes, the conflict spans the time it takes the bus to roll down a few blocks. Sometimes, I surrender. More often, I start winning the armrests. I begin expecting to get the armrest.

These memories seem so silly to me now. Was there really a time when I thought it was unladylike or just plain weird to have the armrest? How was it possible that I both believed I could be president and at the same time that I shouldn't take up space?

But it was, and not just for me. For this was my generation's inheritance from the women's movement, from the civil rights movement, even from the gay liberation movement: the expectation of being included and the inability to imagine what that would actually feel like.

I am wondering why feminism as a body of ideas, of questions, of assertions, attracted me so much in college. Yes, it was about my *piernas* and elbows, but other girls heard the same lecture from the same professor and felt nothing in them stir. Why did my high school friends join the sororities, while I signed up for the Feminist Collective? Why for that matter was it my mother and not her brothers or sisters who first left Colombia?

"I got the invitation," my mother answers. "I knew this lady who had worked with me in Colombia, and she said, 'If I ever get to the United States, I'll send for you.'"

I'm willing to concede that I'm a memoirist, which is to say a romantic, that I search for meaning where there is in fact only a flat piece of paper, an invitation. Still, I can't suppress the little voice in me that says: Oh, but it must mean something, Mami. You were brave. You wanted to know this other world.

What is it in me that refuses to believe in the mundane? That wants to believe the United States or feminism is indeed a country where a woman can have a better life and not simply another piece of land where a woman can work and live and make a home?

In Texas, a social work professor recently described to me her students who go on to identify as feminists and work for social change like this: "They're the kids who come to your class and get more pissed off each week."

And so it was with me as a litany of questions began intruding into my days and nights during college: Why do advertisers sell cars by showing bikini-clad women bending over automobiles? Why are the women on *Sábado Gigante* skits the ones with fake boobs? Why are all the jokes on Spanish radio about men who are feminine?

My sister and I want to know what my mother dreamed of before, as in before us.

My mother stares at us, confused, embarrassed. She hasn't understood the question. My sister, a social worker, adds, "Did you dream of going to school? Of buying a house?"

Now a smile touches my mother's lips. She understands and looks at us as if we really are silly girls. "A house? No." She shakes her head. "I never dreamed of having a house of my own."

She is a practical woman.

When my father proposes to her on a park bench in North Bergen, her answer is "I don't have papers"—not the frenzy of "Yes, I love you," or the cautiousness of "I need to think about it," but the practical. *No tengo papeles.*

She wasn't a citizen. She wasn't even a resident. On paper, she wasn't even a tourist anymore.

The Feminist Collective at my college has organized an event to talk about sex. Sitting in a circle, we're told to write on an index card the best moments of our sex lives and the worst and to do so anonymously. We scribble our answers and the moderator shares them aloud. The best moments include multiple orgasms, gentle lovemaking, the sort of thing you read about in *Glamour.* The worst includes index card after index card of sexual abuse.

While I have yet to read feminist books that describe the "aha" moment— that moment when a person realizes their experiences are not just personal but part of a much larger tapestry—this is my aha. I glimpse for the first time that it's not just me and maybe one other friend but many of us who know sexual violence. This isn't a secret but a matter to be discussed, shared, and even protested.

So I march. During the Take Back the Night march, I walk alongside students and professors, chanting, cringing at the boys who howl at us, aware that the only Latinas are me and Fanny, relieved that she's there all bold and beautiful. Later that night I listen, only listen, as white women tell their stories. A few boys sit with us, and one of them wants to know what he should do. He's upset. He has a girlfriend, a sister, a mother. "What do I do?" he pleads.

He's told to listen, to be there with her, and then something even more strange: to not rescue her. To consider the possibility that men are told to rush in and fix the problem, but the woman in his life isn't a problem. She isn't even broken.

My mother loves to tell the story of how she took me to Canada.

I am nine and twelve and nineteen, and each time annoyed. "That doesn't count!" I interject.

The lawyer said it did count.

In those years, the mid-1970s, the border with Canada wasn't a solid mass, nothing made of granite, but rather a door that swung open, that allowed women like my mother to claim they were out of the country so they could be sponsored by their American husbands or in this case a Cuban husband turned American on paper.

"You were in Canada," she croons, even now, so many decades later. "*En la barriga.*"

Naturally, I love the notion that my impulse to save my mother began at the border when she was almost five months pregnant with me. In that most primitive of states, I must have felt her pulse quicken when immigration officials examined her face. I must have felt the pressure in her throat and then that splendid release when the door swung the other way and she was on her way back to New Jersey in the car with my father driving.

"What did they say?" I ask about the agents. How did they want her to prove that she was really married, that it wasn't fake?

She tilts her chin into the air. "What could they say? I was pregnant. What more proof is there?"

I shake my head, grinning despite myself. My mother hasn't heard the term *anchor baby*, and if she did, she would insist that this is not what she meant.

It's me. It's me who is hearing it that way, who enjoys imagining a time when my mother could show off her swollen belly to white men in uniforms with that universal gesture of smug arrogance only pregnant women are entitled to. It's me who loves the image of my mother almost five months pregnant and snapping, "What the hell are you looking at?"

But the truth is she was probably scared. She hates places where people wear uniforms or suits: hospitals, embassies, banks. Besides, she says now that it was other way around, that crossing the border into Canada, I was the one who kicked in protest. I was the one who wanted to be heard, to be felt, to be taken into account.

It's late in the afternoon. The sunlight is showering the college library table with its golden light. It's my last year of college, and I am reading and taking notes. The author is Mitchell. That's her name. Juliet Mitchell. A feminist writing about Marx and socialism. In her book she's describing the role of women at home and at work, how the family was the unit of production before factories sprung up, before mass production ravished Western Europe, before capitalism began its treacherous rise. *Familia* itself, she suggests, may be a construction, nothing real and solid but an idea of how we should live.

She's writing a version of history—our communal memoir, as Patricia Hampl calls it—that I haven't read before, and I am mesmerized, not only because of the content but also the fact of its existence, of a story I haven't heard before and yet a story that makes sense to me.

Tía Chuchi laments people who became communists in the 1960s and 1970s. "It's all because of the friends they had," she says. "The friends get them into it, wash their brains."

I disagree. "There has to be something already in a person that makes them open to it." A person may already be asking why the hospital clinic doesn't have more doctors, why the women in the waiting room are Latinas.

"It's the friends," Tía insists, putting down the novel she's reading. She's enraged with the protagonist of the novel who is becoming a revolutionary in Uruguay. "I'm so angry I could shake this girl."

My mother wouldn't shake anyone over politics. The most she would do would be to frown at the girl in the novel and ask with a worried look: "Do you think that's the best thing to do?" referring to storing rifles under her mattress.

I can't help but feel a fondness still for that day at the college library, the book by Mitchell, the moment when I lifted my head from those pages, and the sunlight poured over me. Outside was the sky, a fierce wintery gray, and a few trees naked of leaves and the school buildings were squatting as always, but the world had expanded, had made room for other stories, other ideas, other perspectives. I did not feel saved, not at all, but changed, deeply changed, as if I had been handed *un obsequio*, a gift.

My mother doesn't remember any feminists in Colombia, but my auntie does. "They marched in the streets," Tía Chuchi says.

I smile and wait for one of her good stories, a story where a feminist risks her life and that of her child to protest the cruelties of a machismo culture.

But my auntie doesn't launch into a good story. "What else?" I prompt. Her eyebrows gather as she tries to recall. "They held signs."

Years later, reading *El Tiempo*, Colombia's newspaper, from the year my mother left the country, I come across this brief article: The week before Mami boarded the plane, there was an Encuento Nacional Femenino. Union leaders, women union leaders, urged for action against illiteracy among women and demanded a large-scale program of family planning.

And this, my favorite line: They were adamant that the problems faced by working-class women were not theirs alone but were the very problems confronting the entire *clase obrera* in Colombia. Women's problems were not to be pigeon-holed; they were men's issues, as well.

When my first poem is published in college, I show it to my mother. I'm proud, even though it's a personal essay masquerading as a poem. "See, Mami? Here you are. See? There's the word *mami*."

She smiles, catching sight of the word standing alone in a landscape of English nouns and pronouns and verbs. Later, she argues with Tía Chuchi, who can't find the word in the poem. "I don't see *mami* here," Tía complains. "There's a *mother*, not a *mami*."

The poem is long. Four typed pages. My mother pulls it toward her. "I saw it myself. Let me look. No, no, it was toward the end. It said Julio Iglesias, too."

After college, sitting in my cubicle at New York University Press, where I have the fancy title of "editorial assistant," I open the *Village Voice* one day, and a stunning black woman is on the cover of an insert. It's the writer Edwidge Danticat with her flawless dark skin and those tender round eyes. She's doing a reading with a group of women writers called Women in Literature and Letters, or will for short. Three Latinas—a Chicana, Dominican, and Colombian—have started the group. They're producing writing workshops and calling themselves "women writers of consciousness."

Standing on the subway platform, I ask my friend Corinne, "What do you think 'writers of consciousness' means?"

"I don't know," she admits. After a pause, she adds, "It makes me think of losing consciousness and being resuscitated."

We laugh and shake our heads, and I sign up for a WILL writing workshop. I don't care what they call themselves; I want to find other women who are writing, and if they're women of color that's even better.

It's Marta Lucia, *la colombiana*, who explains the consciousness part. I try following her words, but they sound like a chemistry experiment or one of those poems that's littered with images but no spine of a story. I smile politely and nod enthusiastically. She's clearly so passionate about her stories, and I don't want to hurt her feelings.

In a separate conversation her *comadre*, Angie Cruz, translates for me: "We believe we can change the world through writing about it."

They give me the titles of books: *This Bridge Called My Back, Borderlands, Loving in the War Years, Sister Outsider*, anything by bell hooks and Ana Castillo. They are feminists—Angie and Marta and the writers of these books (all of this is taken for granted)—but a different type from what I met in college. These women talk about women on welfare and women in *fabricas*, women who move back and forth across borders, men who are awful to their women and men who are afraid, even men who tremble and want to be loved. They talk about men, for men too have to be liberated.

At one of the first WILL workshops, I squeeze onto a sofa along with other women in a borrowed room at New York University and listen to a South Asian woman in her twenties read her story.

It's about a girl whose family home is burned down in an act of racial hatred. The girl's father is distraught and enraged; the girl is standing apart, watching the scene. She hated the house in a way similar to how she hates her father, who lorded over that home, over her girl life, over her mother.

I listen in shock. It is the first time I have known someone close to my age writing about loving and hating where you come from, about what happens between a girl and the father in this world, about the terrible things that the father does and the awful things the world does to him, and the mother standing in that bitter silence, mute. Running clear under the story is the emotional truth of the relationships, the love the girl feels for her parents, for their home, an emotion that is nevertheless bound to hatred, anguish, and despair.

For me, this had all been a very private matter. But here is a woman, a South Asian woman, sitting right in front of me, having written about what I knew to be just my own life.

The memory flares up of the day a city official came to our home. It was some kind of inspection since my father was itching in those years to expand the house, and the white man arrived with a clipboard, stepping into our small home, examining windows and fire alarms, all the while scribbling notes.

It was a very old house. It had no basement, no closets, no doors on the bedrooms. The living room was a tiny box of a room. The kitchen was the main room on the first floor.

Standing in our kitchen, the city official muttered, "This house should be condemned."

"What did he say?" my mother asked me in Spanish.

"*Nada.*"

It was nothing for I didn't know the Spanish word for *condemned*. I didn't know how to find words that would say, this photograph on the wall, this pot of black beans, this radio that we listen to each day—he's saying none of this matters. It should be not thrown away but bulldozed.

I was twelve or thirteen at the time, and a hatred swept into me, leaving me angry not with the city official but with my mother and my father. I blamed them for the house, for this man with the clipboard, for this cruelty.

My mother only has one harsh word to utter about her own mother: she took in the strays.

Her mother gave birth to twelve children, one of whom died. But informally Abuelita took in other children. Anyone who walked through her front door was given a boiled egg, a tea, an *empanada*. This frustrated my mother to no end. "I'd bring her cakes and pastries, and she'd given them to whoever showed up." She scowls, as if the memory didn't belong to the long-ago past but to yesterday.

My mother was working then at the factory in Bogotá. She had her own money. She could buy her mother these treats, and I wonder if this wasn't her way of saving her mother. If she didn't want to free her mother of the poverty of earlier years by gifting her with sugar and dough and butter.

Sometimes, I think I understand my mother's first days at the factories because it's how I felt the first year I worked in an office after college: Shocked.

To begin with, it's a bizarre feeling to walk into a space occupied neither by embroidery machines nor cash register machines, but an open floor plan where desks snuggle up to walls, bookshelves bulge with books and magazines and manuscripts, and I have my own phone with multiple lines and even voicemail with its startling red light.

It's at an office job where I first come across an issue of *ColorLines* magazine. I can't remember the cover now, just that it said something about race and culture and that it was still a new idea for me that you could take the magazines home.

I had worked at McDonalds and a ShopRite supermarket and a Jenny Craig's, and at those jobs there was an unspoken accusation that we would steal. We being anyone who worked there. And we did.

We snuck extra burgers to our friends; we went home with nail polish that cost us fifty cents instead of three dollars and fifty cents. We stole for ourselves and our families and our friends and sometimes even strangers not because we needed to but because we could. It was the tiniest taste we had of power.

But here, in an office in New York City, a person could take home a magazine and it was expected that you would bring it back and somehow this made you want to bring it back.

I went home with a copy of *ColorLines* magazine, and it was in those thin pages where I first read that maybe women and men of color didn't live in poor neighborhoods because there was something intrinsically wrong with them. It's not that anyone had ever said this, but it was understood from the way other people talked about us and our homes and in the ways we talked about ourselves. This magazine, however, held a different story.

Elected officials and city administrators created policies in black ink about where mass transit lines would be, about what kind of housing would be built and where, all of it, if not inspired, then at least molded by ideas about race, about class, about what sort of people should live where and have what kind of services.

It was there in fine black ink that women, widows really, white widows actually, should be unmarried to receive help. Then the fights for black women to receive that help, and then more ink for the litany of accusations: loose, whores, welfare queens.

I read these articles and began ever so slowly to understand that words did not just metaphorically shape our days but did so quite literally.

My mother would never use the word *hell*, not even *diablo*. She doesn't believe in vulgarities.

The closest she comes in Spanish is to say, "I'm sending him to the PM." PM is shorthand for *puta mierda*, which is like saying, "I'm sending him to fucking hell," except that it sounds worse in Spanish because the word *puta* is so strong in the mouth like spit flung at a child. And *mierda* is a low rumble, the beginning of a growl or a hiss, an animal's word really.

I asked once. I don't know how old I was, but I asked. "*Qué's* PM?"

It was an auntie, of course, Tía Dora or Tía Chuchi, who grinned, so amused, so defiant, and whispered: she's so tired of your father that she's sending him to the *puta mierda*.

For years, I interview people who are undocumented. I write about a teenager who desperately wants to go to arts school, a mother in Manhattan who was deported, a man who is trying to get official identification cards for his community in Staten Island. I report the story of a woman who is filing her income taxes in the hopes of creating a paper trail if amnesty becomes possible again. I write about women who are undocumented and under house arrest with their American-born children.

Along the way these women and men share their feelings, their humiliations, their dreams. They want me to know most of all that they will survive. They will.

But it's Alberto who talks about the fear.

He's writing a memoir about growing up undocumented, about the fear of teachers discovering his status, the fear his family had of being known, the ways in which undocumented immigrants are everywhere—not just next door or in the fields, but in literature, in the stories we tell. He's all grown up now Alberto. He's a father, a writer, a feminist—*un profesional* as my mother would say—and he's the first person I've heard talk about this fear.

I share his story with my mother. She listens. She nods. She sighs.

"It's awful *ese miedo*," she says, her eyes shifting to another place, another time.

For the first time, I hear what she doesn't say, the fear in her voice, and I understand that Alberto's fears were hers also.

I call my sister that night. "Did you realize that Mami was undocumented?"

The phone line is silent. Then: "Yeah, I guess so."

"Did you ever think about it that way, that she was undocumented?"

"No," Liliana says, and then as if to explain it to herself and to me, she leans back on family folklore: "She had a tourist visa."

I try now to reconstruct her days in my imagination from what Tía Chuchi has told me: hearing on the radio about immigration raids, being afraid that it could happen to her, sending dollars home to her mother, taking money to a friend whose husband had been detained.

I try to imagine days that didn't stroll by or stretch out before my mother, but instead menaced her with their quiet mornings, and in the middle of all that an offer, not of love, although it may have been that, but also an offer to stay.

My mother would hate everything I've written here.

"Why can't you write about something nice?" she would lament. She *has* lamented.

She'd want me to tell you that she let me drag her to a museum exhibit of contemporary Cuban art in Miami one year. She followed me around politely. She kept her opinions to herself about those paintings with their strange women, their distorted views of the ocean. She'd want me to tell you that she was patient. She tolerated my passion for the peculiar. She thought of bringing her sister to the exhibit later. "She'd like this sort of thing," she noted. She'd want me to emphasize that she said this without judgment because she doesn't believe in saving anyone from poor taste in art. She thinks it's best to let people be who they are.

She'd want me to tell you that she's a good mother.

Of course, I ask. I want to know what she'd want me to say if I was writing about her life.

"I like to travel," she declares. "I like gardens, flowers."

Her favorite place, the place she still thinks about, is London because somehow, despite the number of dark-haired children, my mother's eyes saw only the ones with blond hair and blue eyes. "They were *cochinitos*," she admits, "but I would have cleaned them up."

Once they were cleaned up, they would have looked like the children of the Jewish woman who owned the first factory where she worked: blond, blue-eyed, worth a mother's love.

My mother tried to clean me up when I was born. She and Tía Chuchi scrubbed my skin with milk. "You were so dark," Tía remembers, as if it were an illness I suffered in infancy.

Before I know that I can pay someone to translate my writing into Spanish, I do it myself. I take my essay from *Ms.* magazine about how much I wanted to give feminism to my mother, to give her what I had experienced, and I draft it in Spanish. I check my spelling. I read it twice. I sigh. It's a crude rendering, and I know it. I have no grace in Spanish, no intimacy with the language, no understanding of it without a reference to English. But it's my first published piece in a magazine, and I want my mother to have it.

Days later when I ask my mother what she thinks of the piece, she says, "*Me dío tristeza.*"

Not I hated it, I was shocked, I think you're crazy. But *me dio tristeza.* It made me sad.

The English translation is not the equivalent of the Spanish. When a woman says she is *sad* in Spanish, it sounds like she has just said good-bye to her child and boarded an airplane *pa' el Norte.* The words in Spanish make you want to look away.

That's what I do and my mother and I don't speak about what I wrote.

I do go back to the original though and read it carefully. There, drifting among the I's and the periods, is the story of how I have left my mother's house, the accusation of how I think my life with its ideas about women's rights and race relations and narrative theory is better than hers, the reality that I haven't told her how my life has changed, how I have changed. I don't know how to do that.

A few weeks after reading the translation, my mother sits next to me at the kitchen table as usual. "What are you reading?"

"A book," I say without taking my eyes off the page.

"Who wrote it?"

I look up, startled. I have spent most of my days since I was nine years old reading books at the kitchen table. I am twenty-five now. My mother has *never* asked me the name of an author.

"It's this woman . . . called Gloria Anzaldúa," I say slowly, afraid to trust this moment. "She's Chicana, like Mexican but born here."

My mother takes a sip of her *manzanilla* tea. "What does she write about?"

I stare at her, slightly disoriented. Before I can think too much about my mother's sudden interest in feminist theory, I am racing, the Spanish words stumbling out of my mouth as I explain Gloria's ideas of the borderlands, of living "in between" as feminists, as Latinas, as women who belong to more than one land and culture. We are neither here nor there, I conclude, almost out of breath. *Ni aquí, ni alla.*

My mother nods. She lowers her eyes to the book's cover; then she looks back at me, waiting for more. The idea begins to bloom in me: My mother knows this.

She doesn't use these words but she knows these ideas. She has lived in between for many decades. She refers to herself as a *colombiana*, and her friends are *peruanas* and *venezuelanas*. These words, these identities, don't refer to a physical geography. They describe the kind of Spanish the women speak, the way they prepare their *arroz* at home, the cities and *pueblos* they refer to when telling stories or telling lies.

All these things that I am trying to tell her, have been trying to teach her about, all these things that I needed words for, my mother already knows.

It's an old adage that we always find the answers we needed were right at home. We had no reason to travel or to struggle. All we needed, we already possessed.

I'm willing to concede that this is the case. But it is equally true that some of us do have to leave home. At least, I had to. It was me I now know—not my mother—who needed the words in English, the theories and the stories *también*. Without that, I might never have come back to her.

It's Christmas Eve, and the palm trees are swaying in the blue-black night. My mother and sister and father and I are at a cousin's house in South Florida. A pig is being roasted in a corner, its pink skin browning in the earth, and someone has turned up the volume on the speakers. The music winds around us, and the women start to dance.

My mother, now in her late sixties, begins an old dance, one from Colombia, from when she was *joven* and beautiful, she says. Her left hand lifts the edge of a large imaginary skirt. Her right hand reaches into the air as if to call forth a lover or the stars. Her feet tip to the left and to the right, and her body follows.

I look at her and think: who the hell is this woman? And then for a brief moment, a pause really, I feel the tie between us break loose and she's a separate woman from me, a woman with her own life, a separate country. Her arm is reaching into the sky like an inverted exclamation point. Her right hand isn't calling anyone to her but is announcing her.

Who Goes to College?

CECILIA RODRÍGUEZ MILANÉS

"You're going to college," my mother told me. Actually it was not so much a statement as a command—that's the way Mami often spoke. My father wasn't part of the conversation because he wasn't home yet from his job as yardman; besides Papi barely finished third grade in Cuba, so school stuff was her responsibility.

"I know that," I must have replied. I was a senior in high school, finishing a semester early because I had attended night school, and while there was no question in my home that I would go to college, I never understand the how, when, or where of it. And what precipitated this encounter one typical sunny Miami day I can't be sure. We were in the Florida Room—a now passé term for an informal living room, usually with lots of windows. Ours faced the busy avenue; *ixora* shrubs and a low-hanging grapefruit tree provided some privacy. I may have said I was going to work full-time now that I was heading to graduation.

"You're going to go to college *full-time*."

Okay, but what exactly did that mean? I had friends who had jobs and went to college at night; hell, I had friends who had jobs and went to high school at night. Anyway, for as long as I could remember my mother worked and went to college. She attended at night while during the day she was first an instructor of sewing and home economics for mostly southern black women in the New Jersey Job Corps and later a substitute teacher and then a teacher's aide after we moved to Miami. When she finally earned her degree, she became a full-time Spanish elementary school teacher. By then we lived in a working-class suburb of small sturdy block houses built in the 1950s; the first inhabitants were predominantly WWII veterans or Jewish retirees, sometimes snowbirds, sometimes yearlong residents. Later these same and subsequent retirees tended to prefer the numerous condos surrounding the city. There were no corner candy stores or bodegas, no sidewalks off the main avenues, no basketball courts, no places to hang out. And even if there were stoops or fire escapes to sit on, it was too damn hot to be outside anyway.

Mami's stance was arms akimbo. That meant I had to step back. I might have said my working would help pay for school.

She emphatically (Cuban mothers like mine don't have a subtle bone in their entire body; her face was drawn and eyes narrowed) reminded me that for years they had been saving for our education. This went on for several minutes during which I tried to formulate what I thought was the most obvious question because I didn't know anything about the application process or securing letters of recommendation or personal statements or even such a thing as open enrollment.

Where will I go?

"Miami-Dade." Again, in a commanding tone.

The junior college nearby, of course—it wasn't practical to send me to a four-year university because I didn't have even a hint of an idea what I wanted to study (*"porque no tienes la menor idea de lo que vas a estudiar"*). And it was true; I was without a plan, a direction, a goal. I didn't even know I could study an "undecided" major. I wasn't a bad student, but I wasn't an ambitious one either. I discovered early on that I was no good at advanced math (or rather didn't have the patience to bother with it) and was disinterested in pretty much everything else except for what I now shamefully admit were materialistic fancies (all that was "plastic," as in the lingo of the day)—so driven by peer approval and socializing that academics weren't anywhere near the top of my priorities, not even close.

So, I was to go to Miami-Dade Junior College. I had never set foot on the campus, though I had often driven by what looked like an army barracks. Behind it were some boxy modern unpainted concrete almost-windowless buildings. No ivy or red brick anywhere in sight—what I imagined "college" looked like (*that* image had been implanted when our parents took us kids to visit Princeton—yes, freaking Ivy League Princeton University). What did I have to do to get into college? Maybe my mother suggested I ask for help at school. Or maybe it occurred to me. I had a guidance counselor like everyone else (though I can't recall any previous interactions with him), and I had heard enough at school to know that I needed transcripts and he would supply them. On my way to see him I passed a brightly decorated room, the college resource room, a place I had never entered. I remember this vividly.

I approached Mr. D without any expectations.

He might have said, "What can I do for you?" He might have looked at my file while asking.

"I need my transcripts."

"Oh. Sure. What do you need them for?" I remember he was surprised.

Either I said, "I am going to college," or, "I am going to apply to college." He must have thought I was utterly ridiculous, requesting transcripts so late in the year; all the well-prepared, well-coached students had their multiple letters of acceptance in hand and here I was asking for transcripts in April.

"Oh. You must be going to Miami-Dade. Are you going to be a court stenographer?"

Maybe I blinked or swallowed hard.

This man didn't know me. At this point I got a funny feeling in my throat and started wincing. I was without words. I didn't plan on being a stenographer though I had at least two friends who were very excited about that career option, but I didn't think I liked his assumption. I mean, didn't my grades, right there in front of him, reveal that I was college material? Was I college material? My parents said I was. I figured out the funny feeling; I was royally pissed. I grabbed my transcripts as soon as I could get them out of his hands and out of his cubicle. I passed the college resource room and noticed, for the first time, the walls adorned by many enticing posters of happy students on beautiful campus grounds as well as various college banners or flags. I stalled a bit at the threshold, getting even more pissed off and ultimately rushed away and out of the suddenly oppressive artificially lit building (not a single window in the whole three-story structure built in 1973 in the Sunshine State).

As an urban youth in New Jersey in the late 1960s and early 1970s, I didn't know anyone who had gone to college; my friends' older siblings went to work or into the military. In my neighborhood, girls were groomed for secretarial positions in the city; boys for all manner of blue collar work.

My mother's going to college was more surprising than an inspiration for our community, but nonetheless her example was one that would shift expectations for girls of my generation. Our move to Miami was timed so that I would start high school down south, though according to me there was never to be an appropriate time. Transplanted, fourteen, and friendless, I could barely stomach my classmates—upper middle class, entitled, tanned, and they talked funny. Of course, to them I was the alien—big frizzy head of hair, pale, poor, and I talked shit.

The first couple of years demanded a war of adaptation; with the odds pitted so greatly against me, I submitted and changed myself to fit the outsider group at school, the dozen or so Latinas. I had to learn new slang—Spanglish and man-oh-man, was I hooked. It took a while, but I made myself over and was allowed "in"—still, I was faking it. I didn't want to be in, I wanted to be the-fuck-outta high school. Like many adolescents, my brain was a seething, explosive mass chock full of confusing contradictions. Was I Cuban enough for them? Nope, the charge of being a *Cubana-arrepentida* (cultural betrayer) was leveled at me if I admitted to liking hard rock or, worse, an "American" guy. Was I like the majority of the school's students? No way—I didn't have my own car, unending supplies of disposable cash, puma shells around my neck or ankle, joints to puff in the stairwells, or any interest in surfing, plastic surgery, or student leadership. No glee club, team, or student organization interested me. The group I felt the most affinity with was the three or four busloads of African American students "invited" in from Liberty City to integrate our shiny new white school. In this incomprehensible environment, I was supposed to think about college?

By the time I got to my senior year, I overheard many classmates' conversations about where they were going—Ivy leagues or big out-of-state state schools. It was another way for them to show off; they flaunted their acceptance letters like they flaunted their Camaros or Trans Ams or ugly expensive clothes (really, if I had that kind of money, I would surely have dressed so fine!). Since my educational and social experience, as well as socioeconomic experience, was so vastly different from theirs, I didn't expect to follow the same path—to me "they" were another kind of animal, or rather, I was so unlike them, I couldn't imagine being in their shoes. Of course, I know now that it was a big mistake, but what guidance could I count on? My mother's experience was not helpful—she studied in Cuba and had to start all over again in a new country, language, and culture. She married, created a family, got a decent job, and *then* went about getting credentialed. One of the high school girls I hung with had already dropped out, gotten her GED, and was happily situated at Miami-Dade and on her way to a well-paying career as a court stenographer. She showed us the machine—it was very cool looking, quiet, sleek, and it contained only a few keys, which set it completely apart from its forerunner, the typewriter. I'm not going to lie, I was intrigued. I loved typing. In my business education classes, I was usually the fastest typist with fewest errors. I loved stationery— pens, paper, clips, desks, envelopes, file cabinets, phones with flashing buttons, electric pencil sharpeners—all the things offices had aplenty. By my graduation in December, I had a full-time job in an agency that sold installment plans for car insurance. I had my very own adding machine that clicked, zipped, and popped with coils of paper flowing over the back of my desk.

"You can work until August," my mother said after seeing how independent I had become with my own money—buying my own clothes, gas, car insurance, and paying for my active social life (nightclub cover charges mostly). We had established ground rules for post–high school life, and I was pretty pleased at being permitted to go out more often and stay out later, but the only caveat was, "Once the classes start, you need to focus on college."

"I have to quit?" I loved my office job with such nice, grown people who treated me like their lovable pet.

"You cannot work full-time and go to school." And that was final.

Miami-Dade Community College, North Campus, in 1978 was a wonderland for me. No semblance of high school anywhere to be found, and maybe that was the most important point. Diversity, before it became a trendy goal for institutions to trot out for impressing official people who act like they care, was everywhere I looked. My classmates came in all sorts of skin colors and included young adults, returning (older) students, foreign students (a lot of Iranians before the overthrow of the shah), recent immigrants from all over the Americas, and the habitual

Miami-Dade types who took two classes a term for years. And there I was now being taken seriously as an adult. Driving on my own to Miami-Dade everyday was a physical and psychic move toward a life of and in higher education. It was an environment where all of my previous "priorities" were starting to be replaced with academic interests. Maybe the most significant condition facilitating this transformation was that my "girls" were no longer around—not unlike it happens to most, once away from the high school crowd, relationships wither. This allowed me the freedom to try and find out what there was in the world, and I strove mightily to find out all I could.

If there were ever a student who embraced the mission of general education classes, it would be me. I was positively charged by the humanities—art and music appreciation amazed me; I was engrossed by the social sciences, especially psychology and sociology, but I struggled to pass algebra (eventually doing so with flying colors after four tries—that was another innovation: I could withdraw from a class and sign up again later). I started out taking basic reporting, thinking that I would very much like a job where I interviewed people, traveled to distant lands to cover stories, and had a byline, but writing objectively didn't seem to be my thing. And yet I did not mind; I made Miami-Dade my home, as much as a commuter student in a commuter school could. I knew where the literature stacks in the library were without looking it up so I could browse the shelves or go to the periodicals to thumb through current magazines I never even knew existed. I watched videos about all sorts of psychological disorders or dramatizations based on short stories by writers I was beginning to admire like Faulkner, Melville, Poe, Porter, or O'Connor. I listened to classical and jazz music in sound booths I didn't have to share with anyone. I attended lectures, film screenings, and plays—all available to me for free on campus.

Which is not to say that I abandoned all my party-girl behaviors—one of the luckiest things for me was that a lot of the cute guys I saw on weekends in the discos went to Miami-Dade North. They would sit along a low wall near the administration building, talking, joking, or checking out the girls, and so it became habit for me to parade by them in the cute new clothes and shoes that I bought with my own money—nothing like flirty *piropos* to puff a girl up. Sometimes it was sobering to see what these guys looked like in the bright daylight. I was no longer an enemy of school or Miami for that matter. The world had indeed opened up for me. Nurtured and mentored by teachers whose impossible workloads seemed contradictory to their caring, I learned to love learning.

When I graduated from junior college, I learned that the only upper-division state school in Miami did not offer what I had finally decided upon as my major of choice—creative writing. As the only daughter of Cuban immigrants, going away to a four-year university was inconceivable—at eighteen, twenty, or any age. I still didn't have any close friends who had gone away to college. The University of Miami was the only local school that offered creative writing as a major.

"It's so expensive," Mami complained when she saw the papers I splayed out on the glass top kitchen table. I detected a tone of acquiescence.

"But it's the only school in Miami that has what I want," I pleaded more for show than in fear of not getting what I wanted. On my side was a four-semester record of outstanding grades with honors; I had stayed out of trouble (remained single and unpregnant); plus, the Pell Grants made my first two years' tuition practically free.

"The counselor said my grades qualify me for lots of scholarship money, and I could count on keeping the Pell Grant," I said with the new confidence I had developed. This time I knew much more. All those years and expectations led to this moment. And even though the transition to a private university would not be as brusque as that from wretched high school to beloved college, I was ready for it.

I'm Living in a Foreign Country

TONI MARGARITA PLUMMER

My mother was born in Mexico, and while she moved to Los Angeles as a little girl and speaks far more English these days, Spanish is her first language. My sisters and I grew up in a suburb of Los Angeles, where the Spanish language was on signs and buildings and menus, spoken in homes, businesses, and churches. It was everywhere. Many of my friends' parents spoke Spanish and very limited English. Those friends were bilingual. But if your parents spoke English, as mine did, for whatever reason, the kids didn't grow up knowing Spanish. It was like that abundance on both ends was too much to hope for. I took classes in high school, could recite the "Our Father" and "Hail Mary," and could make very small talk with my older relatives. But it wasn't until college that I would speak Spanish regularly.

I'd left California for Indiana and now wanted to go even farther and study abroad. I was wait-listed for London and considering Athens. But being a philosophy major who would be practical for once, I decided to use the opportunity to finally really learn Spanish. And even as I wanted to get away, I wanted to feel like I was going somewhere familiar. Since moving to the University of Notre Dame, I realized I missed Spanish. I joined the Spanish choir, just to hear the language on a regular basis. I wasn't a homesick person, but somehow I was homesick for Spanish. I'm still not sure why. I'd never been particularly interested in either hearing it or speaking it. Spanish was something I'd taught myself to tune out, because, I figured, I didn't understand it. But once it disappeared as my background music, I sought it out. It was my way of keeping home close by. The university had a program in Puebla, Mexico. But that was too close for me. That's why I ended up spending the spring semester of my junior year in Santiago, Chile.

Santiago was definitely one of the more offbeat programs, and we were a small group of twelve sophomores and juniors. The girls outnumbered the boys two to one, and most of the boys expressed intentions to join the priesthood. That was Notre Dame for you.

We were all to live with families, in order to be completely immersed. We referred to the members of our adopted families as the Chilean counterparts to our own families. They were our Chilean mothers, our Chilean brothers. Mine was a boisterous, friendly family, accustomed to housing students. Soon after I arrived, two more students made it a full house: a boy from France and a girl from Canada.

My Chilean mother was divorced with four children, two living at home and two away at school. I got to meet the two away children: the daughter studied geography in the desert up north, and the son studied veterinary medicine in the valley region. The daughter used so much slang I found it hard to understand her. I was to learn that Chileans added -po to the ends of words and dropped their s's. This wasn't Mexican Spanish. The accent could sound even Italian at times. Instead of saying *Adios*, everyone said *Chao!*

The two "children" who lived in the house were the oldest, a son who had studied economics, and the youngest, a daughter in high school. They had a German last name, as was fairly common in Chile.

As for my Chilean mother, she couldn't have been more different from my real mother had she tried. They both spoke Spanish and were single parents, but that was where their similarities ended. My Chilean mother was not religious, though she would tell me to pray for her when I went to Mass. She attended once with me, but she enjoyed flirting with the priest, I think, more than anything else. When we watched the orgy scene in *Eyes Wide Shut*, instead of making a face, she exclaimed at how beautiful the bodies were. Perhaps wanting to live vicariously, she suggested I hook up with the French student, to "get practice." Such instruction from a middle-aged woman embarrassed my Catholic/American sensibilities. But she was a fun character, and I relied on her for food and entrance into the house, as I had no key of my own. Luckily, she was always at home, and she had been to cooking school and made some wonderful dishes. My favorites were the beef empanadas she made from scratch. She also introduced me to *manjar*, which seemed to fill every Chilean dessert. It was similar to *dulce de leche* but more creamy than sticky, and was divine! *Manjar* and I would reunite years later at a supermarket in Jackson Heights, Queens. For birthday parties, of which there were many, my Chilean mother would make a tower of creampuffs filled with *manjar* and drizzled with caramel. There were also dishes with strange pairings, like spaghetti with a fried egg or whole hot dog franks on top. I learned to drink tea with every meal and to reuse my teabag.

At first my Chilean family wasn't quite sure what to make of me. I claimed to be American, but I wasn't blond, nor was I snotty or difficult. To reconcile this disparity, they pointed to the fact that my mother was Latina, which meant I was not a typical American. I quietly took offense on behalf of my country. While I called myself Latina, I also absolutely considered myself American. But I can't deny I appreciated being accepted as something closer to one of them.

Within twenty-four hours of arriving at my new home, I made my first language blunder. As she set the table, my Chilean sister told me the dog Chapi had run off. Thinking she had said the dog was lost, I said, "Like me!" wanting to poke fun at my cluelessness. But I had misunderstood and had actually confessed to being in heat. They had a good laugh and then reminded each other to speak more slowly in front of me.

Santiago was a South American Los Angeles, sprawling and earthquake-prone; it could have a foreground of palm trees swaying in the sunshine and a background of snow-capped mountains. It boasted a variety of terrains like my beloved California, including the beach and the desert. Even geographically, Chile was located on the southwestern-most part of the continent, stretching skinnily along the Pacific Ocean. My Chilean brothers were surfers. February was their summer. They almost immediately took me to the beach.

But I was also there to study, or to pretend to. We all had to take a Spanish test in order to be placed in one of two Spanish classes. I tested the second best, which I would like to attribute to some sort of intuition I'd honed growing up around Spanish speakers, relying on what sounded right. There was one other Latino in the group, a native speaker from New Mexico. I was in the higher-level Spanish class, and we all took the other mandatory class on Chilean culture. I also took classes in poetry, film, and one on Platón. The classes were all in Spanish, but the professors took it easy on us *extranjeros*, and so they were not too difficult. There were a few class trips, which included visits to Valparaíso, a port town, and La Isla Negra, the site of Pablo Neruda's home.

As much fun as it was, it was also one of the loneliest times in my life. I was away from all of my close friends at school and didn't connect to any of my current classmates as easily. I spoke to my family only once in the entire time I was there, because of the high cost. There were also the cultural differences. Once my Chilean mother called me *gorda* (fat), and, overcome, my eyes started watering at the table. She thought I was crying over the lack of familiar food! Later she called me *negra* and apologized shortly after. I guess she didn't know that I would rather be called *negra* than *gorda*. These were words I'd heard tossed around in my own extended family and never cared for. My mother had had to endure these kinds of names from her grandmother who raised her, and here I was now experiencing them for myself.

In the house I spoke Spanish, but with my fellow Domers (Notre Dame students) I too often allowed myself to slip into English. It was just too tempting to be able to say whatever I wanted, however I wanted, without being limited by a smaller vocabulary and vague attempts toward proper grammar. Other students felt similarly. Who knew the simple act of speaking could feel so liberating! At one point my Chilean mother told me I had not progressed as much as the French and Canadian students, which I didn't like hearing. But the Frenchman was already a very accomplished speaker before he ever arrived in Chile, having grown up by the Spanish border, and I suspected the Canadian was much more disciplined than I was. I felt a pang of irrational guilt at being outdone by non-Latinos. But I didn't let it get to me too much, because I continued speaking English with the Notre Dame kids. They were my refuge, the closest thing I had to home. I infiltrated different cliques. One liked to go to Mass, then to the market, where we would buy stuff for sandwiches and a spinach salad. I hung out with my Chilean sister, too, who made for a delightful younger sister. She even liked to borrow my clothes.

At the time, the elderly and ill Pinochet had been sent back to Santiago from England, having been found guilty of crimes against humanity. Chile had only recently become a democracy, and you could sense it.

There was a reserve in the people, who had been forbidden to congregate and had been given curfews. Family members had gone missing without explanation. And still there was no consensus on Pinochet. The political views within my own Chilean family ranged greatly. One brother swore off politics, refusing to even vote. The other praised Pinochet for the greater economic stability he'd accomplished in the country. The youngest sibling was called *una comunista* for listening to folk music about *los desaparecidos*. She loved reggaeton and boys with dreads. She would take me to weed-soaked concerts where it cost three dollars maybe to see the most popular bands in Chile, which all featured the rapid strumming of the *charango* and the high notes of the *zampona*. It was a music that had no contemporary American comparison. It reminded me of 1960s music, overtly political. The young people loved it, even though it spoke of events that had happened years ago. It struck me as a strange, after-the-fact sort of protest. But the previous generation had not been allowed to speak out, and they didn't seem to want to now.

I'd brought from home a Walkman and tapes of Bob Dylan, Joni Mitchell, and Tom Waits, which I'd listen to over and over again. I played Joni for my Chilean sister, who loved her voice. I sent her *Blue* later. I recorded my Chilean sister's CDs onto tapes for myself and wrote out all the Spanish lyrics when they were given in the liner notes, otherwise making out the words as best I could. I memorized "La Maza" and "Gracias a la Vida" so that I could sing them aloud as I walked home from school on an empty street. I got the gist of what was being said in these songs, but I didn't make it a special point to translate every word. I was like my Chilean brothers in that way, I suppose. They would sing along to Led Zeppelin and Pink Floyd, without knowing what they were saying. I loved the music, and I wanted to hear my voice singing it. If I couldn't speak Spanish effortlessly, then at least I could sing it with ease. Those songs gave me a voice when mine felt limited. I'd never been interested in Spanish music at home, avoiding the radio stations in Los Angeles and considering my mother's old records as music not intended for me. But now Spanish music was cool! I danced to it at discos. I went to a Maná concert, where flags of Mexico and Chile flapped together, and there was talk of brotherly love and flowing rivers of tequila and *pisco*. I bought CDs of Violeta Parra, Victor Jarra, and Silvio Rodriguez.

At the end of the semester I went with some others on a trip to

Bolivia and Peru. We climbed the steps of Incan ruins, touched the beautiful blue water of Lake Titicaca, searched for ATMs, and lent each other money in the current currency. We drank *maté* and chewed coca leaves. The tour guides would automatically look to me, the sole Latina, when describing services. But the best Spanish speaker among us was actually the blond, blue-eyed guy from Rochester. In these simpler, more rural areas, the Spanish was easier to understand. People spoke more slowly and without any of the city slang we'd heard in Santiago. I'd learned that how much I could understand really depended on the speaker. It varied greatly from person to person. And here in these tiny, remote areas, life had greater clarity.

In my thoughts on Latin America, I had never considered the indigenous cultures that still lived there. The women we saw during our travels especially fascinated me. They wore thick, colorful striped skirts of many layers, long dark braids, and somber-colored, brimmed hats that sat high on their heads. Beautiful cloths secured babies to their backs. Some of the indigenous didn't speak Spanish, only Quecha or Aymara. At an outdoor grill, where we waited for our meat to cook, a little girl translated for her grandmother. At Machu Picchu I wandered alone, among the tourists and student travelers, finally succumbing to the effects of the high altitude as everyone else in our group already had. The sick feeling came upon me, and when it released me I was sitting on the grass, the Andes surrounding me like sleeping giants, on top of the world.

I left the Chilean winter for the Californian summer. Our mother took us to Las Vegas to celebrate my and my sister's birthdays. I was turning twenty-one. There, in a Las Vegas lounge with puffy white leather sofas, after a semester's worth of wine and cocktails, my mom and I had our first legal drink together. Fresh off a trip spent living out of a backpack, staying in hotels without running water, the ridiculous opulence of Las Vegas hit my senses like a freight train. When we went out to eat, I had to resist my now-automatic inclination to speak Spanish with every stranger, having assumed for months that every waiter and every salesperson spoke Spanish.

After graduation, I went straight into grad school. At USC, I workshopped a short story I wrote about Machu Picchu and nearly burst with pride when my teacher, Hubert Selby Jr., said he liked it. "The Mountains Speak Aymara" would become my first published short story. I wrote it from the perspective of an older, white man, maybe because it was simpler to play off that contrast. But I think I also felt like him, like an outsider wanting to be let in. I even gave him a variation of my name. In the story, Anton writes down the Aymara words he hears. It's through speaking the words that he'll feel connected to the place, that he'll find something real.

The nostalgia I feel for Mexico is now accompanied by similar feelings for Chile, which are more concrete in a way. I've never spent any substantial time in Mexico. I've visited there, but never walked the streets on my own or taken the subway on my own. To this day I have a predictable weakness for Chilean wine, alpacas, and Andean music. My eyes pop at the sight of *pisco* on a menu. But I can also communicate more easily with my Mexican relatives, and I can better navigate Mexico itself. On the streets of Manhattan Spanish-speakers stop me to ask for directions, and I'm usually able to help them. I still don't call myself fluent, by any means. But what was once intimidating and alienating isn't so much anymore.

A few years ago I traveled with my mother in Mexico, just the two of us. On a bus trip from Puebla to Huatulco, we spoke entirely in her first language. We gossiped in Spanish. We laughed in Spanish. We even got lost in Spanish. I understood her perfectly. And she understood me. I left my mother when I went to college. She not only let me, but enabled me to leave, in a way she'd never been allowed to herself as a young woman. I like to think I came back even more devoted to her, and to the heritage she gave me.

My Stalker

LORRAINE M. LÓPEZ

We didn't have a word for it then. These days I think that if there had been a word, things might have played out differently. Because the right word, even if it is a familiar word used in a new way, at the right time can convey ideas and attitudes, an entire social stance on an issue that alters the way in which it is perceived. Timely and apt terminology stimulates studies and programs, training seminars, marathons, T-shirts, even candlelight vigils. For lack of the right word in every day use, I believe, years were lost to me, and instead of earning my bachelor of arts degree in four years as I was on track to do, I didn't complete the degree for more than a decade. I entered college as a freshman when I was seventeen, and I graduated over a dozen years later, a senior when I was thirty. All for want of a simple word, a familiar word used a new way. A verb, the transitive form. To stalk: 1: to pursue by stalking; 2: to go through (an area) in search of prey or quarry; 3: to pursue obsessively and to the point of harassment.

My fourth year of college I was stalked by a coworker at my work-study job in the library. Like the B-movie villain who promises to be the protagonist's worst nightmare, vowing to be there when she goes to bed at night and there when she wakes up in the morning, my stalker seemed omnipresent. He was outside the classes I attended, waiting for me to step out the door when they ended; he was on the telephone when it rang in my apartment; and, of course, since he was my supervisor who determined the hourly schedule at the library where I had a part-time job, he was usually there when I reported to work.

My stalker, an unstable young man, was also a student at the state university I attended. He claimed to have been institutionalized for mental illness as an adolescent after threatening to kill his adoptive family, subsequently released into foster care, and then placed in a boys' home before being admitted to the university. His earliest memory, he told me, was witnessing his biological father strike his mother with a hammer. Welfare workers discovered him and his two younger sisters in a tenement apartment, abandoned by both parents, dysfunctional alcoholics who'd left them unattended for days. The three siblings, no more than toddlers, had been found with distended bellies from malnutrition, infested with parasitic worms and body lice. Such a narrative would compel sympathy in almost anyone, but when I first heard this story from him, I found it over-the-top, incredible. *Liar*, I thought at the time. *Everything you say is a lie.* Later, I would be ashamed of my rush to harsh judgment, almost immediately reversing my antipathy. Clearly, education comes slowly for me. I am still learning to listen to myself.

In those days, when there was no word in our vernacular for this obsessive behavior, stalking more easily disguised itself as a flattering infatuation or even romantic love, the flames of passion many young girls dream of sparking in a man's heart. But this is not a love story. A stalker no more loves his quarry than a cheetah is enamored of the gazelle it aims to chase down and sink teeth into. Like predatory animals, stalkers select their prey carefully, searching out the infirm, the young and inexperienced, or the old and enfeebled. In my case I was young and very naive, in addition to living away from family for the first time. I was soft spoken, socially awkward to the point of shyness. No doubt I seemed passive and vulnerable, traits far more attractive to predators than good looks, sex appeal, and charm.

In fact, this, my last and most dangerous stalker, was not my first. A nontraditional student, somewhat older than me, a fellow English major, whom I'll call Barry here, was my first stalker. When he could, Barry kept pace with me wherever I walked on campus, and when I was unavailable, he sought out my younger sister to talk to her about me, or rather about his feelings for me. He had a gaunt face with a beak-like nose, he wore his blond hair in an outdated crew-cut, and he tended to hunch forward, assuming a stance suggestive of a slouching buzzard. Barry wrote poems for me and petitioned persistently for a kiss. But the poems he claimed were inspired by me featured a "dark lady," when I am a brunette but fair skinned, and in these he described the "dark lady" presiding over bullfights or strolling some hot, dusty *zocalo* in Mexico, drawing admiring glances as she passes. In these poems this "dark lady's" essential trait, apart from "darkness," is silence. She's given to inexplicably "mournful glances" and occasional sighing, but she never utters a single word.

Had he known me, Barry would have realized that in those days I was a vegetarian for ethical reasons, and I have always deplored the mistreatment of animals. I would never choose to attend a bullfight, much less preside over such a thing. Had he troubled to find out, he would have learned that my family has resided in the United States since the 1600s, and at the time I had never even set foot out of the American Southwest, rendering my stroll through his imaginary *zocalo* especially absurd. But these poems, this dogged pursuit, and the obsessive attention were never about me. They were always about Barry, his loneliness and longing, his desire to fetishize what he found temptingly exotic, a young woman of Mexican American heritage who—ashamed of a lisp—didn't speak much, even in one-on-one conversations, providing an ideally blank page whereupon he could inscribe his fantasies about bullfights and sleepy Mexican pueblos. In me he found a girl who blushed easily, someone who seemed far too timid to tell him to fuck off.

In fact, it took tremendous determination for me to tell Barry, with excruciating politeness, that I'd rather he left me alone. When I finally did this, his reaction was immediately visible and alarming: his gaunt face went stony, his eyes flattened, and he compressed his thin lips. He wheeled away from me without a word. Afterward Barry acted out in the Shakespeare seminar we took together. From one class meeting to the next, he transformed from an enthusiastic returning student into an arrogant bully who was sarcastic and insulting to the professor, a kind man with the wisdom to address the affective aspect of this behavior, rather than to be provoked by it. Clearly Barry was displacing the anger he felt toward me in a performative way that I found both humiliating and threatening. My reluctance to confront him this time trumped my need for this class credit; I withdrew from the course.

Shyness, vulnerability, a preference for retreat over confrontation—

these traits, I am sure, drew my next stalker to me, in the same way Barry had been compelled by them. But in this case the attraction, at first, was mutual. Unlike the homely Barry, with his corny crew-cut, my next stalker was handsome and confident, and since he was my supervisor, I respected his authority and sought his approval. Also, in contrast to Barry, he didn't bother to install me in what he felt to be a culturally appropriate fantasy. A Latino himself, he had no need to do this. My selling points were strictly those that made me ideal prey. In those days, the comet's tail of the sexual revolution, my social awkwardness and timidity masked the paradoxical sense of sexual freedom I enjoyed. My body belonged to no one but me. I used it freely with whomever I wanted, whenever I wanted. My next stalker was first my lover.

And since my body belonged to no one but me, he had no claim on it, even if we had been intimate. He, in fact, was living with another woman, and I had other lovers. The night he attacked me, I was returning to my apartment, holding hands with someone else. Now the situation comes into sharper focus. Even these days the question of culpability insinuates itself; the dynamic subtly shifts. While we can't quite say that assault is what a faithless woman deserves, a slightly different picture emerges here. How shy, one might ask, is a young woman who takes many lovers? But promiscuity (what it's called when women behave like men) is not necessarily incompatible with being timid, hesitant, and unsure of oneself. And aren't we all contradictory creatures? We recognize the types: the filthy-minded neatnik, the honorable thief, the sentimental assassin. Why not a shy seductress, the timorous and quaking vamp?

So, yes, I was walking to my place with another man when the person who would become my stalker spotted me. Unseen, he trailed us into the courtyard. When we were inside my apartment, he knocked. I opened the door, and he forced his way in. He began shouting at me, accusing me of lying to him, calling me names, and he spit full in my face. He pushed me into a wall, ripped my shirt. Too stunned to intervene, the man I was with backed away in shock. Then my stalker hauled back and punched me in the face with such force that I blacked out.

I remember the police. Two tall, beefy white men in dark blue appeared at the threshold of my apartment, and I remember shivering, though it was a summer evening, warm enough for shorts. I was wearing cut-offs and a gauzy white blouse that was now torn and blood splattered. My date, who'd shrunk away during the assault but later called the police, now stood beside me while both of us answered questions the officers asked. And then, inexplicably, my attacker returned on his bike. He was arrested, handcuffed, taken away in a squad car, and I was driven to a nearby hospital emergency room, where I was photographed and X-rayed, my nostrils plugged with gauze and my nose taped. Light-headed and face throbbing, I returned to my apartment and climbed, fully dressed and still shivering, into bed.

In a few days I received a phone call from one of the other supervisors at the library. At first Caleb inquired kindly about how I was doing, but soon enough he got to his point. He asked me to drop all charges. Though usually pliant as can be, I was aghast. I couldn't recognize my face in the mirror. My nose had perceptibly shifted right of center. Purple bruises raccoon-ringed both my eyes. At the grocery store and gas station, people gaped at the Technicolor spectacle of my swollen face, many wincing and some asking if I had been in a car crash. It was easier to nod at this than to attempt explaining what I couldn't yet fully comprehend. Caleb told me on the phone that our coworker who attacked me wasn't doing too well in lock-up, and he said that Cheryl, the woman who lived with our coworker, was worried sick about him. Even so, I refused to drop the charges.

The next day a meeting was called. A group of male supervisors, including the library director, met with me at Caleb's house, ostensibly to spare me the difficulty of appearing on campus with my broken-looking face, but now I think this was to prevent other staff members from seeing what one student worker had done to another. In Caleb's dim and dusty living room, the men sat in dinette chairs arranged in a circle. I joined them, taking a seat nearest the door. One by one they persuaded me that dropping charges would be the first step in putting this unpleasantness behind me. Finally, one of the supervisors told me this: "If you don't drop charges, we will have to report this incident in both of your personnel files."

I was twenty-one. I had no idea what this meant. It sounded damning and permanent. It sounded like the kind of thing that could prevent me from graduating, from teaching school, as I had planned, from finding any kind of employment for which I would need references. It didn't seem to matter to these men that I had been the one attacked. They let me know this violence would be held against me unless I played along, unless I declined to prosecute my assailant. Too stunned to speak, I just nodded.

Later my stalker would tell me that one of the supervisors said that I had looked like I was "out in left field, really spacey and not with it" at that meeting. He told me this as if to prove I was lacking in conviction about my stalker's culpability in the attack. One man's perception of my being "spacey" somehow evinced my uncertainty about what had really happened and who was to blame. He also told me that the policeman who arrested him said that he understood "how angry some bitches can make a guy." Now I believe that if the officer said this, he did so to elicit an admission from him, but back then my stalker threw it at me as further proof that I had gotten what was coming to me. Again and again he offered support for his claim: I had provoked the attack, I had deserved it, and others knew this as well as he did. My stalker also complained that he had missed classes while he was in jail, admitting that he had told his professors he'd been arrested for getting into a fight "with two guys." But if he felt justified in attacking me, why couldn't he have explained to his teachers that some bitch had made him so angry that he'd knocked her out?

All of these things he told me just days after he'd been warned by administrators at the library to have no contact with me. Despite the fact that the incident went unreported in both of our files, he was ordered not to speak to me or contact me in any way. But the first day I returned to work, he was there, in the back sorting area of the library where I was assigned to work. I gasped at the sight of him, and he tossed a balled-up piece of paper at me. It was a handwritten apology, which blamed his deep feelings for me. With this, the stalking gained momentum. From that day on until the semester's end, he usually turned up wherever I happened to be on campus, from work to the cafeteria to my classes to my car in the parking lot.

If I wanted to sleep through the night, I had to unplug my phone because he would call and call and call, the phone ringing through to the first light of dawn. The only place he left me alone was in my apartment, since I'd told him the manager had taken out a restraining order on him and that he would be arrested if he as much as set foot

Rapunzel's Ladder

JULIA ALVAREZ

Rapunzel, here is a ladder for you to climb down from the ivory tower. A phrase woven out of three words, strong enough to hold anyone who feels stuck in an old paradigm:

Social justice education.

When I first heard the term, I felt one of those "aha!" moments. So there was a name for the unease I had long experienced in the classroom as a student and later as a teacher. A name for why I often felt like an outsider in the academy.

Now I understand why. Though the academy welcomed me, the content of the education that I got as a student and that later I was asked to pass down to my own students often did not include people like me. Or it labeled us in ways that marginalized us. Or it disappeared us altogether under the righteous blanket of "universality." As a female, as a Latina/Hispanic, as a scholarship student, and later as a non-PhD faculty member with a mere master's in creative writing, I felt institutionally marginal.

What's more, most of what I was learning in those pre-multicultural days, including how I was being asked to learn it, did not include my own style and story, my ways of perceiving and moving in the world. I learned to live a double life in those ivory towers, to impersonate the exemplary minority who was lucky to have been chosen, who could be cited as a credit to the institution, not to mention a check mark in that critical box of diversity that schools were scrambling to fill at the time. But all the while, I was plotting my escape.

It was not until the day I gave up tenure to become a full-time writer who now teaches on the side that I felt a baffling sense of both terror (I was leaving behind the structure that had been the only home I knew in this country) and relief (I was released from a home that had never felt like home). Perhaps the best way to describe my unease is to compare my academy self to Goldilocks in the house of the three bears. The dimensions of every piece of furniture did not acknowledge or accommodate my proportions. The windows were far too high for me to see out of or to open. I gasped for air in that stuffy space, wondering why no one else was complaining. What's more, I lived in fear of being found out and—the scholarship student's nightmare and later the untenured's terror—of being thrown out.

Having made my confession, I worry about overstating my case. I was, after all, nourished in academia. Even when the institutional structures and canons lagged far behind, there were always individual teachers and texts and classmates and courses and colleagues who taught me a way around things or made exceptions. But the fact that an alternate way was considered an exception branded this bending of the status quo as "problematic."

What's amazing to me is how many of us felt the same way. Not just women, not just Latinas, not just minorities, not just scholarship students. Institutions, bless them, often start out as responsive living structures. But the problem is that they become codified, claustrophobic, limiting, and we have to keep reinventing them. And they resist reinvention. In fact, "they" dig their heels in and fight back.

And yet, a learning institution has, as its raison d'être the mandate to be a place of constant, vibrant revision; a place where knowledge and tradition can be held up to the scrutiny of time to ensure that they are still useful to the needs of the world, can still nurture our spirits, can still respond to who we are now and who we must become in order to survive. Here, too, the new arrivals in the field of time meet head on with the challenges they will soon be facing as the next generation at the helm of our human family.

In evaluating my own education, I want to walk softly and throw away the big sticks. Why? Because it matters too much that this be a space for all of us. There is no future in blame, which just ends up being more of that old bifurcated thinking, a reactive *us*-ing and *them*-

in the courtyard. That fall semester, which was to be my penultimate semester before graduation in the spring, became unbearable for me, worse still when I discovered I was pregnant. In December I dropped out of school. I moved from my apartment, I got married, and I changed my name. I was twenty-two when I left college and twenty-eight when I returned. It took me two more years to graduate because I had to reestablish residency, and I decided to pursue credit toward a teaching credential.

These days the university appears to be my permanent professional home. I am an author and a professor of English who teaches in the Master of Fine Arts program at a prestigious university in the South. I'll admit there's a vestigial trace of the shy girl I once was, but now I feel a sense of belonging as I stroll on the campus of the university that houses me. Here I am encouraged to write and to speak, to make my thoughts and observations known. I often travel to other universities, bookstores, and conferences to read my work and to speak to audiences composed of people interested in what I have to say. I'm surprised at my ease in public speaking, the confidence of my voice. Nowadays, I'm even fond of my lisp.

Perhaps the more interesting story transpires in the time between my first foray into academia and my tenure as a professor of English: a narrative of marrying, divorcing, raising children, returning to school, graduating, teaching in middle school, completing graduate school, remarrying, and teaching at the university level, while writing, writing, writing all along. But that story is too complex and unwieldy to capture here, where it proves more manageable to focus on how my experiences in academia, in negative and positive ways, have shaped, defined, and even book-ended my adult life.

As for my stalker, he still works at the state university library where we first encountered one another. Recently he sent me a congratulatory message at my campus e-mail address when a book of mine won a national prize. It's no surprise he found me. Anyone can find pretty much anyone else on the Internet these days when we have so many words in daily use that we never dreamed of using back when I first started college. *Cursor, modem,* and even *e-mail* are some examples of these. Others like *stalker* have taken on new meaning, as have *mouse* and *spam.* Despite the ease of Internet technology in reconnecting people, the message itself, after all these years, stunned me, like a fist popping through my computer screen. In it my stalker wrote that he was proud of my accomplishment. I marked the message as spam before clicking it into the file labeled by another familiar word used somewhat differently here, though it still ripples with the same satisfyingly apt connotations: I sent it to *trash*.

III.
Inside These
Academic Walls

ing that makes a battleground of learning, a space where someone will be left out.

And my life in academia was never a matter of cruel imposition, colonizing of my mind; it was more of an absence. Small omissions, fine points, miniscule matters of tone or perspective, which might seem like splitting hairs to bring up now.

But the devil (I was taught) is in the details. Indeed, it is in those fine points that we can make a difference. Strand by strand, we can plait a ladder down from our ivory towers and ask ourselves what would an education look like that holds itself accountable to the very values it seeks to promote? An education that is not just about proficiency in content. An education whereby we create community and conscience. An education that can do what Keats claimed only for poetry: embody negative capability, that ability to entertain dualities and "to be in uncertainties, Mysteries, doubts without any irritable reaching after fact & reason." Education as "a vale of soulmaking."

An education that puts Rapunzel in a tower, removes her from her roots, her family, her community, and her own self does not do justice to what education is all about. In fact, such an "education" does violence, however unwittingly, to that effort to comprehend, connect, question, and make whole that is the very life of a learning institution. How to create an academy that takes on its acknowledged role of helping form an integrated self, body, mind—in a word: a soul? After all, we call schools *alma maters*, mothers of our souls.

I want to go back to a defining Rapunzel experience in my own education. All through my American schooling, I had a serious academic problem: I couldn't take exams. I'd show up, all right, overprepared and determined that this time it would be different. But as I began to read the questions, a terror would seize me that I couldn't seem to control.

Back then (early 1960s), we didn't have a term for what was going on. Now, no doubt, I would be diagnosed as suffering "panic attacks." When I finally finished my formal education, I packed away my exam phobia in that Pandora's Box of memory where we happily leave behind our past damaged selves, hoping they'll crumble away into dust and disappear.

But recently I was forced to revisit that time in my life. I was working on a nonfiction book on Latina adolescence, *Once upon a Quinceañera:*

Coming of Age in the USA, and my editor suggested that I include some of my own experiences as a teenager coming of age in my new country. I tried writing about that time without bringing *it* up, but somehow I could not avoid dealing with a problem that had marked my whole adolescent life.

Learning about social justice education has helped me see this problem in a new light. Granted that my extreme response had a lot to do with my own temperament, with the fact that when the problem began, we were recent political refugees from a grim dictatorship and had barely escaped with our lives. But could my academic breakdown also have been a way my psyche was registering its bafflement at finding itself, like the canary in the mineshaft, in a noxious environment? Could it be that my spirit was responding to an education that was asking me to leave out too much of who I was? That my young Rapunzel self, who had not yet heard of social justice education, was scrambling down from that ivory tower before the witch's scissors descended and cut off all my hair?

When my family arrived in this country in 1960, fleeing the dictatorship of Trujillo in the Dominican Republic, education became a matter of survival. School was the place to learn the skills that would allow us entry into an alien culture. Those were the early days of the civil rights movement, pre-bilingual education, pre-everything but the old assimilationist model of immigration. From the start my American education was not about adding to and, therefore, expanding my heritage or preserving my native language, but replacing it with something *better*. In fact, the harassment in the playground confirmed that fact. My sisters and I were pelted with pebbles, taunted as "spics," told to go back to where we came from.

Our rescue came in the form of boarding school. My older sister and I won scholarships at Abbot Academy, an elite prep school north of Boston. Abbot Academy was just beginning to concern itself with bringing diversity to its all-white, Anglo-Saxon, Protestant student body. But diversity was that early, well-meaning but ultimately condescending variety of "diversity," a kind of missionary pedagogy in which a few girls from different backgrounds (Jewish, African American, "foreign") were given the privilege of being converted into Abbot girls. All the while, our difference was held up as proof of the liberal-mindedness of the institution.

At Abbot, education became not just classroom learning but a total immersion. I was soaking it in: how an elite fleet of girls dressed, talked, worked, played, lived, learned. Since Abbot was a prep school, the main mission of our education was to prepare us for college. This goal was always before us as the reason we were learning. Sure, the inscription on the front gates read "Enter into Understanding that Ye May Go Forth Into Nobler Living," and this might be what we ultimately hoped for, but who could see that far summit for all the ivory towers looming before us? One of them would end up being the college Abbot helped us get into.

What now seems odd is that the skills we were being taught in the classroom—to be smart, ambitious, competitive—went against the feminine virtues and social graces promoted by the school and outlined in our Abbot "Blue Book." We were to behave in a manner befitting young ladies—with all the mind-numbing implications of that phrase in that pre–women's movement time. But what seems even odder was that no one remarked on this gulf. No one seemed to acknowledge that each of us was being asked to be a divided self.

If this was so for our Anglo classmates, it was even more so for my sister and me. An even larger gulf was growing between what we were absorbing at Abbot and our Dominican Catholic culture and *familia*. In fact, almost everything I was learning was bringing down a whole belief system and way of life.

Take the content of just two courses. In European history we were learning about the corrupt practices of the medieval Catholic Church: the Inquisition, rival popes, the selling of indulgences. I was shocked and shaken. I didn't know *how* to take in these new facts and integrate them with what was still the guiding faith of my father's and mother's lives and my own life. How to throw out the baby of unexamined dogma but not the bath water of a spiritual life?

In American history our teacher lectured on the Monroe Doctrine, presenting the eight-year (1916–24) U.S. Marine occupation of my country as an effort to rescue an unruly people from debt and bloodshed. I wasn't totally sure what *unruly* meant, but it didn't sound good. Had my father been lying when he talked about those same marines as invaders who had put in place the thirty-one-year dictator who had forced my family to flee the country?

And it wasn't just the content of my courses that distressed me. It was the whole competitive style of learning that set us against each other to see who would come out on top. I had grown up in a familial culture, where I didn't operate as a sole agent but was always a part of a "we," a community effort. Even after we came to this country and were living as a nuclear family in Queens, my sisters and I were a unit, constantly talking in our shared bedrooms, trying to make sense of what was happening to us.

I wish I could report that I was a young Joan of Arc at Abbot, holding firm to my faith and pride in my culture and language. But no, I began to feel that as the gatekeepers of the dominant culture, my teachers were right, and I was wrong. Since this was boarding school, there was no matrix of home and culture and community that I could return to daily to affirm and feed that other self. Moreover, I was terrified I'd lose my scholarship, be sent home in shame to my parents, end up in a worse place—that other rougher, public school playground where the kids threw stones and didn't allow me entry into even rhetorical understanding, but hollered that my spic sisters and I should go back to where we came from.

And so, by sheer effort, I disciplined myself to become a good student. I was going to make my parents proud. I would vindicate us by showing the Americans that we were not just an unruly lot. Thinking back, I feel a pang for that young Rapunzel—how much was riding on her education! Where was the freedom of spirit or fun of learning? Not to mention the outright contradiction of vindicating "us" by becoming "them"! A few summers ago at our fortieth-year reunion, my Abbot roommate recalled how every day I'd draw up a detailed schedule that I would follow religiously: 6–6:15 a.m.: wake up, get dressed, brush teeth; 6:15–6:30 a.m.: study vocabulary list, reread English assignment, review Latin translation, and so on.

But although I could follow a rigorous schedule and be transformed in the crucible of the classroom, back in my dorm room at night, it was a different story. I had trouble sleeping, worrying about all I had to learn or what I had already learned that was a mortal sin to have learned. I was terrified that the devil would come after me. In fact, all through high school I slept with a crucifix under my pillow, a crucifix I was careful to keep hidden from my roommate, who already teased me enough about being a nut and a grind. I had come from a country and culture steeped in Catholicism and *santería*, demons and spells, beliefs and practices now termed "primitive superstitions." I could not so easily cut myself from these deep roots, which indeed had their negative aspects, but were also the only way I knew to feed my soul and nurture my spirit.

Soon, these demons—whom I renamed "the furies" in order, I think, to contain them, to make them literary—began to stray from the private space of my bedroom at night. They'd show up at the most inopportune time: the moment of reckoning when I had to be at my most competitive: exam time. I'd sit down to a test, and a sense of dread would descend on me. A distracting voice would start up in my head, *You're going to mess up!* I would try to ignore the voice, to force myself to concentrate, but panic would seize me, my breath would come short, my head would begin to spin. The discomfort was so great that finally I would bolt out of the room, leaving behind my dumbfounded teachers and disgusted classmates.

I felt ashamed. I couldn't explain what was going on. Why was I self-destructing in this way? "You don't have any reason to worry," my teachers kept reassuring me. I had high grades going into finals. I was at risk of dropping out when the administration found a way to calm the furies. All through my time at Abbot, I took my final exams in the infirmary, and until we got the problem under control, my mother drove up to school and sat on the other side of the door waiting to take me home when I was done.

Now I see how unprepared I was to receive an education that did not take into account all it was destroying inside me. Something in me was refusing to make that leap to the other side of that widening gulf my education was creating between an old life and a new self. My mother had to be there to reassure me that I could still have "us" even if I succeeded as a "me." My spirit was up in arms.

In his insightful and controversial memoir, *Hunger of Memory*, Richard Rodriguez writes of a similar painful gulf in his education.[1] As the young Richard becomes increasingly successful in school, he learns to keep his home life and culture "repressed, hidden beneath layers of embarrassment." It's only now as a grown man writing his memoir that he acknowledges "what it has taken me more than twenty years to admit: *A primary reason for my success in the classroom was that I couldn't forget that schooling was changing me and separating me from the life I enjoyed before becoming a student*" (45).

As his memoir attests, Rodriguez is haunted by his education. Researching the literature on pedagogy, Rodriguez finds a description in Richard Hoggart's *The Uses of Literacy* of the type of student he became: "the scholarship boy."[2] (This term enlightens Rodriquez, much as the phrase *social justice education* enlightened me.)

The scholarship boy is a student who has come "up" from the lower ranks. (Hoggart, a Brit, was writing in the 1950s.) He moves between antithetical environments, his home and the classroom. With his family, the boy has "the intense pleasure of intimacy, the family's consolation in feeling public alienation. Lavish emotions texture home life. Then, at school, the instruction bids him to trust lonely reason primarily" (Hoggart, quoted in Rodriquez 46). Unlike his upper-class or middle-class classmates, the scholarship boy goes home and "sees in his parents a way of life not only different but starkly opposed to that of the classroom" (47). Hoggart describes the increasing toll his education exacts on the scholarship boy: "He has to be more and more alone, if he is going to 'get on.' . . . He will have, probably unconsciously, to oppose the ethos of the hearth, the intense gregariousness of the working-class family group" (47).

Add to the scholarship boy's social and economic class difference an ethnic, racial, cultural, and language difference, and you've got an anxious student; an over-achieving boy; a girl running out of exams: "Here is a child who cannot forget that his academic success distances him from a life he loved, even from his own memory of himself. . . . To evade nostalgia for the life he lost, he concentrates on the benefits education will bestow upon him. . . . Without the support of old certainties and consolations, almost mechanically, he assumes the procedures and doctrines of the classroom. . . . Success comes with special anxiety" (49).

This does not sound like the education of a student but, rather, like the breaking of his spirit.

Where my own experience differs from that of Richard Rodriguez, and what has made him a controversial figure with many Latinos and educators, is his belief that this is an inevitable process. But to think so is to have totally absorbed that other, dominant point of view. Granted, as Rodriguez himself acknowledges, education always contains loss. It is painful to leave behind our gated understandings of the world, our little security-blanket ways of thinking, our historical and cultural and familial biases. It hurts to expand the self, to forge a soul. But education need not be a violence against the self, a core Rapunzel self held hostage forever.

And this is precisely the challenge to social justice educators who labor in the classroom to create more inclusive models: how to grow the spirit with the mind, how to help our students not just with content but with the process of integrating that content into an *alma* whose *mater*, after all, the academy claims to be.

As for my own story, this problem not only marked the course of my American education; it determined the course of my life. What I mean is that without this problem, I probably would not have sought out those courses (creative writing: all the "exams" were take home!) and teachers (writers, many of whom were disaffected with the academy, exceptions themselves) who would allow me to express what I had learned in a way more simpatico with my temperament and background. I probably would not have embraced a major (English) in what was, after all, a second language if I had not found in that major a "minor" (creative writing) where poetic license was the rule.

And so, my breakdown in the educational process proved to have a happy ending. To the academy's credit, I was allowed to stay on the strength of recommendations from my teachers, who found enough merit in my writing and hard work to overlook my inability to perform under pressure. As my education "progressed" in college and later in graduate school, I regressed less and less. This was not just a matter of my own maturity, but the academy itself was changing, loosening up, challenged by the student activism of the 1960s, the civil rights movement, the women's movement, affirmative action, the culture "wars" in departmental curriculum and faculty. In the student-centered, open classroom movement of the late 1960s and early 1970s, professors began encouraging creativity among students, even in traditionally conservative disciplines, like the sciences. (I recall writing a series of poems on the Vermont landscape for my geology class.)

Years later, these examination fears showed up again when I came up for tenure. Again I was being tested, forced to perform and prove myself for visiting evaluators. (Note for future soul-searching: what is the place of tenure, a ranking system that encourages hierarchy and preservation of the status quo, in an academy committed to social justice education?) Granted, these evaluators were colleagues, whom I knew would be fair, my department was "behind me," and I had great student evaluations as well as a first novel coming out with a good publisher. But since when had hard work and a well-laid groundwork stopped my furies from running riot over my confidence?

What saved my soul that semester and garnered me tenure, I still believe, was that I had recently married. Rooted at last in my own home and life, I could withstand the pressures of performance. Many times during that "tenure semester," I'd ask my husband, "What if I don't get tenure?"

"Don't worry, we'll figure something out. No matter what, we'll have each other." This was another version of my mother posted outside the performance door! I came through—not exactly with flying colors—but this time intact, body and soul.

And yet, like Richard Rodriguez, I've remained haunted by my education. Curiously I not only stayed in the academy by becoming a teacher, but I also returned to teach at the two schools that were the most significant in my own education: Abbot Academy (now absorbed into Phillips Andover Academy) and Middlebury College. It's almost as if I needed to go back, in part to understand what had happened to me there, but also out of a sense of responsibility to those coming after me. If nothing else, I could contribute what had been missing for me—the presence of others like me. As Sandra Cisneros writes at the end of *The House on Mango Street*, "I have gone away to come back. For the ones I left behind. For the ones who cannot get out" (110).[3]

Indeed, as Richard Rodriguez acknowledges, "if because of my schooling, I had grown culturally separated from my parents, my education finally had given ways of speaking and caring about that fact" (72). I came "home" to the academy because that was the only home I knew in my new country, where I became an American self. Abbot Academy and Middlebury College were my alma maters, mothers of my soul, however problematic that mother-daughter relationship was. The academy was also where I found my calling, where I learned to navigate this craft of writing through the Scylla and Charybdis of *either-ors* and integrate all those disparate selves, if only on paper, with the promise of more.

In fact, even after I gave up tenure, I found a way to come back. The academy, which had always seemed so gated and exclusive, fashioned a place for me as a writer in residence. It turns out there is no witch in Rapunzel's tower, or if there once was a witch, she doesn't live there anymore. More and more, administrators, faculty, and especially students, who are increasingly diverse themselves, are demanding an education that reflects and does justice to the multiplicity and richness of the world in which we all live. With the rapid advances in technology, that world is now literally on campus, in our students' dorm rooms, before them on a screen, at their fingertips. With this incredible broadening of possibility comes an even greater challenge for educators: how to help our individual students so that they do not lose their way, swept up in this deluge of information. How to help them integrate all they are learning into a meaningful whole, a whole they will keep making and remaking for the rest of their lives. For there should never be an end to education, a segregation of learning into a determined set of years in our lives. As I like to tell my workshop students, one of the best reasons to be a writer is that you are always having to learn new things.

There are those who worry that bringing such issues as social justice to the academy threatens to politicize neutral ground. That the value of academic discourse is in its impartiality. (Another righteous-sounding term like *universality* that stifles all further discussion.) In fact, the academy already has deep-seated and often unconscious biases that should be examined, discussed, held up to the light. As Chaucer's Wife of Bath reminds us, "Who peynte the leon, tel me who?" In other words, if the picture of the hunter slaying a lion had been painted by the lion, what would the scene look like?

What would an education look like that includes both the lion's and the hunter's points of view? In a pluralist society, indeed a pluralist world, how can education not do justice to this multiplicity if we are indeed preparing our students for their lives in this complex world?

At the close of each meeting of the board of Shelburne Farms, a local nonprofit sustainability farm and learning center, we always have an agenda item called, "blue sky." This is a time when we cast aside bureaucratic concerns about funding, adherence to precedents, and instead "dwell in possibility," as Emily Dickinson once wrote; we allow the institution—through our dreaming—to reimagine itself.

What would it look like, an academy that has social justice at its center?

It would be inclusive, providing a welcome home for traditionally excluded others so that the concept of "others" becomes moot, and the focus is community, participation, comprehension.

It would put a student's whole well-being at the center of the process, remembering that in addition to passing on information, the academy is also helping to form and inform a whole person, a humane being who is always learning, always enlarging his or her understanding of the world.

It would allow for play because learning is fun, and labor done with passion can be exhilarating, liberating.

It would commit itself to change by looking at the ways it might consciously (or unconsciously) be promoting and prolonging stereotypes or biases that ill serve its mission to educate each and every one of its members.

It would reconsider the ways in which it promotes hierarchy and resistance to change in order to preserve a status quo through its process of tenuring.

It would embody the principles it professes to value. For instance, putting in place environmental practices that it teaches in its classrooms must be observed if we are to survive as a planet.

It would find ways to connect the classroom with the local and global community so that students do not experience learning in a gated community disconnected from the world.

It would never forget the others, the vast majority of the world's population who don't yet have the opportunity and the luxury of an education. It must hold itself accountable to them, remembering that the ultimate blue-sky wish of social justice education is a world that is also socially just.

Rung by rung: this is how we begin climbing down from Rapunzel's tower.

NOTES

1. Richard Rodriguez, *Hunger of Memory: The Education of Richard Rodriguez* (New York: Bantam Books, 1983).

2. Richard Hoggart, *The Uses of Literacy: Aspects of Working-Class Life with Special References to Publications and Entertainments* (London: Chatto and Windus, 1957).

3. Sandra Cisneros, *The House on Mango Street* (Houston: Arte Publico Press, 1983). Quote is taken from the recent 25th anniversary edition: New York: Vintage Contemporaries, 2009.

Derrumbando Muros along an Academic Path

NORMA ELIA CANTÚ

Let us do work that matters, vale la pena, it is worth the pain.
GLORIA E. ANZALDÚA, *THE GLORIA E. ANZALDÚA READER*

For one of my birthdays, as a twenty-something, filled with curiosity
and seeking to know what my future held, I had an astrologer friend of
a friend draw up my astrological chart. I knew little about such things,
but as an avid reader I had gathered enough knowledge of how it worked
to be dangerous. Mr. Uribe, solemnly read my chart, prepared a multicolored piece of art that predicted that I would have a hard time getting
through my undergraduate work, but that if I chose to go on to graduate
school it would be easier. He likened the path through my undergraduate work to one where I would scale walls and overcome numerous
hurdles. Indeed, at the time, I was having a hard time getting through
my undergraduate program. It felt as if I were truly scaling walls and
breaking through impassable terrain, *derrumbando muros*. I was working full-time for Central Power and Light Company (CP&L) and taking
night classes at a community college, for we had no university in my
hometown of Laredo, Texas. I could not see how it would be possible to
attain my goal of a bachelor's degree. My desire to learn impelled my
continuous registration for courses at the community college; I had
repeatedly asked to be transferred to the CP&L office in Kingsville, Texas,

where I could continue on to the degree in teaching to which I aspired so fervently. I was repeatedly denied the transfer.

In addition to problems of access, I faced other obstacles at home: my family was in dire economic straits; my brother had been killed in Vietnam; my father was on the verge of disability retirement due to severe crippling arthritis, and the needs of my younger siblings tugged at my heart. I wanted so much for them; I wanted to help my parents with the constant worries over money; I wanted the younger girls to take dance classes; I wanted to get Christmas gifts for everyone—make their wishes come true; I wanted to get my mother new furniture: a dining room table, a sofa. *En fin*, I was torn between pursuing my dream of higher education and my *compromiso*, my allegiance to my family. I needed to work, so I didn't see how I would ever leave to get my degree. In fact, as I sometimes joke, because I could not go to the university, the university came to me.

In 1970, when Kingsville's Texas A&I University opened a branch in Laredo, I was among the first to register. As I continued working full-time and taking night classes, I struggled with class demands. I had little time to prepare, to read all the assignments, to write the papers, and to prepare presentations. When things got really tough, I would remember Mr. Uribe's words and how the stars had predicted that the path was supposed to be difficult; somehow knowing this inspired me. I felt confident that regardless of all the obstacles I was facing, I would succeed. Too soon, I faced graduation and the sinking realization that what I had prepared for—to be a high school English teacher—was not what I really wanted. I had completed student teaching at a middle school and had encountered enough frustration with the Texas public education system of the 1970s that I knew teaching in the public schools was not for me. Now what?

One balmy March evening in the semester when I was to graduate, my English professor, Dr. Alan Briggs, asked what I was going to do after graduation. I confessed that I was looking at graduate schools—I had browsed through a few catalogs in the library and had written for information from Stanford and UT Austin. Dr. Briggs encouraged me to talk to Orlan Sawey, the chair of the Department of English in Kingsville and suggested I apply there. Coincidentally Dr. Sawey was in town for a meeting, and Dr. Briggs arranged for me to meet him. I didn't realize it at the time, but I was being interviewed for a teaching assistantship and to be admitted to the MA program in Kingsville.

When Dr. Sawey offered me a teaching assistantship for the fall, I was a bit confused but feigned enthusiasm, hiding how perplexed I was. Subsequently Dr. Briggs explained that because he knew I wanted to go on to a graduate program, he had asked Dr. Sawey to talk to me and consider me for their MA program in English. I accepted the offer with trepidation but also with a sense of excitement, keeping Mr. Uribe's words as a point of reassurance that the graduate school path would be easier to travel.

I was twenty-six, and my father was not happy that I was deciding to leave the family home to continue my education. He was conflicted because all along, his message had been education, education, education, and here he was upset because I was pursuing higher education. I think he feared that I was growing away from the family and that I would never come back. In the way of parents who fear that their children will become strangers to them, he held on to all of us. Especially after my brother, Florentino Junior, was killed in Vietnam, my father had become even more protective of his large brood. But I did go to Kingsville, where I spent two years as an MA student in English at Texas A&I University enjoying my tiny apartment—actually a room attached to the rear of a house rented by Gustavo, my friend from Laredo who was back from Vietnam and also pursuing an MA in English. I was there to get my master's degree, and the living conditions—including the Texas-sized roaches that would fly when I turned off the lights—would not deter me from my goal. No matter what we did, the landlady and I, we just couldn't get rid of the *cucarachos*. I never learned to live with them as she suggested I do.

Kingsville was not far from Laredo, but it was a world away. For the first time I lived alone, without children or elders around. It took some getting used to; I missed my family so much. To fill in the void, I volunteered with the Newman Club, the Catholic chapel on campus, to visit the elderly. I translated the mass for the English-speaking Irish priest. The elderly *mejicanas* loved to sit and chat. Mrs. Betancourt was one of my favorites—she told me stories of her family's demise from prominent Tejano landholders to peons working in the King Ranch. She encouraged me and made me promise I would continue with my studies as far as I could go. She passed a few months after I left Kingsville. The senior citizen housing where she lived was across the street from the cemetery, a fact I thought morbidly ironic. Ever practical, she thought it fitting.

One of the first classes I took at Texas A&I University was nineteenth-century British poetry with Hildegarde Schmalenbeck: Tennyson and Browning. I loved it. As I was finishing my MA, it was Dr. Schmalenbeck who put the idea of a doctorate in my head. Not surprising, I chose British nineteenth-century fiction as my area of expertise. When Victor Nelson came down to South Texas to recruit for Stanford University I spoke to him. But I felt discouraged and dismissed; still I applied—and was rejected. However, encouraged by a classmate and friend, Ute, I had also applied to other schools. I was accepted at a number of them: Kent State, Wisconsin, Ohio State, and others I've forgotten. All in the Midwest. I chose to attend Nebraska because it was the only university that had a Chicano in the English department faculty, Ralph Grajeda. I was about to send my acceptance letter to another university when Ralph called and left a message with the secretary in the department; we talked, and he urged me to attend Nebraska. *El destino* intervened once again.

One Sunday evening in April, I called home from the pay phone a few blocks away from my apartment, as I did every week, to happily share with my parents the news that I had accepted to go to Nebraska and that the funding was generous; my father went into a rage. He was not happy that I was going on with my studies beyond the MA. After all, the plan had been for me to return to Laredo and teach at the community college. I walked all the way home in tears. I cried myself to sleep. But I never considered changing my mind. Although his words had cut deeply—how I was ashamed of where I came from, how I didn't love my family, how I had betrayed them—I knew it was out of fear, fear for what would happen to me out in the world, away from family. Fear for what he couldn't control. Years later, while driving with my parents to Kingsville for an event, I reminded my dad of that phone call. He couldn't remember it. Now that I am the age he was then, I understand that he might have forgotten the incident that had so scarred my soul.

The Sunday following that painful conversation I dialed the same number we have had for over fifty years, hoping that the party line was not busy. I waited with dread in my heart for my father to accept or reject the collect call. He accepted the charges and greeted me with the usual love in his voice. I was flabbergasted. What had changed? I asked my mom when she took the phone, and she explained that they had received a high school graduation announcement from distant relatives. We had family in Lincoln, Nebraska! I would be okay. In fact, my dad's cousin's daughter's husband, Frank Godinez, an army lifer, was an NCO instructor with the ROTC on campus, and they lived a few blocks from campus.

It was a blessing! I stayed the first year with my cousin Gela, her husband Frank, and their four kids, who ranged in age from ten to eighteen; it was their oldest daughter, Violanda, who had graduated from Lincoln High School the previous June. That fall I walked to and from the university along a tree-lined street with sidewalks, thoroughly enjoying the fall colors and the crisp fall weather. I was in heaven. But, I didn't have the clothes for the weather that was to come and began visiting thrift stores looking for boots, for a winter coat, for woolen sweaters, and for gloves and hats; *en fin*, getting ready for the snows that came on Thanksgiving weekend.

Mr. Uribe had been right, but he had also been wrong; there were many challenges, but relatively speaking, graduate school was easier than my undergraduate schooling. I struggled; it was not an easy road at all, but I still loved graduate school, and having family there was a blessing. The racism, the sexism, and the isolation of being away from my family was devastating. Over the four years that I lived in Lincoln, I encountered people who just didn't expect someone like me to me there. For instance, one time I lost my university ID and went to get a new one, and the clerk kept looking for my name in the janitorial staff list even though I clearly explained that I was a TA in the English department; more than once I was asked what country I was from and was overly scrutinized when I answered Texas; or when I had a student drop my class claiming that a Mexican could not teach him English. At one point someone painted a swastika on my office door; I was scared and stopped staying in the office to work after 10:00 p.m.

Despite the struggles, I still look back at those years with fondness. In Nebraska I met wonderful people from the community and visiting writers—feminists like Audre Lorde and Adrienne Rich as well as Chicanos like Tomas Rivera, Alurista, and Lalo Delgado. I became closer to my cousin and Tía Trine, my father's cousin, who lived in Omaha. I experienced so many new things: weather, food, flora, and fauna. I finally knew what four seasons feel like: hot, humid summers; blizzards and ice storms in winter; gorgeous crisp falls; and chilly, even cold, springs.

I suppose I was getting an education—in the Aztec concept of education—I was shaping face and soul, learning to be in the world. It was in Nebraska that I first called myself a Chicana during a visit to a rural school district, where I was hired by the Nebraska Department of Education to help the faculty and staff deal with newly arrived Vietnamese students. When I was introduced as "Spanish," I reacted. When I asked him why, the person who introduced me explained that he didn't want to offend me by calling me "Mexican," and he asked what he should have called me. I loudly and proudly answered, "Chicana." It was in Nebraska that I learned to drink tequila, too. It was there that I saw the connection between the oppressions of isolation and poverty that we had on the border and the poverty on the reservations, as I had students who came from Rosebud and from other reservations in western Nebraska and the Dakotas. It was in Lincoln that I first had a best friend who was black, Nena. It was with her that I learned to speak back at racist comments, to be fearless and call folks on their racist attitudes.

I was never intended to survive in higher education as a student— perhaps if I had gone directly from high school to undergraduate and graduate school, I wouldn't have been strong enough to resist, to persist. But I followed my own path, and I believe that it prepared me on various levels so that I could survive the alienating and often hostile environment I encountered along the way. Mr. Uribe was right, the undergraduate years were arduous, but they tempered and seasoned me for what was relatively easier, graduate school. But I was never expected to survive in the alien country that is academia as a graduate student either. Yet, along with giving me an excellent academic preparation, several professors believed in me and instilled in me that words and knowledge can be used to effect social change. Such knowledge made me the activist scholar that I am.

As an assistant professor back in my hometown, I worked with a local feminist women's group, Las Mujeres, on a transnational annual

Primavera conference;[1] I joined other women to build a literacy project, a refugee assistance center, an Amnesty International chapter, and on and on. I worked tirelessly to make a difference in the lives of those who had not survived academia, who had not had access to higher education, who had not been as fortunate as I. Back then, in Laredo, both as a professor and administrator at Texas A&M International University, later as a professor at the University of Texas at San Antonio, and now as a professor of Latina/o studies at the University of Missouri in Kansas City, I heed the words of Chicana lesbian theorist Gloria Anzaldúa, and I aim to do work that matters. For me this means being an activist scholar and doing scholarly activism.

The persistence of racism and sexism as well as inequalities at various levels in academia spurs my continued desire to do work that matters and make it a better world for those who come after. In a sense opening doors is not enough; we must ensure that scholars of color can enter and make changes as if it were their home, which it is. I usually use the metaphor of a home when speaking about my linguistic binguality—how English, as my second language, felt like it was not my home; I felt like a visitor in a stranger's home until I felt comfortable enough to change and relax in it, joke and curse in it—then I knew English was my home. In like fashion, academia was a stranger's home where I felt like an outsider, an imposter when others assumed or treated me as if I belonged there. What I have strived to do with my work in academia is to make it my home and to welcome those who might not have been welcomed in the past, especially women of color and, in particular, Chicanas like myself who never imagined that they could belong in front of a university classroom, or publishing books, or speaking at conferences.

Although during my academic career I have encountered instances of what the book *Presumed Incompetent* documents, I am not dwelling on these but merely acknowledging that in the mainstream academic world, and indeed for many of my sisters who work at HSIS (Hispanic-serving institutions) or HBCUS (historically black colleges and universities), the situation remains that we as women of color must work twice as hard to be considered half as good.

In addition to his predictions about the challenges of undergraduate and graduate school, Mr. Uribe also told me I would be a successful writer, but not exactly as a poet and not exactly as a novelist. I remember that he scratched his right temple as he studied the chart; then he looked up to tell me that he was not quite sure what genre it would be, but I would be a writer. No doubt he was referring to the work I would write almost fifteen years later, *Canícula*, not exactly poetry, but also not exactly fiction, and to my autobioethnographic work that I continue to pursue. The beautiful multicolored chart that Mr. Uribe prepared so many years ago is now housed in my archives at the University of Texas at San Antonio. Along my path I would refer to the laminated chart; I often think back to the solace I felt from "knowing" that I would make it. Now I am the one who can help those who decide to travel down the academic road into this world that is academia. As an adviser for our doctoral program at UTSA, I would invariably ask, "Why do you want a PhD?" No one asked me. Sometimes my students elicit prophecies similar to Mr. Uribe's, albeit without the astrological chart. "You will make it!" I reassure a student going through a difficult time. "It may be hard, but remember why you are here, remember that you belong here, remember that you have come a long way and that you *will* make it," I remind another. Mostly it is my Chicana students who come to me with doubts, with insecurities, with what has been called the imposter syndrome for women of color in academia.[2] My hope is that later, when the doubts creep in, as they undoubtedly will, when the student asks, why am I doing this? she will remember my words and know that as a woman of color, as a Chicana, as a working-class white student, or as a student from the barrios of South Texas, she does belong in academia, she has a right to be whoever she wants to be, to do work that matters, and that she *will* make it.

NOTES

1. See Cantú, "Las Mujeres."

2. What has been called the imposter syndrome was first studied by Pauline Rose Clance and Suzanne Imes in the late 1970s. Their article, "The Imposter Phenomenon in High Achieving Women: Dynamics and Therapeutic Intervention," could certainly be applied to women of color in academia who exhibit the same kinds of internalized experiences.

BIBLIOGRAPHY

Anzaldúa, Gloria E. "Let Us Be the Healing of the Wound: The Coyolxauhqui Imperative—La Sombra y el Sueño." In *One Wound for Another: Testimonios de Latin@s in the U.S. through Cyberspace (11 de septiembre 2001–11 de marzo de 2002)*, edited by Claire Joysmith and Clara Lomas. Mexico, DF: Universidad Autónoma de México, 2005.

Cantú, Norma E. "Las Mujeres." In "The Handbook of Texas Online." Texas State Historical Association. http://www.tshaonline.org/handbook/online/articles/vilo3 (accessed June 11, 2013).

Clance, Pauline Rose, and Suzanne Imes. "The Imposter Phenomenon in High Achieving Women: Dynamics and Therapeutic Intervention." *Psychotherapy Theory, Research and Practice* 15, no. 3 (Fall 1978): 1–8. http://www.suzanne imes.com/wp-content/uploads/2012/09/Imposter-Phenomenon.pdf (accessed June 11, 2013).

Gutierrez y Muhs, Gabriella, Yolanda Flores Niemann, Carmen G. Gonzalez, and Angela P. Harris, eds. *Presumed Incompetent: The Intersections of Race and Class for Women in Academia*. Boulder: University Press of Colorado, 2012.

On Becoming Educated

JOY CASTRO

In graduate school in the 1990s, I am introduced to a feminist professor of law. We're in a bagel shop. It's sunny. Wiry, with cropped sandy
hair and glasses, she looks exactly like my nascent concept of a feminist. She's working on an article about a little-known provision in the
Violence Against Women Act, which President Clinton has just signed
into law. The new legislation makes employers responsible for providing workplace protection for women whose partners have threatened
them with violence. In the past, violent men had ignored restraining
orders to assault and even kill women at their workplaces. This new
legislation requires employers, if notified that a targeted woman is in
their employ, to provide appropriate security rather than leaving it to
the individual woman to defend herself.

I know about men who hurt women. Our mother had fled the state
to escape our stepfather, who had beaten her and us for years. I had
run away at fourteen and been on my own since sixteen. This is mar-
velous, I tell the professor. Her article will help protect thousands of
women—hundreds of thousands, maybe. I think of my mother, my
friend Cindy, my neighbor Diana. Battering happens in every stratum
of society, but under the poverty level, domestic violence increases by a
factor of five. In the trailer park and barrio and rural towns where I've
lived, I've seen my share.

But the professor grimaces and shakes her head. Her article, she
explains, is for a law journal, an academic journal. Only other scholars

will read it. But since this new legislative provision isn't widely known, I suggest she could write an article for a mass-market women's magazine, one that will reach millions of women. Not *Ms.*, which is hard to find, but the kind of magazine available at drugstores and supermarkets, the kind that sits in stacks at inexpensive beauty salons, *Cosmopolitan* or *Redbook*; the kind that reaches ordinary women, women who might be getting beaten. She could save actual women's lives. Her face wrinkles. That's not the kind of article she writes, she explains with exaggerated patience. Someone else will do that, eventually. A writer who does commercial, popular articles for a general audience. Her own work, she says, will trickle down.

I take a graduate course in feminist theory. Our professor, educated at one of the world's most prestigious universities, is intimidatingly brilliant in the seminar she runs like a Socratic inquisition one evening a week. I admire her; I like her; I want to be her—but as the semester winds on, my eagerness dissipates because I don't understand Toril Moi or Luce Irigaray or any of the feminists (after Virginia Woolf) whose work we're reading. I'm a first-generation college student, here by fluke on fellowship, and the theorists' English seems foreign to me, filled with jargon and abstractions at which I can only guess. They say nothing about wife beating or rape or unequal wages or child molesting, which is the charge that finally got my stepfather sent to prison. They say nothing about being a single mother on $10,000 a year, which is my own situation. The feminist writers respond to male theorists—Lacan, Derrida—whose work I haven't read. I can't parse their sentences or recognize their allusions, and I don't know what they mean or how they're helpful to the strippers and dropouts and waitresses I know, the women I care about the most, to my aunt Lettie, who worked the register at Publix, and my aunt Linda, who cleaned houses.

It's true that the complexity and jargon are alluring, like another country, safe and leisured, with a strange, beautiful language that means only abstract things, where a dozen bright young women and their interlocutor can spend three hours conversing around a big table in a comfortable, air-conditioned room that looks like a corporate boardroom in a movie. But I climb the stairs each week in grim frustration.

bell hooks's piece "Out of the Academy and into the Streets" appears in *Ms.*, and I'm relieved that someone has expressed the inchoate things rumbling inside me.[1] I make photocopies and take it to my professor, asking if we could please read and discuss it in class. She takes the copies and says she'll see.

One evening, our discussion has strayed to Stephen Greenblatt, who, I'll learn later, is the paradigm-shifting Renaissance scholar who initiated New Historicism, a scholarly approach to literary texts. At the time, I know none of this; he's just another male name. I have no context, but the professor and some of the older students seem to have read his work, perhaps in other classes. The professor is intense, lively. She presses her fist to the seminar table. "How do we, as feminist theorists, *respond* to Stephen Greenblatt?"

"What if we don't respond?" I say in frustration. "What if we just keep working on issues that are focused on actual women, issues we actually care about?"

Her eyes are wide. "You can't just *ignore* Stephen Greenblatt," she says. The oldest graduate student, the smart one I admire, shakes her head and smiles faintly.

I disengage. At the end of the term, I write my paper on Woolf's *A Room of One's Own*, the only book that was clear to me.

We never do discuss the piece by bell hooks.

In a different class, a graduate seminar on multicultural literature, our professor assigns Gloria Anzaldúa's *Borderlands/La Frontera: The New Mestiza*.[2] I enter the seminar room that day with excitement. For the first time in my graduate career, I've encountered a text that speaks passionately to me, a text radical and thrilling, an author whose feminist, ethnic, sexual, and working-class concerns correspond to my own, a book that acknowledges real-world prejudice, poverty, and sexual violation, that mixes poetry and history, memoir and argument. I have fallen in love. In cursive, I've gushed onto the title page of the black paperback: *The most incredible book I've ever read. It speaks straight to me.*

At last. I can't wait to talk about it.

But the professor, whom I've always admired, opens class by apologizing for having assigned the book at all. He'd included it, he explains, only because he'd heard it was important. But if he'd read it first, he would never have put it on the syllabus: it was too disjointed, too polemical. Students quickly chime in with their discomfort over the book's "angry" content.

I'm confused. My professor and classmates hadn't stumbled over W. E. B. Du Bois, Zora Neale Hurston, or Maxine Hong Kingston, but Gloria Anzaldúa is somehow too different, too much.

It's the anger in the text, I learn, that bothers them. "She's so *angry*," they keep saying. For the whole session, I find myself arguing in defense of the book's worth, trying to articulate the difference between being angry by temperament and expressing justified anger in response to violation.

The experience is both alienating and illuminating. *Did you think we weren't angry?*

Maybe if you're a distinguished professor of law, the notion of your name next to a piece in *Cosmo* makes you cringe. Maybe if your educational pedigree is immaculate, the remedial intellectual needs of people who grew up with food stamps aren't your problem. Maybe if you're a well-meaning professor teaching ethnic literature, Anzaldúa's anger is the only thing visible. Maybe you can't feel the burn of every injustice she inherited and lived, much less appreciate the elegance of her complex aesthetic.

At the time I didn't realize that these small incidents were negotiations of power, contests over whose perspectives mattered and whose voices would be permitted and welcomed at the table. At the institution where I did my graduate work in the 1990s, Third World feminism, women-of-color feminism, and transnational feminism hadn't yet trickled down.

In 1997, PhD in hand, I began my first academic job at a small college: 850 students, all men, in a town of 15,000 in rural Indiana. Wabash College prided itself on its maintenance of tradition. Men constituted not only the entire student body but also most of the faculty and almost the whole administrative structure.

Students asked, while I was sitting at my desk in my office, whose secretary I was. Alumni at luncheons asked what a "purty young thing" like me was doing there. All-campus e-mails by drunk freshmen asked for the best place on campus to beat their meat. I taught there for ten years, the only tenure-line woman in my department for the first nine. I earned tenure; I chaired my department. We hired three women. I also got to teach women's literature, including Latina literature, and feminist theory to classrooms of thirty-five men at a time. Farmboys and lawyers' sons took my classes. Some came with the expressed intention of debunking feminism. Some wanted to know, when we read the novels of Jean Rhys, why we had to read a book by a slut. Some questioned women's right to vote. Yes. When I taught Gloria Anzaldúa's *Borderlands/La Frontera*, I was under no illusion that its insights would be met with joy.

I value those voices, those questions, that red-state hostility, because they taught me how to make feminism's insights relevant to people outside a closed, snug room of agreement. I learned how to make feminist theory, and critical race theory, and observations about class privilege relevant, exciting, and even needful to people who had no material reason to care. I learned diplomacy. I learned not to back down.

As academics, we can forget the urgency and hunger people have for the knowledge we hold. We can forget that even those who claim to be hostile may need what we offer to help them make sense of a complicated world. Academics don't share a monolithic experience. Many of us are adjuncts or lecturers, forced to piece together work with few benefits and little security, while the fortunate percentage of us with tenure-track positions have to hustle to build our vitas and merit files as our institutions require. Either way, the thick busyness of our lives can induce a sweet, privileged forgetfulness, a smug sense of how worthwhile our work of "knowledge production" is. Over the years I've known many dedicated and creative teachers, eager to reach and engage every student, yet I've also known many academics who view students as an obstacle to their real work of research, or who see teaching as a process of simply culling the best from the herd.

But I speak now as one of that herd. The herd is made up of smart, desperate, and intellectually eager individuals—if they are met halfway, if they are spoken to with respect and in language they can understand. They have not been to Harvard, and if we make them feel stupid, inadequate, and ashamed for not knowing its vocabularies and sharing its assumptions, they will retreat. (My brother, living in a trailer with friends and putting himself through college, dropped out after a year.) If our concerns seem too abstract, effete, and irrelevant, they will turn away in disgust.

Yet we need them. Their voices are vital. The academy—as we fondly, misguidedly call it, as if it were some great, unified thing—is lumbering along amid eviscerating budget cuts, pressures to corporatize, to streamline, to justify its existence to hostile anti-intellectual factions and a skeptical public, to become purely instrumental, a machine that grants job credentials to twenty-two-year-olds so they can get on with their lives. In the face of such intense and varied pressures, the academy must find ways to preserve itself as a place for thought to flourish—yet *everyone* needs to be invited to think. The discussion has to matter to everyone, and everyone's voice must be heard.

Last spring my son graduated from Oberlin College, and in only a few more months I'll have paid off my own enormous student loans. That is, I believe deeply in the intellectual benefits of higher education and have willingly indentured myself to attain them. On the other hand, I loathe the academy's blind spots.

A few years ago Stephen Greenblatt—*the* Stephen Greenblatt—said in an interview, "I've been at this for 40 years. And, as an academic, I've been content with relatively small audiences, with the thought that the audience I long for will find its way eventually to what I have written, provided that what I have written is good enough."[3] On the one hand, there's a lovely quiet confidence in the long view Greenblatt takes, a modest surety of purpose, but it's also a position freighted with an absence of urgency. That unacknowledged absence is a luxury, a privilege that too many academics ignore, not at their own peril, but at the peril of others, others like the women who would have been very grateful to learn about that provision in the Violence Against Women Act about employers' responsibilities to protect them. "The audience I long for will find its way eventually to what I have written," Greenblatt states. *Eventually.* There's no rush. And the burden of finding knowledge, you'll note, is on the audience. Seeking the audience out is not configured as the thinker's job. *Eventually, if I am superb enough, the chosen few will manage to discover my work.*

Sitting on my sofa on a Saturday morning, writing, it still surprises and honors me that an editor has asked me to write for a prestigious college's online journal. I was raised to be seen and not heard. Now someone wants my voice? That's the key, I think: to remain surprised, to remain honored. Our public voices are an extraordinary privilege. We can make the choice to carry with us and be shaped by the voices we've heard—the strippers and dropouts and battered mothers—and we can act so that what we do will matter to them. We can continue to choose—no matter what islands of remove our positions may afford us—to keep inviting those voices, to teach free classes to the poor, for example, and to listen to what the poor tell us when they read our cherished texts. We can teach texts written by poor women in our classrooms. We can remember that torture and abuse traumatize humans into silence, and that humiliation and subordination train people into reticence, but that their voices, those valuable voices, can be fished to the surface again, if we are patient, if we are kind. If we care.

In graduate school professors said you had to choose one thing or the other: you could be a creative writer or a scholar, not both. The creative writing professors said you had to choose a genre: poetry or fiction, not both. You could be a feminist professor in a classroom or a feminist activist on the streets, not both. It was all too reminiscent of the old divisions long demanded of us: you must think or feel, not both. You must be a mind or a body, not both. You can be pretty or smart, not both. You can have a family or a career. Why did intellectuals in the 1990s continue to invest in such reductive binaries? Why the urge to bifurcate, to build retaining walls between the multiple truths of our experience?

They were wrong. It isn't necessary. Today feminists publish scholarship and creative work. We write for general audiences and trained specialists in our field. I publish in glossy magazines, and the local newspaper, and academic journals; I publish scholarly articles, and poetry, and fiction, and memoir.

For me, all of feminism's waves and permutations—as well as the voices that contest it—are essential. All of our varied feminisms seek a more just world, and there's no need to limit our efforts to particular spheres, no need to cut ties with parts of ourselves. While I serve on the advisory board of a university press with other professors, vetting scholarly projects for publication, I also serve as a mentor to a Latina-Lakota teenager whose mother, a meth addict, lost custody.

She lives with her father, stepmother, and two brothers in their small mobile home in a trailer park. When I drive to see her, it feels like I am driving into my own past.

NOTES

1. bell hooks, "Out of the Academy and into the Streets," *Ms.* 3, no. 1 (July/August 1992): 80–82.

2. Gloria Anzaldúa, *Borderlands/La Frontera: The New Mestiza* (San Francisco: Aunt Lute Books, 1987).

3. Stephen Greenblatt, "Meet the Writers: Stephen Greenblatt," 2004 interview, Barnes and Noble, BN.com.

La Silla

RUTH BEHAR

When we left Cuba, we settled on a street in Queens that was lined with rows of six-story red brick buildings. Chain-link fences surrounded the patches of green lawn in front of each building. Jabbed into the dirt were signs that read, "Keep Off the Grass." Those may have been some of the first words I learned in English.

The sea-drenched streets of La Habana, shaded by frangipani and royal palms, were far away; so too the bright lights and skyscrapers of Manhattan that my mother had dreamed of. Mami thought those brick buildings in Queens were ugly, but she didn't dare say that aloud. We'd followed in the path of her older sister, Sylvia, whom Mami looked up to. Just before the Revolution began in Cuba, my aunt Sylvia married my uncle Bill, an *americano*, and moved into one of those brick buildings.

Only years later did Mami admit how disappointed she was to discover that this was the America where we'd landed. What mattered was to reunite our family. My parents and Mori and I lived in an apartment on the sixth floor. Sylvia and Bill and my cousins, Danny and Linda, lived on the fourth floor. Baba and Zayde lived on the third floor with my uncle Miguel, then in his late teens. We children roamed in and out of the three apartments freely, as if no doors separated them.

I was the oldest of the four children, three years older than Mori and Linda, and two years older than Danny. I was the first to go to school. Because I was so miserable—suddenly finding myself unable to speak to my classmates because I didn't know English—I insisted we play school after I returned home. Re-creating my school day in the world of make-believe, I could be in charge rather than being a loser. As the only one who knew anything about school, I insisted on being the teacher; Mori, Linda, and Danny were the students.

By the age of six, in first grade, I felt very grown up. As an immigrant child, I'd lost interest, or possibly faith, in dolls, but I begged my parents to buy me a blackboard. Papi wasn't keen on the idea, but Mami advocated on my behalf, and they got me a blackboard that teetered on rickety wooden legs. It came with a drawer for storing the chalk and eraser. Just like my real teacher, I had an envelope with gold stars. I'd paste them on the "assignments" of my "students" if they did well and behaved in class.

Linda received all the stars. She was obedient. Mori daydreamed. Danny never sat still. Eventually the two boys formed an alliance and wrecked my classroom, becoming hopelessly unruly. No amount of threats that they'd never earn a gold star brought them into line.

What painful recognition I feel gazing at pictures of myself then—an uncertain smile, hair uncombed. I wore knee-high socks that sagged, black-and-white loafers a size too big. I had a plaid skirt with a lumpy hem. Mami rolled it up and sewed it with loose stitches, so she could let it down as I grew taller. For some mysterious reason, I liked to button my blouses all the way up to the top, primly, so they pinched my neck. I looked the part of the frumpy schoolteacher.

So why does it come as a surprise to me that I did eventually become a schoolteacher? It is my teaching that supports my travels, and when I'm not on the road, I'm standing in front of the room lecturing to students. But the truth is I'd prefer to sit in the corner and not have to speak. I'm more a listener than a talker. And I don't forget my humble roots as a shy immigrant child who spent a year in the dumb class.

I had a high school teacher, Mrs. Rodríguez, who told me I was smart and should go away to college. A Cuban immigrant, she'd taught literature at the University of Havana, but when she came to New York her degree was worthless. To make ends meet, she became a Spanish teacher at Forest Hills High School, slowly accruing the credits for her PhD in literature in night courses at NYU. She introduced me to the novels of Gabriel García Márquez and the short stories of Jorge Luis Borges and inspired me to write poems in Spanish. As Mrs. Rodríguez's favorite student, I was invited out each week for a kitchen sink ice cream sundae at Jahn's on Queens Boulevard. I loved hearing Mrs. Rodríguez speak her melodious Spanish. She sang when she talked, and she bared her heart to me during these outings but never let me forget *she* was the teacher. With a gentle wink of her blue eyes, she'd correct me if I failed to address her in the formal *usted*.

I kept it a secret from Mami and Papi that I spent so much time after school with Mrs. Rodríguez. It upset Papi that she was giving me advice about my future. He didn't want me to go to college. He believed that a good girl stayed in her father's house until a man came along and married her.

Mami understood me. She sneaked money out of the checkbook so I could pay the college application fees.

Once the acceptances arrived, with scholarship offers to boot, I expected Papi to change his mind and be happy. Instead he was furious. I shed many tears over dinners of *arroz con pollo* during my last few months of high school, failing to convince him it was important for me to get an education. My mother shed many more tears in the bedroom with my father, who admonished her for giving in to my wishes. Late at night, sleeping with my ear pressed against the wall of the bedroom I shared with Mori, which adjoined theirs, I heard Mami's cries.

Finally Papi relented and let me go. But there was rage in his surrender. And maybe also love, though I couldn't understand that back then. Love for a daughter who was leaving home. I set off for Wesleyan University, just a few hours away in Middletown, Connecticut, filled with feelings of doom. Even with a scholarship, college was expensive, and Mami let me know in our weekly phone calls that my studies were proving to be a financial strain on them. Two months into college, I met with the dean and figured out a plan to take summer tutorials so I could graduate a year early. After finishing college in three years (including spending a semester abroad in Spain), I went straight to graduate school, supported this time by a full scholarship. At twenty-six, I earned my PhD.

Mrs. Rodríguez said I was smart, but I never believed it. I feared I needed to stay in school in order not to grow dumb. But in school, to this very day, I often feel so dumb! Attending a symposium recently with faculty and graduate students at my university, I felt pathetically tongue-tied, unable to think of anything smart to say.

But now my colleagues, demonstrating huge kindness and generosity, have nominated me for a collegiate professorship, a named chair.

Rather than run out and shout the news to everyone in sight, I keep it to myself. I am not at all sure I deserve such an honor.

I don't tell even Mami and Papi.

Months pass and finally, at the airport, returning from an academic event in Atlanta, and with a little time to kill, I decide to give Mami and Papi a call in New York.

Mami, as always, answers the phone.

"*Me van a dar una silla. Lo llaman así—un* chair."

"*¿Y Ruti, te van a pagar más? ¿Te suben el sueldo?*"

"*Un poco.*"

Mami doesn't think I earn enough money. When I started teaching and Mami asked about my salary, she lamented, "*¿Por eso te estás quemando la vista?*" For that you're burning out your eyes?

"*¡Alberto!*" she calls to my father, who is down in the basement.

Papi is watching a football game. He hates to be interrupted but picks up the phone.

"Hello, Ruth."

He calls me Ruth lately, not Ruti, my childhood name. I wonder whether he does it to emphasize the distance between us, the unforgiveable mutiny I enacted when I left home over thirty years ago. But maybe he's just acknowledging, finally, that I'm no longer his little girl.

"I just wanted to tell you—they're giving me a chair."

"*¿Que es eso—un* chair? *No entiendo.*"

I try to think of how to explain it to him, stumbling so much I stutter. "*Es algo muy importante.* It's the highest honor they give professors at our university."

"And they call it like that—*una silla?*"

"That means it's permanent. They want me at the university forever."

"Okay. Talk more to your mother."

He clicks off. No words of praise. No words of congratulations.

I know Papi never forgave Abuelo for forcing him to give up his dream of studying to become an architect. With his gorgeous penmanship, Papi would have designed the most beautiful houses. But Abuelo demanded he help him peddle blankets door to door, so Papi ended up studying accounting, the only subject offered during evening classes in the 1950s at the University of Havana. Coming to the United States soon after, and having to start life over as a penniless immigrant, he worked seven days a week to support my mother, my brother, and me, working at a desk job from Monday to Friday and fumigating apartments in Spanish Harlem on weekends. Eventually he moved up, becoming a traveling textile salesman, selling the *shmates*, as he often put it, that nobody in the United States wanted to buy to merchants in Latin America.

Perhaps Papi resents my education? Perhaps he thinks it's a pity so much precious knowledge has been wasted on a woman? Perhaps I've never shown sufficient appreciation for the sacrifices he made for me as a father? I can only speculate about what he thinks, what thorns are scratching at his heart. Such a long time being his daughter, and I still can't read my father's silences.

Hearing the gate agent announce over the loudspeaker that the first-class passengers can board the plane, I leap to my feet, glad to line up with the other privileged travelers. On domestic flights I'm sometimes upgraded to first class, my reward for traveling so much. Between the plush seating and getting plenty of water to drink on the flight, I'll get schoolwork done. There's always more schoolwork to be done when you're a teacher.

As the plane rises into the sky, I pull out my red pen and the writing assignments of my students. I see ways they can improve, ways they can say what they want to say more clearly, more forcefully. I figure the plane can't possibly crash so long as the students are awaiting my response to their work.

I concentrate well when my head is in the clouds. I scribble dozens of comments on the margins of the papers. I remember to say something positive to each student. Everyone gets a gold star—for effort, if nothing else.

As we touch down, it dawns on me that what Papi wants is a gold star—from me. And as old as I am, a middle-aged woman now, I'm still waiting for a gold star—from Papi.

IV.
In Tribute, In Time

The Weight of Paper

BEATRIZ TERRAZAS

It's the kind of North Texas afternoon in which the heat tops one hundred degrees and the humidity has us panting. Still, because it's late summer, there's the sweet anticipation of bass-drum beats heralding a new football season and school year across America. For me there's also the thrill for my cousin's daughter, Veronica, who sits at my kitchen table explaining the roommate situation for her college freshman year. She attended the same high school from which I graduated thirty years prior, and as I did then, she is now moving on to college classes, college football games. Her embrace of a new mascot—go Bears!—has been immediate and complete.

"They matched us by major," she says of the young woman with whom she will share a dorm. "But I've changed mine since then."

"Really? To what?" I can't imagine what could have toppled medicine from its spot as her top choice. As far back as elementary school she dreamed of being a pediatrician.

"Neuroscience," she says. It seems that now she may want to go into medical research rather than medical practice.

My heart quickly expands with pride, feeling as if it might burst like an overblown balloon. This is a child who attended my wedding as a screaming newborn. Who visited my home and kicked a soccer ball at a nearby park. And who one Christmas engaged in a forbidden game of ball with a cousin in my living room and accidentally beheaded a ceramic St. Joseph in the nativity scene. Now, just a day shy of her eighteenth birthday, she is a burgeoning scientist encapsulated in cheerleader legs and flawless summer skin. She is risen from the same Mexican roots as I, blood of my blood. Her grandmother is my *tía*, my mom's sister. And when Veronica insisted on coming from El Paso to Baylor University in Central Texas for her undergraduate degree, the family selected my home, less than a two-hour drive from the university, as a sort of headquarters for the college move. Though I don't have kids, my proximity also means that during her college stay she can rely on me and my husband to help out in case of an emergency. So now we sit at my table, her father exhausted from attending parent orientations and shopping for dorm furnishings, both of us not a little dazed and dumbfounded by the possibilities for this girl once she has that college degree.

The thing is, I know the weight of a piece of paper. My parents traded a life in Mexico for one such paper. Later I would realize this trade involved a more brutal reneging of soul than of land, but with my first awareness of American citizenship and what it meant, I understood their naturalization as a key to a universe replete with opportunities they'd never known. Thus, my siblings and I inherited a legacy of more paper; we were expected to earn good grades on school report cards, a high school diploma, and, finally, the ultimate paper, a college degree. All of which were to open more doors for us.

Which is why the opportunities before Veronica stir a sense of pride within me. But beneath the excitement run currents of something else: a drop of envy as she begins her journey, and a measure of apprehension at how it might change her life. Blame my own education, how hit or miss it seems looking back on it, and how its perceived deficiencies can still haunt me to the point of paralysis. Not to mention how it has challenged my own relationship with my parents. With barely an elementary school education themselves, my parents pushed and prodded my siblings and me into graduating from high school and college. It wasn't a choice. As in other Mexican households, my parents were *la ley*. We *would* go to college. As immigrants, my parents knew that in order to have better jobs and livelihoods than they did, their kids had to get an education. But I don't think they realized the battles we would face along the college road—within ourselves and without—nor how that goal, once reached, would enlarge a gap that opened between us and them the moment they chose to come to this country. It wasn't language that would divide us in the future, though certainly there would be times when English would crowd the Spanish out of my mind and leave me stuttering. It was more a matter of our family's culture, values, and even religion ceding ground in my life to new, sometimes seemingly treacherous ideas and philosophies. Occasionally the chasm between us would feel so wide we would see one another and think, "Who is that?"

My father has never spoken of the dreams he had for his life in America. Or rather, to my great shame, I've never asked. But I know that he grew up poor in the state of Chihuahua, that his toys and sometimes even the shoes he wore as a boy were crafted by his own hands. I know that he worked as a *brazero* in the fields around Las Cruces and El Paso, and that from there his life expanded to include my mother and us kids. That eventually he moved into construction work and after that opened up his own business. My mother, on the other hand, harbored dreams of becoming a nurse but was limited by an education that didn't extend beyond grade school. From the state of Durango she came to Juárez with her family, and there she worked in a *farmácia* selling Crema de la Campana, filling prescriptions, and administering shots that she'd learned to give patients by puncturing the skin of an orange with a needle.

Despite her lack of education—or perhaps because of it—my mother is the one who I most recall exhorting me to focus on school. Distractions? Not allowed. Not in the form of friend or foe. I didn't do sleepovers at friends' homes, and I wasn't allowed to stay out late. If other kids didn't like me or made fun of me, I was to ignore them. One girl in junior high tested me dearly. I don't remember exactly what she did, only that she disliked me intensely and would say things to rile me, to pick a fight. In a final effort to provoke me one day, she stole the key to my gym locker. I set my jaw and, per my mother's instructions, pretended not to care. I don't recall how long this went on—days probably—but finally one afternoon she tossed the key at me from across the room and said, "*Tóma, métetela.*" She never bothered me again.

High school was a different kind of challenge, with groups self-segregating into cliques: the beautiful and the popular; the ones who smoked dope; the letter-jacketed jocks; the brains who garnered As in the toughest classes. Unless you counted band nerds, I belonged to no group. But the distinction that I most felt as my high school years slipped by was that other kids—mostly white kids, mind you—knew from Day One which university they would attend, what they would study, and what degree they'd have in hand at the end of those four years. It was as if they'd been assigned a role for adulthood, complete with a roadmap for getting there, and they were simply fulfilling it by studying biology and calculus, joining the math club, acting in theater productions, or competing with the debate team. I'm sure this was largely due to the fact that their families had a long history of college attendance. Their university careers were a given.

As the oldest among my siblings, I would be the first in our family—among the first generation, in fact, on both sides of my family—to graduate high school, let alone college. But a college degree was a nebulous thing. My parents knew I needed one, but they didn't know the first thing about how to apply to a school, nor on what basis to select one. So I stumbled through high school a little blindly, working toward that magical piece of paper that would unlock my future.

My English and composition teachers were encouraging; I could write. I also had a knack for art and enjoyed taking photographs, though no one ever suggested I write or shoot for the school paper or yearbook. I wasn't so great at math, nor at science, though I enjoyed biology classes tremendously, and sometimes I thought I could be a doctor. One of my biology teachers was a favorite among my brainier peers. He, too, was kind, and encouraging, but I didn't fit in with the others in his classes.

Where I did fit in was the elective classes where many of my brown-skinned peers ended up. I could take dictation like nobody's business, eighty words a minute on the typewriter and sometimes up to a hundred words a minute in shorthand. Looking back, I wonder if I was pushed in that direction by a well-meaning but misguided counselor; after all, I was in the top 25 percent of my class, which is to say that I was a decent student, but not stellar. Had I been in the top 10 percent, like my sister who would come along later, I would have been harder to ignore. But I'd done nothing to distinguish myself, and not having a precedent for higher education, I'm sure I floundered when teachers asked what I'd like to study after high school. I really didn't know.

Maybe that's why I don't recall a single teacher or counselor ever telling me that I could attend a university outside of my hometown. Somehow I graduated high school and was admitted at the University of Texas at El Paso. I stumbled around there, too, changing majors a couple of times in the quest for the right degree, for the piece of paper that would unlock the doors to my future, before finally settling on something that seemed to combine my writing talent with a love of all things visual: journalism. I did well, got mostly As and Bs, even made the dean's list a couple of years. I was in the band, performing in woodwind choirs and clarinet choirs, all of which for three straight years earned me a scholarship that paid for most of my tuition. It's not with regret that I look back on my years at the UTEP and the degree the school conferred on me, a bachelor of arts in journalism. I'm proud of UTEP and the education it offers. Rather, I look back at those years with a question: how much more expansive might my education have been had a single person in high school encouraged me to look beyond my hometown? Would knowing that I had a choice of where to go to college have made a difference in my life? Would a private school or an out-of-state school have opened doors I didn't know existed back then? And more than that, would it have given me the kind of self-confidence that sometimes I find in short supply?

Because thirty years later there are nights when I run through hallways and up and down stairwells in my dreams. I am on campus, looking for and not finding the classroom where a math professor is giving a final that I need to take and pass in order to get my degree. Sometimes it's a history class. Other times it's English. But the result is always the same: I am roused by a sense of terror that somehow I got off track and missed getting that degree. I have to fully awaken and remind myself that I did graduate, and that no one can take away what I've already earned.

There are also waking moments of withering doubt. Such as the day when I was exchanging e-mails with an organizer of a literary festival. She had read a memoir piece I wrote for a national women's magazine and liked it so much she wanted me to lead some workshops for high school students as part of a literary festival. Unlike my own high school, this was a predominantly white school in a part of Texas where old money dwells. The community is distinguished enough that parents can organize their yearly event around literary stars the likes of Anchee Min, Michael Chabon, and Billy Collins. This year, it would be Tobias Wolff.

I was honored. And terrified. Even as I said that yes I would do this—because it was a paying gig and because sometimes I must do the thing that scares me most in order to keep vanquishing the nightmares and the anxieties of not measuring up—even as I said yes, the doubts rose. Much like my junior high bully, a voice spoke within me, taunting, humiliating.

Poser!

Faker!

Fraud!

Who do you think you are, teaching privileged white kids who are going to attend Harvard and Yale and Princeton? You, whose claim to an education is from the University of Texas at El Paso, the hometown school that you attended because no one ever told you that you could aim higher? When you say, "UTEP. I graduated from UTEP," what do you think those kids are going to think? What can you possibly have to offer them?

I was tempted to e-mail my contact and renege. But I made myself deaf to the voice, reminded myself that an education is only as significant as what you do with it, and that the piece of paper bestowed on me by my hometown school, UTEP, did indeed open doors for me. As a journalist I've been witness to some profound moments of global history that I've helped share with others: a group of Japanese women attending a United Nations conference on women in Huairou, China, excitedly posing for a photo with Betty Friedan, late feminist activist and cofounder of the National Organization for Women; indigenous activist Rigoberta Menchú talking to a group of journalists in her hotel room at the same UN conference; the late Pope John Paul II waving from behind the bullet-proof glass of the "pope-mobile" as it glided along Cuba's Malecón. I've covered political conventions and photographed U.S. presidents, Hollywood stars, and professional athletes. My camera and reporter's notebook have also been a window to some intensely personal moments: a mother crying as she keeps vigil by the bed where her sixteen-year-old lay dying; a firefighter carrying through the woods a dead child he pulled from a flooded creek; a sheriff weeping in court after being exonerated of a crime; art patrons exclaiming over the vivid rendering of Georgia O'Keeffe's flowers on canvas.

A simple sheet of paper—a bachelor of arts in journalism—became my entry into a universe where I was privileged to bear witness to human triumph, pain, love, and glory. Without that piece of paper with its university seal embossed in gold, what world would I now inhabit? How much smaller might it be?

If my parents' success can be measured by their kids' college degrees, then they did pretty darn well. My brother and sister both went on to finish graduate school. I did not, choosing instead to devote myself fully to daily journalism; I thrived on the intensity of deadlines and travel and coming into contact with every manner of human life and emotion. And in 1998 I would receive a Nieman Fellowship, a non-degreed year of study for journalists at Harvard University. But if there is a downside to my parents' achievement it's that nothing is gained without something being lost. They gave me the books and the knowledge that they never had so that I could better myself. But in doing so, they ensured that at some points in my life I would view them as provincial people clinging to cultural mores and religious dogma that made no sense in a modern world. We argued, for instance, about things such as contraception and abortion. How could contraceptives be wrong? I challenged my mother. Didn't she think that I had a right to decide on what went on with my own body? And what do you mean abortion is morally wrong even in the case of rape? Wasn't the pressure of bearing a rapist's baby heaping one wrong on top of another? I viewed the issues through the lens of increasing choices for women, which I'd begun to explore during my university years. She viewed them through a narrower lens of religion and family. She couldn't believe that I'd turned my back on her teachings. And when I moved six hundred miles from home to launch the career made possible by my degree, it was if I were turning my back on the biggest tenet of our culture, family. "Se me hace cosa de otro mundo," I recall her saying. She was right. I was moving into another world made possible by education, and I didn't know how to do so without leaving parts of my old world behind.

Later I wanted to share career highlights with my parents, but I faltered in explaining the magnitude of these experiences. When I was on a team at the Dallas Morning News that won the Pulitzer Prize in 1994 for a project examining violence against women around the globe, I struggled to describe the honor. How to explain that this project sought to show violence against women through the human rights prism, and how to explain the triumph of being a part of something so much bigger than my own life and having that rewarded by a Pulitzer Prize? There were, of course, career moments that defied any explanation at all: Why photograph gang members with guns? Why get in my car to chase tornadoes? Or stand out near a creek through most of a cold, rainy night, fingers frozen, in order to document the spot where a child was found murdered? These moments I didn't mention at all.

Once, during my Nieman year at Harvard, a small group of Latina students in the Graduate School of Education invited me to spend time with them. They'd joined together so they could share the personal struggles inherent in being ethnic minorities at an Ivy League school. A familiar ache announced itself in my heart as one of the young women said that going home during holidays was wonderful, but it was also awful. She loved her family, but now when she was at home, she was shocked by their ignorance. Ethnic terms, for instance, were a problem, and she found herself correcting terms her mother had used all her life: "*No es chinito 'Ama, es asiatico.*" I knew exactly how she felt. In seeking an education, we had evolved. We didn't quite fit in with our families anymore, but we didn't quite fit in with mainstream society, either. In between these worlds, we were now forced to carve out a new space where we felt comfortable, where we did fit in, at least with one another. We were not alone.

These are the things I ponder as my cousin's daughter embarks on her university adventure. I remind myself that her experience is already different. She is an extrovert with the self-confidence born of playing team sports and serving on teen boards. Her mother has an accounting degree, and she has two cousins who recently graduated from college and another who will start next semester. Her support system is broader and stronger than mine was twenty-five years ago. Still, leaving home is stressful. She's tired. I can see on her face that she wants these last moments with her family to be over, and at the same time she wants them to last forever.

There are so many things I want to say to her. I want to tell her there will be moments in the next few years when she wants to rid herself of all of us because we are too old-fashioned or set in our ways, or because we don't understand her, and that it's okay to feel that way. I want to tell her that no matter what, her parents have sacrificed time and money and pieces of their own lives to get her here, so she mustn't forget that. I want to remind her that due to Alzheimer's, on most days my mother doesn't remember my name but she always, *always* remembers to wave at the UTEP campus when she goes by on the freeway because that's where her two daughters went to college. I want to say, "See how much this means in our family, this newfound legacy of education?"

But in the end, I say only this: "Remember, I'm less than two hours away from you. If you need anything at all—if you get homesick, or just sick—call me. I am here for you."

And maybe that's all she needs to hear right now, because she says, "Don't worry, you're at the top of my call list."

EPILOGUE

A few months after writing this piece, I e-mailed it to Veronica. It was an offering of family history I thought she might one day want. I didn't want her to feel obligated to respond; nor did I want her to embrace my story as her own. I wanted her to rejoice in how far we've come as a family, and to realize that there are horizons beyond horizons out there waiting for her and that she will reach them if she just keeps moving forward. She responded with a lengthy, emotional message. I'd unwittingly tapped into something she'd felt but had not yet verbalized, what with the stress of moving, living with strangers, making new friends, pulling all night-study sessions for final exams. She said the essay nearly brought her to tears and that it's difficult "going to a predominantly white school" where most kids have money. It's difficult to "not conform," she wrote, which I take to mean in part that it's hard to not want what others have. She said that she, too, fears one day not fitting in with her family or the friends who chose to remain in El Paso.

The latter part of her message was the toughest to absorb. She's a strong young woman and will come to terms with the ever-present issue of money and its power over our lives. She's already learning to look beyond ethnicity and race for our universal humanity. But education and how it transforms us? That's a trickier issue.

Must we always leave something or someone behind in order to move forward? My mother once confessed to me that having her U.S. citizenship approved all those years ago had been a bittersweet triumph. "It happened so fast," she said. So fast that when the moment for her oath came, she wasn't ready to renounce her homeland, yet she had to do so. I looked in her face and saw a heartbreak I didn't yet understand. It would be years before I realized the impact her sacrifice had on my life. In her blood, Veronica probably understands it already.

The last thing she wrote was this: "I love you and you're still the top of my phone list :)"

To My Younger Self

ERIKA MARTÍNEZ

You never imagined yourself living in Santo Domingo on a Fulbright Fellowship. But you'll be there heading east on Avenida 27 de Febrero toward the intersection with Avenida Abraham Lincoln. After thirty years, the green, yellow, and red of the Super Mercado Nacional sign will be the same. This intersection represented the center of the city for you as a child because your mother did her weekly grocery shopping here. With the Fulbright, this will once again be the center of your life because the largest bookstore in the city is right next door. If you'd stayed on the island, maybe your parents would still be married, and perhaps you'd have a better relationship with Mami. You've always wished that, like your cousins, you'd lived in your childhood home into adulthood, that you'd been educated in Spanish, that you'd had more time with your grandparents. As the traffic light turns green you'll realize maybe you wouldn't have attended the one public university in Santo Domingo with a major in literature; you wouldn't have lived the experiences that led you to become a writer. Emigrating to the United States, after all, made it possible for you to study languages, literature, and creative writing.

Until the fellowship you won't see the ways Mami influenced you to seek a better life through education. While growing up you'll hear from your younger sister and brother that Mami boasts about your scholastic achievements to aunts at parties, and you'll feel a sting, as if lemon juice trickled into a tiny cut on your finger making it feel like a deeper gash. At first you'll wonder why she's never told you herself that she's proud of you. Then, you'll be annoyed because you think she has no right to take credit for what you feel you've done on your own.

For years you will think that the decision to go to college was yours. You will look back at middle school and think that Mr. Wilson, your ninth-grade biology teacher, was the one who planted the seed in your mind. He will take you to the hallway, return your first exam of the year with a grade of 98, and tell you that you should go to college. As you return to your lab table you'll glow like the morning sun. His voice, suggesting you attend the college fair at the high school in a few weeks, will echo in your mind.

The night of the college fair will fall on Mami's day off from cleaning bathrooms at the Long Island Lighting Company. Even though her sunken eyelids reveal the exhaustion from her day shift at the U.S. Tape factory, you'll convince her to take you. You'll make your way through the library, the cafeteria, and the gym filled with tables displaying catalogs and think that you are just like all the other students, but you are not. Your peers will follow their parents who read consumer reports about the top colleges in the country and have lists of questions about admission requirements. You will be the one navigating through the rows of college representatives and listening to their pitches. By eavesdropping on other conversations you'll learn which questions to ask. Mami will follow close behind without speaking.

When you sign up for mailings you'll think Mami is quiet because she doesn't know the language; in fact, you are accustomed to leading her through schools, hospitals, and government buildings, always translating English to Spanish and interpreting the unsaid. You won't realize that this time she may be silent because she didn't go to college—it was difficult for her to finish high school at the age of twenty-two, and at that time, in Santo Domingo, there was only one university to attend. Mami no longer talks about her past or your future—at most, you see her in the morning before she leaves for work and at night before going to bed. In those few minutes she only gives you orders: to watch over your little sister and brother, to make dinner, to go to the Laundromat before you run out of clean clothes, to call the landlord and complain about the malfunctioning boiler, to buy money orders at the post office to pay the rent, the electricity, and the telephone.

In your home there are no family dinners where you can tell Mami how your day went at school. When you were in third grade she used to ask if you did your homework when she returned from work, but she doesn't do that anymore, perhaps because you are a good student. She doesn't tell you that education is important; she figures you know. She moved the family from Union City, New Jersey, to Long Island to live in better school districts, but you won't find this out until you are in your thirties when you hear her talking to your aunt. Since the relocation you've thought she moved the family to the suburbs so that you would be far away from Papi after the divorce. But she believed that the best schools in Union City were private, which she couldn't afford.

You know that even with several jobs it is hard for Mami to make the rent and buy food and clothes, yet you keep wishing for a mother who goes to your track meets, attends your school concerts, and helps you with your homework. You want someone like your best friend's mother who gives you a ride home after most extracurricular activities. When Mami does arrive at school, you are embarrassed because you are one of the last to be picked up in a little green Datsun that is older than you. You know what your reality is—your mother is a blue-collar worker earning not much more than minimum wage. At a later age you won't be proud of the shame you feel right now, but you will be glad you hoped for something better.

You think that maybe if you'd stayed in New Jersey living among other Latin American immigrants you wouldn't yearn for an English-speaking mother who works nine to five at an office, comes home to help you with vocabulary, and buys you new outfits at the beginning of every school year. You hate being one of a few Latinas in a Long Island school where no one knows about the Dominican Republic. You hate being different, but this will prepare you to live on campus later. In college other students of color will face this isolation for the first time. You will already be accustomed to not fitting in. Feeling marginal won't stop you from seeking higher education.

You've had aspirations since you were little. As an eight-year-old you walked home from work with Mami one fall afternoon and talked about your future. Every time you jumped into a pile of brown maple leaves you told her all the things you could be—a lawyer like your uncle in Santo Domingo, or a doctor like your grandfather, or even the president of the United States. She watched you stomp the leaves until they no longer crunched beneath your feet. That will be the last time you remember her listening to your desires. Her pause told you she considered each possibility. Her smile let you know she believed in your potential.

You dream of being a professional who earns enough money, and to become one you have to go to college. Your biology teacher didn't have to say, "You should go to college." But you needed to hear that he believed in you. As an adult you'll be sorry you didn't have more people like him in your life to make up for what Mami could not be or do. You'll appreciate that he had high expectations for you and that he told you about the college fair—you will attend every year until you graduate.

When you go to high school for tenth grade, you'll see gold stars posted on the windows of the guidance counselors' offices for every senior accepted into a college. As more stars appear with different universities written below students' names, you'll make note of the ones you could add to the list you've been considering since the college fair. You'll notice the attention given to the stars with Yale and Cornell written on them. At first you'll aim high; you'll think about going to Princeton or the University of Pennsylvania. Mami will not know about your ambitions; you'll share these with Mrs. O'Neill, who sits beyond the golden stars—the guidance counselor assigned to work with students whose last names fall between the letters *M* and *P*.

Mrs. O'Neill will tell you about the importance of SAT scores for college admissions. After you take your PSATs she'll tell you where you can aspire to go; her list will not match yours. She'll encourage you to consider state schools, but you dream about private colleges. You'll need an advocate to tell Mrs. O'Neill you should not be underestimated, but you don't have a mother like that. You no longer remember the Mami in Santo Domingo who persuaded the Colegio La Salle administration to skip you from first to second grade. The Mami who was a preschool teacher at the Colegio San Judas Tadeo before coming to New York is a different person today. She works with her hands now and is too tired to speak. You hear her voice only when she shouts at the sight of your room littered with college catalogs and dirty McDonalds uniforms. The Mami who taught you to read and write before you started school will not appear in your memory for many years. She would push you to apply for those dream colleges and universities despite what Mrs. O'Neill says. You'll make due and continue to seek out assistance from your assigned guidance counselor. But maybe the old Mami will be there inside you because for tenth, eleventh, and twelfth grade you'll select classes that will look best on your records: AP history, AP English, AP Spanish, AP politics, AP physics, French 5, precalculus.

You'll know that taking honors classes, getting the best grades, and participating in extracurricular activities will be requisites to get into schools and to get scholarships. You'll ask Mrs. O'Neill about how to finance your education since Mami will not be able to pay for it. She'll suggest the ROTC program, which allows you to get a degree before requiring service in the armed forces. You will add colleges that have ROTC programs to your list. She'll also tell you about the Educational Opportunity Program at state schools that helps students from historically disadvantaged backgrounds go to college with financial aid and academic assistance. You'll add the four top SUNY schools to your list even though you'll be sure to discard them because they're too big; you'll already feel lost in a high school with three thousand students enrolled in grades ten through twelve.

You will take your SATs, and upon seeing the results Mrs. O'Neill will encourage you to take them again, but you doubt your score will improve. You'll hear your classmates talk about their Saturday SAT prep courses and how they study for hours. They'll take the exams again and again until they get the scores necessary for acceptance into schools like William and Mary or Boston College. You won't be able to enroll in a prep class—it's unaffordable. The days when Mami tutored you after school are in your early childhood past, left behind in Santo Domingo. You won't know how to prepare for the tests on your own, and you won't have the time to prepare because you'll be involved in Spanish club, French club, track and field, not to mention working at McDonald's. It won't make sense to peel the wrapper off another exam. You won't want to be at school on another Saturday morning with a number 2 pencil slipping from your sweaty grip. You won't want to feel your stomach cramp as the minute hand on the wall clock ticks as if connected to a bomb ready to detonate your future.

The SATs will haunt you at your ROTC interview. After the officer reviews the form you'll have filled out upon arrival, he'll suggest you sign up for the next test date because your scores aren't high enough. He'll talk to you about what you said you'd do if you didn't get the scholarship.

You'll confirm that the EOP program is your backup, and he'll tell you to change the answer on the form to indicate that you would apply for a two-year ROTC scholarship so that you're more likely to get the award. They'll want to make sure you are interested in becoming an officer. But you'll be trying to figure out a way to go to college without enlisting first; you won't know how to pay for the first two years.

You'll talk about college tuition and fees with Susan Barnes, a manager at McDonald's who'll become your first woman-of-color mentor. You will tell her things you think Mami won't understand. You'll grow closer to Susan as she guides you through the promotion process from crew trainer to crew chief to in-store manager. She'll admire your ability to balance cash drawers during closing shifts at midnight and will think you are going to study business management. While she trains you to do end-of-shift paperwork, she'll make you rethink working for the armed services. You'll tell her about your ROTC interview after a dinner rush, and she'll take you behind the salad display. You'll stand close enough to smell spearmint in her breath when she says, "Erika, they'll teach you how to kill people."

In your senior year of high school you'll decide to apply to Lafayette College and New York University, and Mrs. O'Neill will insist you pick a safety school. During your counseling session, a former student will visit, and she'll ask him to convince you to apply to Ithaca College. You will look at them straight-faced because you'll know Ithaca as a great party school and will have heard that many football players want to go there. Since you've been in the upper track at school, you've watched classmates compete for the best grades to stay in AP or honors classes so that they can get into excellent universities; they disregard those who go to community college or technical schools. In this way you'll have begun to look down on those who don't attend top institutions or who don't continue their studies at all. By now, without knowing it, you'll have bought into the elitism of the U.S. educational system, believing that people are smarter if they go to Ivy League schools. You'll want to place yourself with, or as close as possible to, what you believe is the more intelligent group, but you'll nod yes, a safety school. The Ithaca application won't require you to produce any additional essays and you'll request a fee waiver so that it only costs you the postage to apply.

Mami will sit you down at the kitchen table one weekend after your shift. She'll look down at her hands, cracked from the tape measures she handles at the factory and the cleansers she uses at her night job, and say, "*Yo te veo con la esperanza de ir a la universidad, pero tu tienes que saber que yo no te puedo ayudar.*" Her low voice will come out in a single tone—empty of emotion. Going to college will no longer be just a hope; you'll be determined to make it happen without her help. You'll tell her not to worry, that you're going to do it somehow. Within seconds you'll get up, head to the sink and start doing dishes with English and Spanish knotted in your throat. You'll be furious. You'll hold back tears of anger, because you'll wonder how it ever crossed her mind to tell you not to expect anything from her. Of course you'll know she can't help because she makes you contribute money for rent every month. You've bought your own clothes since ninth grade and don't eat at home any more because she cannot afford the groceries and doesn't think she should have to feed you if you work at a restaurant. Your anger will drive you even further to go away to college.

Seven gold stars will appear with your name written above each school to which you applied. You'll make your way through the financial aid forms, get copies of your income tax return forms and Mami's, and send in the requisites. You'll think you are going to Lafayette College: it is far away but close enough for affordable trips home on the holidays; it is small and the campus looks like those on the Ivy League catalogs you have eyed since ninth grade. You'll attend a pre-frosh weekend for students of color and fall in love with the school. It will be confirmed: this is where you want to go. You'll visit NYU and like it too, but it is a different kind of experience. You will want Lafayette. You won't visit Ithaca—it's unnecessary.

Your financial aid letters will arrive in the mail. Ithaca's EOP program will fund all expenses and disburse part of your Stafford Loan to cover books and transportation. NYU's award will defray most of the costs, but you'll need Mami to apply for a PLUS Loan to pay the remaining fees. NYU won't be an option, not because Mami said she wouldn't help, but because there is no way she'll be eligible for a loan—she doesn't even have a bank account. Both of these packages will be more than the SUNY offers; even though their tuition is lower, they'll award less financial aid, and you'll have to pay more out of your own pocket to attend. Lafayette won't give you financial aid. They'll say you can attend using federal aid you are eligible for—the Stafford Loan and Pell Grant—and won't understand that it will be impossible to come up with the other $22,000 annually. Your mother has never made more than $15,000 a year and never will.

When Mami and your cousin with a car drop you off at Ithaca College it won't seem like you had a choice, even though you've considered college since middle school. Seven acceptance letters will not have meant seven possibilities; only one will have been an option. You will make it despite tuition increases and decreases in financial aid. By the final year you'll be working forty hours a week on campus as a resident assistant, a teaching assistant, a reader for a blind student, an intern for a sociology professor, and off campus at McDonald's. You won't let the work compromise your grades—for your last semester you'll get a 4.0. You'll tell Mami some of your difficulties when you are forced to ask her to apply for a PLUS Loan the final year. She'll sign the forms you fill out under the condition that you'll repay the bills yourself as soon as they arrive. She'll never know the total amount you borrowed to get your bachelor's degree.

After four years, your family will come to graduation weekend. The commencement speaker will tell the class of 1995 to turn around and face the people in the bleachers. "It is time to thank your family and friends, send them your love because without them you would not be here today." In the crowd of over five thousand people above, you'll look in the left-hand corner to where your family stood during the procession. You'll spot Mami's hair freshly dyed jet-black and eyebrows filled in to match. Dressed in black, to mourn her mother's recent death, she'll seem small and frail. You'll be glad your sister drove her the six hours to be there, that you found her a room to rent on campus for the night so that she could be present. She will not have seen the campus since she left you in your freshman dorm four years earlier. You'll wave furiously, blow her kisses with both hands, and blink away your warm tears. You'll think back to the conversation you had with her after work when you were still in high school and say, "This is it, Mami, I did it just like I said I would."

Following the ceremony she'll give you a gold ring with your birthstone on it—*peridot*. She'll also give you a frame sold by the school, matted with two spaces, one for your diploma and the other for a picture of Ithaca's

1970s buildings on the top of South Hill. It will look expensive. You'll choke as you imagine how much she spent. You'll begin to recognize the sacrifices she's made; she'll still be working two jobs. Instead of aching for the mother that she couldn't be, you'll begin to see Mami as someone who gave you all she could.

Thirteen years later, when you come to Santo Domingo on the Fulbright to conduct research for your books, it will be most important to partake in family meals like the ones you wished for while growing up. Aunts and uncles will tell you what Mami was like before she left the island. At the dinner table your *tía* will say, "*Yo admiro mucho a Mercedes. Ella trabajó tanto para que ustedes se hicieran profesionales.*" She'll commend Mami for overcoming adversity to raise children who would become accomplished adults. Appreciation for Mami's hard work will replace the shame you felt while growing up. Even though your family valued an education, it didn't change a person's worth. You'll remember the frame Mami gave you for your diploma. It will have hung in your home office above the bookcase because she worked so hard to buy you that for graduation, but now you'll realize it was for all the work she did throughout your life. The photograph of Ithaca College's grey buildings among the fall-colored trees will remind you of your privilege to pursue the dreams you told Mami about long ago when you stomped on the brown maple leaves.

After Yale

LI YUN ALVARADO

I've started dreaming in Spanish, which has never happened before. . . . I'm afraid to lose all this, to lose Abuela Ce-
lia again. But sooner or later I'd have to return to New York.
I know now it's where I belong—not *instead* of here, but
more than here. How can I tell my grandmother this?

PILAR IN *DREAMING IN CUBAN* BY CRISTINA GARCÍA

As the singing draws to a close, the cousins urge her to make a wish.
She leans forward and shuts her eyes. There is so much she wants,
it is hard to single out one wish. There have been too many stops
on the road of the last twenty-nine years since her family left this
island behind. . . . Let this turn out to be my home, Yolanda wishes.

YOLANDA IN *HOW THE GARCÍA GIRLS LOST
THEIR ACCENTS* BY JULIA ALVAREZ

That world in Brooklyn from which I derived both comfort and anxiety was home, as was the other world, across the ocean, where my father still wrote poems. As was the other world, the one across the river, where I intended to make my life. I'd have to learn to straddle all
of them, a rider on three horses, each headed in a different direction.

NEGI IN *ALMOST A WOMAN* BY ESMERALDA SANTIAGO

SENIOR THESIS

High on adrenaline and caffeine
the air thin, my head light
I wrote you.

Te escribí.

When no one else
was writing
I wrote.

Combed the stacks
for the slightest references
the quietest whispers

proof

that these words had left
una huella
no solo en este corazón.

I wove your stories together.
Broke each down.
Built new connections.

Cristina, Julia, Esmeralda,

I grew with your girls. Found myself
in their struggles. Hope
in their victories.

I wrote for you.
Elevated these "new" stories.
Pushed the boundaries of old canons.

Te escribí.

Pilar, Yolanda, Negi,

like me, you navigated
familias de sal y sazón,
and a white white world.

Escribí
about summers on the island,
winters in English only hallways.

I wrote

surrounded by ivy,
scowling gargoyles,
massive stone walls.

Recounted
your histories,
relived my own.

I birthed
fifty pages
¡En español!

And when four
months had passed,
each page written,

I crawled
into bed. Cradled
my exhaustion.

I cried

fat, wet tears
sobs built over four
years—more.

I slept long.

My breath heaving,
then slow. And when I woke,
just a whisper:

thank you

for our words
these truths
and this sweet sweet

release.

. . . .

Te escribí—I wrote you
¡en español!—in Spanish!
una huella / no solo en este corazón—a footprint / not only in this heart
familias de sal y sazón—families made of salt and spice

APRIL 2009 ~ SEVEN YEARS AFTER COMMENCEMENT ~ YALE UNIVERSITY

I wrote // surrounded by ivy / scowling gargoyles / massive stone walls

I am on stage wearing snug jeans that flare over my black faux-leather boots. My sleeveless black blouse has a plunging neckline accentuated by a large shell necklace resting across the fading brown hue on my chest—I have not been in Puerto Rico since Christmas. My bangs are parted, slicked back, and pinned carefully under a cascading crown of curls that frame my lightly powdered face. My lips are filled in with Almay's coffee #210. I hardly ever wear makeup, but on stage, this carefully chosen outfit, glossed lips, and powdered face are a must—a sign of respect for my audience. I look past the stage lights toward the shadowed faces in the crowd: Yale University Latino alumni spanning the classes of 1977 to 2012. It is the first night of the first Latino Alumni Reunion.

Tomorrow we will wander from old haunt to old haunt. We will listen to panels of Latina and Latino scholars, professionals, and volunteers.

I will pass Justice Sonia Sotomayor in the hallway and snap a picture next to Justice Carlos Moreno. Tomorrow the founders of the Puerto Rican and Chicano Cultural Centers will be honored by generations of eternally grateful alumni. Tomorrow we will dance in a dining hall and then migrate to one of my class's favorite bars, El Amigo Felix, and finally to La Casa (the site where the former Puerto Rican and Chicano Cultural Centers merged into one Latino Cultural Center) for the after-after-party.

The following day, sleepy but inspired, we will gather to plan. To continue the process of building a National Latino Alumni Association that will enable us to connect and support each other. An association that will help us leverage the power of our collective action.

But for now, I am on stage, reading a poem.

DECEMBER 2001 ~ SENIOR YEAR ~ FARNAM HALL, OLD CAMPUS

High on adrenaline and caffeine / the air thin, my head light / I wrote you.

The call came on a Sunday.

By some stroke of luck, I was sitting by the white touch-tone phone (complete with springy cord), and not off at some organization's meeting. Or at the library researching. Or crying in my best friend's dorm room about my devastating breakup. Or coaching one of my freshmen counselees through the trauma of first semester finals week at Yale. I was there, in the dust and paper-filled common room I shared with the other two freshmen counselors, as if I had been waiting for that call to come.

When I heard my senior essay adviser's voice on the phone, my stomach dropped. Why was he calling? On a Sunday? On the Sunday after I submitted my senior essay—a week late.

Despite my best efforts, I had gone to see my dean two days before the essay was due. Nose running, breath tight, I walked into his office and, tail between my legs, explained, "Dean C., my essay is due on Friday, and I almost have enough pages but I need a few extra days and some sleep to make it better. I think I just need until Monday. I hate to ask, but can I have a dean's excuse?"

I had always prided myself in my ability to work to deadlines, rarely asking for extensions. This was only the second time in my four years at

Yale that I asked the dean for permission to turn in an assignment late. I was embarrassed that my body had failed me at this critical moment in my college career.

"Take a week," Dean C. said. "Go to bed, get better, then finish the essay by next Friday."

AUGUST 2000 ~ JUNIOR YEAR ~ MAMI'S HOUSE, NEW YORK CITY

when no one else / was writing / I wrote

I leafed through the massive "blue-book," carefully noting which of the thousands of classes I would "shop" this fall before choosing the five for which I would officially register. Yale's "shopping period" was a blessing and a curse for a meticulous student like myself. Before each semester, I would draw color-coded schedules of all the classes that interested me, creating full days of "shopping" class after class. By junior year, I had refined my technique, quickly skipping over the math and science sections, and focusing on my major interests like sociology, Spanish, and political science. By sophomore year, I declared a sociology major, but staring at a "shopping" list full of Spanish classes junior fall made me I realize what I had to do. I would take two or three Spanish classes each semester over the next two years. I would write two senior essays, one in Spanish in the fall and one in English to complete the sociology major in the spring. I would be a double major.

When I arrived at Yale freshman year, I knew I wanted to take at least one Spanish class each semester. Inspired by my AP Spanish literature class in high school and aware that I would not visit Puerto Rico each summer as I had while growing up, I decided to use Spanish classes at Yale as a way to read wonderful literature while improving my abilities in my family's mother tongue. Speaking, reading, and writing in Spanish made me feel closer to my other home and to my cousins, many of whom, like me, were in college, but on the island.

Besides the family connection, I loved literature. I had even considered majoring in English, but after one semester in a freshman English class at Yale, I decided against becoming a member of the English department. Whereas a TA taught my advanced freshman English class, professors taught all my Spanish classes. Also, as a student in a smaller department, I knew I would receive the kind of personal attention that would help me excel. And even before I knew the name Harold Bloom, Yale's English department seemed a little pretentious to me. Looking back, I realize that I steered clear of the English department because of something I was intuiting then, that the English department lacked faculty and student diversity, that it was overwhelmingly white. Ultimately I personally chose to study Spanish for some of the same reasons my friends chose to major or second major in disciplines like African American studies, Ethnicity, Race and Migration, Latin American studies, East Asian studies, or even American studies. We chose these disciplines because they were the ones in which we had a chance to see ourselves mirrored back in the materials *and* in the professors who taught that material.

My sophomore year at Yale, I met Dr. Irizarry. He was the Puerto Rican professor teaching the introduction to Latin American literature course, a prerequisite for taking advanced level Spanish classes. Dr. Irizarry was a tenure-track professor at Yale who earned his BA from the University of Puerto Rico, or "La Upi," as everyone in Puerto Rico calls it. "La Upi" is the same university system where several of my cousins earned or were earning their degrees. Here was a Puerto Rican professor who understood my three cultures: mainland, island, and academia-land without words. I had found my newest mentor and a piece of home at Yale. By senior year, I had taken two of Dr. Irizarry's courses and had asked him to act as my senior essay adviser.

OCTOBER 2008 ~ SIX YEARS AFTER COMMENCEMENT ~ SAN JUAN, PUERTO RICO

like me, you navigated / familias de sal y sazón / and a white white world.

I was earning an MA in English with creative writing at Fordham University when I attended my first Puerto Rican Studies Association conference. The morning before picking up my registration at the graduate center where the conference was being held, I explored Old San Juan. My family comes from Salinas, a small fishing town on the southern coast of the island, and I had never had time to myself in the old colonial capital. I envisioned what it might be like to experience Viejo San Juan as a resident instead of as a tourist. I pictured myself lounging in an internal garden in one of the old-fashioned colonial homes, or leaning over one of those wrought iron balconies. I saw myself writing poems while breathing in the thick humid air that always tasted like salt. I imagined living a drive away from my grandparents instead of a flight away.

As I walked into the open courtyard of the graduate center, I spotted Dr. Irizarry. Though we had stayed in touch since graduation, we hadn't seen each other since. We hugged and exchanged the standard Puerto Rican "kiss-on-the-cheek" greeting before he began introducing me to his friends and colleagues. I was surrounded by trilingual Puerto Ricans who, like me, spoke mainland, island, and academia-land. Dr. Irizarry, who had mentored me throughout my Yale career, was now welcoming me into this new family, one I had been in search of for years.

Dr. Irizarry was no longer at Yale, and I wondered what Yale had done to fill what I understood to be a great void. I once had the opportunity to ask Yale's president, Richard Levin, about the university's efforts to recruit and retain Latino and Latina professors. As an alumna active in alumni organizing, I was elected to serve as an at-large delegate to the Assembly of the Association of Yale Alumni. The assembly meets once a year and is meant to "provide an open forum for representatives of Yale volunteers to weigh in on Yale's role in a variety of issues." One of the perks of attending the assembly each year was having some access to leading officers of the university. At an assembly event I approached President Levin and asked him what the university was doing to recruit and retain more Latino and Latina professors. He hesitated, looked around at the others who wanted to greet him, and then cited one popular young tenured Latino professor in the history department. "Yes, I know him, we're friends," I responded, "but what about other departments?" Before being ushered away by another alumnus with a question, he went on to briefly explain that there are not enough Latinos and Latinas with PhDs and that many of those who have their doctorate are not far enough along in their careers to get tenure at an institution like Yale.

Yale is not unique in these concerns and constraints, but it remains unnerving for me to see these old institutional systems at play. The tenure process, among a variety of other factors, quietly and effectively keeps our most elite institutions' faculties homogenous even as student bodies become increasingly diverse. Too often, universities and even liberal arts colleges prioritize a faculty member's ability to publish over his or her ability to teach and support undergraduate and graduate students.

I was lucky. Dr. Irizarry happened to be at Yale just as I was seeking a mentor. I was also intentional: I chose a department that was likely to have Latino and Latina professors. My friends earning an English major had to take "Spanish" classes taught in English if they wanted to study works by Latino and Latina authors written *in English*, because Professor Irizarry was the one qualified to teach those courses at Yale. How many Yalies missed out on working with Professor Irizarry or professors like him because of the university's lack of vision and its lack of commitment to actively diversifying its faculty, especially in regards to Latino and Latina professors?

A decade after my graduation, Dr. Irizarry and I are still friends and now colleagues. As I study, read, research, and write my way through Fordham University's doctoral English program, I still rely on Dr. Irizarry's mentorship and support.

DECEMBER 2001 ~ YALE UNIVERSITY ~ SENIOR YEAR

I birthed / fifty pages / ¡En español!

Fall of my senior year I worked closely with Dr. Irizarry to choose my essay topic, create a working bibliography, structure my essay, and complete drafts in a timely manner. I knew I wanted to write about Latina-authored texts that considered migration between the Caribbean and New York City, and I chose to write about: Cristina García's *Dreaming in Cuban*, Julia Alvarez's *How the Garcia Girls Lost their Accents*, and Esmeralda Santiago's *When I Was Puerto Rican* and *Almost a Woman*. As I researched and wrote, I found myself writing about myself. I found a surprising comfort in being reminded I wasn't alone. Pilar, Yolanda, and Esmeralda, like Dr. Irizarry, became my mirrors.

Writing the essay was an overwhelming experience. I set out to write thirty-five pages—in Spanish—and ended up with fifty. The sociology essay I would write in the spring to complete the requirements of a double major would be a walk in the breeze compared to the cathartic experience writing my Spanish senior essay had been.

I finished and turned in the essay, *"tarde pero seguro"* as they say in Puerto Rico, and a few days later the phone rang.

"Li Yun," Dr. Irizarry said, "I just finished your essay and I couldn't wait to call you. It is one of the best undergraduate essays I have ever read. Graduate-level work. I'm giving you an A. I'm very impressed, and you should be very proud."

I was speechless. I must have said thank you. Whether I actually cried or only came close is one of the details that have been lost to memory.

With that phone call, I knew I had done it. I had made it through Yale. I knew I would graduate with distinction in the Spanish major, knew I would complete my coursework, and knew I would write the second essay. With Dr. Irizarry's phone call, all those things were just items on a "to do" list, waiting to be checked off. Any doubts that had surfaced throughout my Yale career disappeared. That senior essay, my crowning achievement, completed and well received, had made it all worth it.

I hung up the phone and called my friend Alvaro.

"Get dressed. We're going out every night this week. I just got an A on my senior essay!"

APRIL 2009 ~ SEVEN YEARS AFTER COMMENCEMENT ~ YALE UNIVERSITY

thank you // for our words / these truths / and this sweet sweet // release.

I finish my poem. After the show, senior after senior approaches me to thank me for my words. They tell me about their own struggles to write their essays and to make them meaningful to their lives and experiences. Over and over I hear what I knew was the case for my classmates and for myself. We saw our senior essays not as just another assignment, but also as an opportunity to create knowledge about our respective communities and lives.

As I listen to the students, I think about my friends who did not complete their essays in time. Friends who participated in our commencement ceremonies in 2002, while keeping their secret—they would not receive their diplomas that day. They planned to complete their opuses over the summer, not knowing it would take them years to finish. For many of my close Latino and Latina friends, the senior essay was not just a hurdle on the way to graduation; it was a reckoning. It was a uniting of multiple languages and identities onto the page. It was a demonstration, proof of our right to be at Yale and of Yale's need for us to be there, asking new questions and shedding new light on old problems. We were there to help carve out space for the trilingual and tricultural students who would follow us. Such responsibility was not taken lightly. For some of us, it took an intense semester of research and writing; for others it took several years of the same. But each one of us, thanks in part to the support we gave each other and the support we found in our mentors, completed our senior essays.

Knowing all of that, I speak to the students in the class of 2009 and tell them that they can complete their essays and that they *must* complete them. That they have a roomful of alumni, reunited for the first time, standing behind them, counting on them to succeed, knowing that they will.

How to Leave Hialeah

JENNINE CAPÓ CRUCET

It is impossible to leave without an excuse—something must push you out, at least at first. You won't go otherwise; you are happy, the weather is bright, and you have a car. It has a sunroof (which you call a moonroof—you're so quirky) and a thunderous muffler. After fifteen years of trial and error, you have finally arranged your bedroom furniture in a way that you and your father can agree on. You have a locker you can reach at Miami High. With so much going right, it is only when you're driven out like a fly waved through a window that you'll be outside long enough to realize that, barring the occasional hurricane, you won't die.

The most reliable (and admittedly the least empowering) way to excuse yourself from Hialeah is to date Michael Cardenas Junior. He lives two houses away from you and is very handsome and smart enough to feed himself and take you on dates. Your mother will love him because he plans to marry you in three years when you turn eighteen. He is nineteen. He also goes to Miami High, where he is very popular because he plays football and makes fun of reading. You are not so cool: you have a few friends, but all their last names start with the same letter as yours because, since first grade, your teachers have used the alphabet to assign your seats. Your friends have parents just like yours, and your moms are always hoping another mother comes along as a chaperone when you all go to the movies on Saturday nights because then they can compare their husbands' demands—*put my socks on for me before I get out of bed, I hate cold floors,* or *you have to make me my lunch because only your sandwiches taste good to me*—and laugh at how much they are like babies. Michael does not like your friends, but this is normal and to be expected since your friends occasionally use polysyllabic words. Michael will repeatedly try to have sex with you because you are a virgin and somewhat Catholic and he knows if you sleep together, you'll feel too guilty to ever leave him. Sex will be tempting because your best friend Carla is dating Michael's best friend Frankie, and Michael will swear on his father's grave that they're doing it. But you must hold out—you must push him off when he surprises you on your eight-month anniversary with a room at the Executive Inn by the airport and he has sprung for an entire five hours—because only then will he break up with you. This must happen, because even though you will get back together and break up two more times, it is during those broken-up weeks that you do things like research out-of-state colleges and sign up for community college classes at night to distract you from how pissed you are. This has the side effect of boosting your GPA.

During these same break-up weeks, Michael will use his fake ID to buy beer and hang out with Frankie, who, at the advice of an ex-girlfriend he slept with twice who's now living in Tallahassee, has applied to Florida State. They will talk about college girls, who they heard have sex with you without crying for two hours afterward. Michael, because he is not in your backyard playing catch with your little brother while your mother encourages you to swoon from the kitchen window, has time to fill out an application on a whim. And lo and behold, because it is October, and because FSU has rolling admissions and various guarantees of acceptance for Florida residents who can sign their names, he is suddenly college bound.

When you get back together and he tells you he's leaving at the end of June (his admission being conditional, requiring a summer term before his freshman year), tell your mom about his impending departure, how you will miss him *so* much, how you wish you could make him stay just a year longer so you could go to college at the same time. A week later, sit through your mother's vague sex talk, which your father has forced her to give you. She may rent *The Miracle of Life*; she may not. Either way, do not let on that you know more than she does thanks to public school and health class.

I was a virgin until my wedding night, she says.

Believe her. Ask if your dad was a virgin, too. Know exactly what she means when she says, Sort of. Try not to picture your father as a teenager, on top of some girl doing what you and Carla call a Temporary Penis Occupation. Assure yourself that TPOS are not sex, not really, because TPOS happen mostly by accident, without you wanting them to, and without any actual movement on your part. Do not ask about butt-sex, even though Michael has presented this as an option to let you keep your semi-virginity. Your mother will mention it briefly on her own, saying, For that men have prostitutes. Her words are enough to convince you never to try it.

Allow Michael to end things after attempting a long-distance relationship for three months. The distance has not been hard: you inherited his friends from last year who were juniors with you, and he drives down to Hialeah every weekend to see you and his mother and Frankie. Still, you're stubborn about the sex thing, and still, you can't think of your butt as anything other than an out-hole. Michael has no choice but to admit you're unreasonable and dump you.

Cry because you're genuinely hurt—you *love* him, you *do*—and because you did not apply early-decision to any colleges because you hadn't yet decided if you should follow him to FSU. When the misery melts to fury, send off the already-completed applications you'd torn from the glossy brochures stashed under your mattress and begin formulating arguments that will convince your parents to let you move far away from the city where every relative you have that's not in Cuba has lived since flying or floating into Miami; you will sell your car, you will eat cat food to save money, you are their American Dream. Get their blessing to go to the one school that accepts you by promising to come back and live down the street from them forever. Be sure to cross your fingers behind your back while making this promise, otherwise you risk being struck by lightening.

Once away at school, refuse to admit you are homesick. Pretend you are happy in your tiny dorm room with your roommate from Long Island. She has a Jeep Cherokee and you need groceries, and you have never seen snow and are nervous about walking a mile to the grocery store and back. Ask the RA what time the dorm closes for the night and try to play it off as a joke when she starts laughing. Do not tell anyone your father never finished high school. Admit to no one that you left Hialeah in large part to piss off a boy whose last name you will not remember in ten years.

Enroll in English classes because you want to meet white guys who wear V-neck sweaters and have never played football for fear of concussions. Sit behind them in lecture but decide early on that they're too distracting. You must do very well in your classes; e-mails from the school's Office of Diversity have emphasized that you are special, that you may feel like you're not cut out for this, that you should take advantage of the free tutors offered to students like you. You are important to our university community, they say. You are part of our commitment to diversity. Call your mother crying and tell her you don't fit in, and feel surprisingly better when she says, Just come home. Book a five hundred dollar flight to Miami for winter break.

Count down the days left until Noche Buena. Minutes after you walk off the plane, call all your old friends and tell them you're back and to get permission from their moms to stay out later than usual. Go to the beach even though it's sixty degrees and the water is freezing and full of Canadians. Laugh as your friends don their back-of-the-closet sweaters on New Year's while you're perfectly fine in a halter-top. New England winters have made you tough, you think. You have earned scores of ninety or higher on every final exam. You have had sex with one and a half guys (counting TPOS), and yes, there'd been guilt, but God did not strike you dead. Ignore Michael's calls on the first of the year and hide in your bedroom—which has not at all changed—when you see him in his Seminoles hoodie, stomping toward your house. Listen as he demands to talk to you, and your mom lies like you asked her to and says you're not home. Watch the conversation from between the blinds of the window that faces the driveway. Swallow down the wave of nausea when you catch your mother winking at him and titling her head toward that window. Pack immediately and live out of your suitcase for the one week left in your visit.

Go play pool with Myra, one of your closest alphabetical friends and say, *Oh man, that sucks*, when she tells you she's still working as a truck dispatcher for El Dorado Furniture. She will try to ignore you by making fun of your shoes, which you bought near campus, and which you didn't like at first but now appreciate for their comfort. Say, Seriously chica, that's a high school job—you can't work there forever.

Shut up with this chica crap like you know me, she says.

Then she slams her pool cue down on the green felt and throws the chunk of chalk at you as she charges out. Avoid embarrassment by shaking your head No as she leaves, like you regret sending her to her room with no dinner, but she left you no choice. Say to the people at the table next to yours, What the fuck, huh? One guy will look down at your hippie sandals and ask, How do you know Myra? Be confused, because you and Myra always had the same friends thanks to the alphabet, but you've never in your life seen this guy before that night.

While you drive home in your mom's car, think about what happened at the pool place. Replay the sound of the cue slapping the table in your head, the clinking balls as they rolled out of its way but didn't hide in the pockets. Decide not to talk to Myra for a while, that inviting her to come visit you up north is, for now, a bad idea. Wipe your face on your sleeve before you go inside your house, and when your mom asks you why you look so upset tell her the truth: you can't believe it—Myra is jealous.

Become an RA yourself your next year so that your parents don't worry as much about money. Attend all orientation workshops and decide, after a sexual harassment prevention role-playing where Russel, another new RA, asked if tit fucking counted as rape, that you will only do this for one year. Around Rush Week, hang up the anti-binge-drinking posters the hall director put in your mailbox. On it is a group of eight grinning students; only one of them is white. You look at your residents and are confused: they are all white, except for the girl from Kenya and the girl from California. Do not worry when these two residents start spending hours hanging out in your room—letting them sit on your bed does not constitute sexual harassment. Laugh with them when they make fun of the poster. *Such Diversity in One University!* Recommend them to your hall director as potential RA candidates for next year.

When you call home to check in (you do this five times a week), ask how everyone is doing. Get used to your mom saying, Fine, Fine. Appreciate the lack of detail—you have limited minutes on your phone plan and besides, your family, like you, is young and indestructible. They have floated across oceans and sucker-punched sharks with their bare hands. Your father eats three pounds of beef a day and his cholesterol is fine. Each weeknight, just before crossing herself and pulling a thin sheet over her pipe-cleaner legs, your ninety-nine-year-old great-grandmother smokes a cigar while sipping a glass of whiskey and water. No one you love has ever died—just one benefit of the teenage parenthood you've magically avoided despite the family tradition. Death is far off for every Cuban—you use Castro as your example. You know everyone will still be in Hialeah when you decide to come back.

Join the Spanish Club, where you meet actual lisping Spaniards and have a hard time understanding what they say. Date the treasurer, a grad student in Spanish literature named Marco, until he mentions your preference for being on top during sex subconsciously functions as retribution for *his* people conquering *your* people. Quit the Spanish Club and check out several Latin American history books from the library to figure out what the hell he's talking about. Do not tell your mother you broke things off; she loves Spaniards, and you are twenty and not married and you refuse to settle down.

We are not sending you so far away to come back with nothing, she says.

At the end of that semester, look at a printout of your transcript and give yourself a high-five. (To anyone watching, you're just clapping.) Going home for the summer with this printout still constitutes coming back with nothing despite the good grades, so decide to spend those months working full-time at the campus movie theater, flirting with sun-burned patrons.

Come senior year, decide what you need is to get back to your roots. Date a brother in Iota Delta, the campus's Latino Fraternity, because one, he has a car, and two, he gives you credibility in the collegiate minority community you forgot to join because you were hiding in the library for the past three years and never saw the flyers. Tell him you've always liked Puerto Ricans (even though every racist joke your father has ever told you involved Puerto Ricans in some way). Visit his house in Cherry Hill, New Jersey, and meet his third-generation American parents who cannot speak Spanish. Do not look confused when his mother serves meatloaf and mashed potatoes and your boyfriend calls it *real home cooking*. You have only ever had meatloaf in the school dining hall, and only once. Avoid staring at his mother's multiple chins. Hold your laughter even as she claims that Che Guevara is actually still alive and living in a castle off the coast of Vieques. Scribble physical notes inside your copy of *Clarissa* (the subject of your senior thesis) detailing all the ridiculous things his mother says while you're there: taking a shower while it rains basically guarantees you'll be hit by lightning; paper cannot actually be recycled; Puerto Ricans invented the fort. Wait until you get back to campus to call your father.

After almost four years away from Hialeah, panic that you're panicking when you think about going back—you had to leave to realize you ever wanted to. You'd thank Michael for the push, but you don't know where he is. You have not spoken to Myra since the blowout by the pool table. You only know she still lives with her parents because her mom and your mom see each other every Thursday while buying groceries at Sedano's. At your Iota brother's suggestion, take a Latino studies class with him after reasoning that it will make you remember who you were in high school and get you excited about moving back home.

Start saying things like, What does it really mean to be a minority? How do we construct identity? How is the concept of race forced upon us? Say these phrases to your parents when they ask you when they should drive up to move your stuff back to your room. Dismiss your father as a lazy thinker when he answers, What the fuck are you talking about? Break up with the Iota brother after deciding he and his organization are posers buying into the Ghetto-Fabulous-Jennifer-Lopez-Loving Latino identity put forth by the media; you earned an A-in the Latino studies course. After a fancy graduation dinner where your mom used your hotplate to cook arroz imperial—your favorite—tell your family you can't come home, because you need to know what home means before you can go there. Just keep eating when your father throws his fork on the floor and yells, What the fuck are you talking about? Cross your fingers under the table after you tell them you're going to grad school and your mom says, But *mamita*, you made a promise.

Move to what you learn is nicknamed The Great White North. Tell yourself, this is America! This is the heartland! Appreciate how everyone is so *nice*, but claim Hialeah fiercely since it's all people ask you about anyway. They've never seen hair so curly, so dark. You have never felt more Cuban in your life, mainly because for the first time you are consistently being identified as *Mexican or something*. This thrills you until the beginning-of-semester party for your grad program: you are the only person in attendance who is not white, and you're the only one under five foot seven. You stand alone by an unlit floor lamp, holding a glass of cheap red wine. You wish that Iota brother were around to protect you; he was very big; people were scared he would eat them; he had *Puro Latino* tattooed across his shoulders in Olde English Lettering. Chug the wine and decide that everyone in the world is a poser except maybe your parents. You think, *what does that even mean—poser?* Don't admit that you are somewhat drunk. Have another glass of wine and slip Spanish words into your sentences to see if anyone asks you about them. Consider yourself very charming and the most attractive female in your year, by far—you are *exotic*. Let one of the third-year students drive you home after he says he doesn't think you're okay to take a bus. Tell him, What, puta, you think I never rode no bus in Miami? Shit, I grew up on the bus. Do not tell him it was a private bus your parents paid twenty dollars a week for you to ride, along with other neighborhood kids, because they thought the public school bus was too dangerous— *they* had actually grown up on the busses you're now claiming. Your dad told you stories about bus fights, so you feel you can wing it as the third-year clicks your seatbelt on for you and says, That's fascinating— what does *puta* mean?

Spend the rest of that summer and early fall marveling at the lightning storms that you're sure are the only flashy thing about the Midwest. Take three months to figure out that the wailing sounds you sometimes hear in the air are not in your head—they are tornado sirens.

As the days grow shorter, sneak into tanning salons to maintain what you call your natural color. Justify this to yourself as healthy. You need more Vitamin D than these Viking people, you have no choice. Relax when the fake sun actually does make you brown, rather than the Play Doh orange beaming off your students—you have genuine African roots! You knew it all along! Do not think about how, just like all the other salon patrons, you reek of drying paint and burnt hair every time you emerge from that ultraviolet casket.

Date the third-year because he finds you *fascinating* and asks you all sorts of questions about growing up in *el barrio*, and you like to talk anyway. More importantly, he has a car, and you need groceries, and this city is much colder than your college home—you don't plan on walking anywhere. And you are lonely. Once the weather turns brutal and your heating bill hits triple digits, start sleeping with him for warmth. When he confesses that the growth you'd felt between his legs is actually a third testicle, you'll both be silent for several seconds, then he will growl, It doesn't actually *function*. He will grimace and grind his very square teeth as if you'd just called him *Tri-Balls*, even though you only said it in your head. When he turns away from you on the bed and covers his moon white legs, think that you could love this gloomy, deformed person; maybe he has always felt the loneliness sitting on you since you left home, except for him, it's because of an extra-heavy nut sack. Lean toward him and tell him you don't care—say it softly, of course—say that you would have liked some warning, but that otherwise it's just another fact about him. Do not use the word *exotic* to describe his special scrotum. You've learned since moving here that that word is used to push people into some separate, freakish category.

Break up with him when, after a department happy hour, you learn from another third-year that he's recently changed his dissertation topic to something concerning the Cuban-American community in Miami. He did this a month ago—*didn't he tell you?* On the walk to the car, accuse him of using you for research purposes.

Maybe I did, he says, But that isn't *why* I dated you, it was a *bonus*.

Tell him that being Cuban is no more a bonus than, say, a third nut. Turn on your heel and walk home in single-digit weather while he follows you in his car and yelps from the lowered window, Can't we talk about this? Call your mother after cursing him out in front of your apartment building for half an hour while he just stood there, observing.

Oh please, she says, her voice far away, Like anyone would want to read about Hialeah.

Do not yell at your mother for missing the point.

Change advisers several times until you find the one who does not refer to you as *the Mexican one* and does not ask you how your research applies to *regular* communities. Sit in bi-weekly off-campus meetings with your fellow Latinas, each of them made paler by the Great White North's conquest over their once-stubborn pigment. They face the same issues in their departments—the problem, you're learning, is system-wide. Write strongly worded joint letters to be sent at the end of the term. Think, *Is this really happening? I am part of this group?* Look at the dark greenish circles hanging under their eyes, the curly frizz poking out from their pulled-back hair and think, *Why did I think I had a choice?*

Call home less often. There is nothing good to report.

Why can't you just *shut up* about being Cuban, your mother says after asking if you're still causing trouble for yourself. No one would even notice if you flat-ironed your hair and stopped talking.

Put your head down and plow through the years you have left there because you know you will graduate: the department can't wait for you to be gone. You snuck into the main office (someone had sent out an e-mail saying there was free pizza in the staff fridge) and while your mouth worked on a cold slice of pepperoni, you heard the program coordinator yak into her phone that they couldn't wait to get rid of the troublemaker.

I don't know, she says seconds later, Probably about spics, that's her only angle.

You sneak back out of the office and spit the pepperoni out in a hallway trashcan because you're afraid of choking—you can't stop laughing. You have not heard the word *spic* used in the past decade. Your parents were spics. *Spics* is so seventies. They would not believe someone just called you that. Crack up because even the Midwest's slurs are way behind the East Coast's. Rename the computer file of your dissertation draft "Spictacular." Make yourself laugh every time you open it.

Embrace your obvious masochism. Make it your personal mission to educate the middle of the country about Latinos by living there just a little longer. But you have to move—you can't work in a department that your protests helped to officially document as *Currently Inhospitable to Blacks and Latinos*, even if it is friendly to disabled people and people with three testicles.

Decide to stay in the rural Midwest partly for political reasons: you have done what no one in your family has ever done—you have voted in a state other than Florida. And you cannot stand Hialeah's politics. You monitored their poll results via the Internet. Days before the election, you received a mass e-mail from Myra urging you to vote for the candidate whose books you turn upside down when you see them in stores. Start to worry you have Communist leanings—wonder if that's really so bad. Keep this to yourself; you do not want to hear the story of your father eating grasshoppers while in a Cuban prison, not again.

Get an adjunct position at a junior college in southern Wisconsin, where you teach a class called The Sociology of Communities. You have seventy-six students and, unlike your previous overly polite ones, they have opinions. Several of them are from Chicago and recognize your accent for what it actually is—not Spanish, but Urban. Let this give you hope. Their questions about Miami are about the beach, or if you'd been there during a particular hurricane, or if you've ever been to the birthplace of a particular rapper. Smile and nod, answer them after class—keep them focused on the reading.

At home, listen to and delete the week's messages from your mother. She is miserable because you have abandoned her, she says. You could have been raped and dismembered, your appendages strewn about Wisconsin and Illinois, and she would have no way of knowing.

You would call if you'd been dismembered, right? the recording says.

It has only been eight days since you last spoke to her.

The last message you do not delete. She is vague and says she needs to tell you something important. She is crying. You call back, forgetting about the time difference—it is eleven-thirty in Hialeah.

Ask, What's wrong?

Can I tell her? she asks your father. He says, I don't care.

Tell me what?

Tuck your feet under you on your couch and rub your eyes with your free hand.

Your cousin Barbarita, she says, Barbarita has a brain tumor.

Say, What, and then, Is this a fucking joke?

Take your hand away from your eyes and stick your thumbnail in your mouth. Gnaw on it. Barbarita is eleven years older than you. She taught you how to spit and how to roller skate. You cannot remember the last time you talked to her, but that is normal—you live far away. Then it comes to you. Eight months ago, at Noche Buena, last time you were home.

It's really bad. They know it's cancer. We didn't want to tell you.

Sigh deeply, sincerely. You expected something about your centurial great-grandmother going in her whiskey-induced sleep. You expected your father having to cut back to one pound of beef a day because of his tired heart.

Ask, Mom, you okay? Assume her silence is due to more crying. Say, Mom?

She's been sick since February, she says.

Now you are silent. It is late August. You did not go back for your birthday this year—you had to find a job, and the market is grueling. Your mother had said she understood. Also, you adopted a rabbit in April (you've been a little lonely in Wisconsin), and your mother knows you don't like leaving the poor thing alone for too long. Push your at-the-ready excuses out of the way and say, Why didn't you tell me before?

She does not answer your question. Instead she says, You have to come home.

Tell her you will see when you can cancel class. There is a fall break coming up, you might be able to find a rabbit-sitter and get away for a week.

No, I'm sorry I didn't tell you before. I didn't want you to worry. You couldn't do anything from up there.

Wait until she stops crying into the phone. You feel terrible—your poor cousin. She needs to get out and see the world; she has never been farther north than Orlando. When she was a teenager, she'd bragged to you that one day, she'd move to New York City and never come back. You think (but know better than to say), Maybe this is a blessing in disguise. When you see her, you will ignore the staples keeping her scalp closed over her skull. You will pretend to recognize your cousin through the disease and the bloated, hospital gown–clad monster it's created. You will call her *Barbarino* like you used to, and make jokes when no one else can. Just before you leave—visiting hours end, and you are just a visitor—you'll lean in close to her face, so close your nose brushes the tiny hairs still clinging to her sideburns, and say, Tomorrow. Tomorrow I'm busting you out of here.

Your mother says, She died this morning. She went fast. The service is the day after tomorrow. Everyone else will be there, please come.

You are beyond outrage—you feel your neck burning hot. You skip right past your dead cousin and think, *I cannot believe these people. They have robbed me of my final hours with my cousin. They have robbed Barbarita of her escape.*

You will think about your reaction later, on the plane, when you try but fail to rewrite a list about the windows of your parents' house in the margins of an in-flight magazine. But right now, you are still angry at being left out. Promise your mother you'll be back in Hialeah in time and say nothing else. Hang up, and book an eight-hundred-dollar-flight home after e-mailing your students that class is canceled until further notice.

Brush your teeth, put on flannel pajamas (even after all these winters, you are still always cold), tuck yourself in to bed. Try to make yourself cry. Pull out the ladybug-adorned to-do list pad from the milk crate you still use as a nightstand and write down everything you know about your now-dead cousin.

Here's what you remember: Barbarita loved papaya and making jokes about papaya. One time, before she even knew what it meant, she called her sister a *papayona* in front of everyone at a family pig roast. Her mother slapped her hard enough to lay her out on the cement patio. She did not cry, but she stormed inside to her room and did not come out until she'd said the word *papayona* out loud and into her pillow two hundred times. Then she said it another hundred times in her head. She'd told you this story when your parents dragged you to visit Barbarita's mom and her newly busted hip while you were home during one of your college breaks. Barbarita's mother, from underneath several white blankets, said, I never understood why you even like that fruit. It tastes like a fart.

Barbarita moved back in with her parents for good after her mom fractured her hip. The family scandal became Barbarita's special lady-friend, with whom she'd been living the previous eight years. You remember the lady-friend's glittered fanny pack—it always seemed full of breath mints and rubber bands—how you'd guessed it did not come off even for a shower. Barbarita took you to Marlins games and let you drink stadium beer from the plastic bottle if you gave her the change in your pockets. She kept coins in a jar on her nightstand and called it her retirement fund. She made fun of you for opening a savings account when you turned sixteen and said you'd be better off stuffing the cash in a can and burying it in the backyard. She laughed and slapped her knee and said, No lie, I probably have ninety thousand dollars under my mom's papaya tree.

Look at your list. It is too short. Whose fault is that? You want to say God's; you want to say your parents'. You want to blame the ladybug imprinted on the paper. You are jealous of how she adorns yet can ignore everything you've put down. Write, *My cousin is dead and I'm blaming a ladybug.* Cross out *my cousin* and write *Barbarita.* Throw the pad back in the crate before you write, *Am I really this selfish?*

Decide not to sleep. The airport shuttle is picking you up at 4:00 a.m. anyway, and it's already 1:00. Get out of bed, set up the automatic food dispenser in your rabbit's cage, then flat-iron your hair so that it looks nice for the funeral. Your father has cursed your frizzy head and blamed the bad genes on your mother's side since you sprouted the first tuft. Wrap the crispy ends of your hair around Velcro rollers and microwave some water in that I-don't-do-Mondays mug that you never use (the one you stole off the grad program coordinator's desk right before shoving your keys in the drop box—you couldn't help stealing it: you're a spic). Stir in the Café Bustelo instant coffee your mother sent you a few weeks ago in a box that also contained credit card offers you'd been mailed at their address and three packs of Juicy Fruit. The spoon clinks against the mug, and it sounds to you like the slightest, most insignificant noise in the world.

Sit at the window seat that convinced you to sign the lease to this place even though your closest neighbor is a six-minute drive away. Listen to the gutters around the window flood with rain. Remember the canal across from your parents' house, how the rain threatened to flood it twice a week. There is a statue of San Lázaro in their front yard and a mango tree in the back. Lázaro is wedged underneath an old bathtub your dad half buried vertically in the dirt, to protect the saint from rain. The mango tree takes care of itself. But your father made sure both the mango tree and San Lázaro were well guarded behind a five-foot-high chain-link fence. The house's windows had bars—*rejas*—on them to protect the rest of his valuables, the ones living inside. You never noticed the *rejas* (every house around for blocks had them) until you left and came back. The last night of your first winter break in Hialeah, just before you went to sleep, you wasted four pages—front and back—in a notebook scribbling all the ways the *rejas* were a metaphor for your childhood: *a caged bird, wings clipped, never to fly free; a zoo animal on display yet up for sale to the highest-bidding boyfriend; a rare painting trapped each night after the museum closes.* Roll your eyes—these are the ones you remember now. You didn't mean it, not even as you wrote them, but you wanted to mean it, because that made your leaving an escape and not a desertion. Strain to conjure up more of them—it's got to be easier than reconciling the pilfered mug with your meager list about your cousin. But you can't come up with anything else. All you remember is your father weeding the grass around the saint every other Saturday, even in a downpour.

Peek through the blinds and think, *It will never stop raining.* Pack light—you still have clothes that fit you in your Hialeah closet. Open the blinds all the way and watch the steam from your cup play against the reflected darkness, the flashes of rain. Watch lightening careen into the flat land surrounding your tiny house, your empty, saintless yard. Wait for the thunder. You know, from growing up where it rained every afternoon from three to five, that thunder's timing tells you how far you are from the storm. You cannot remember which cousin taught you this—only that it wasn't Barbarita. When it booms just a second later, know the lightning is too close. Lean your forehead against the windowpane and feel the glass rattle, feel the vibration pass into your skull, into your teeth. Keep your head down; see the dozens of tiny flies, capsized and drained, dead on the sill. Only the shells of their bodies are left, along with hundreds of broken legs that still manage to point at you. If you squint hard enough, the flies blend right into the dust padding their mass grave. And when your eyes water, even these dusty pillows blur into an easy, anonymous gray smear.

Your hands feel too heavy to open the window, then the storm glass, then the screen, to sweep their corpses away. You say out loud to no one, I'll do it when I get back. But your words—your breath—rustle the burial ground, sending tiny swirls of dust toward your face. It tastes like chalk and dirt. Feel it scratch the roof of your mouth, but don't cough—you don't need to. Clear your throat if you want; it won't make the taste go away any faster.

Don't guess how long it will take for the clouds to clear up; you're always wrong about weather. The lightning comes so close to your house you're sure this time you'll at least lose power. Close your eyes, cross your fingers behind your back. Swallow hard. The windowsill's grit scrapes every cell in your throat on its way down. Let this itch convince you that the lightning won't hit—it can't, not this time—because for now, you're keeping your promise. On the flight, distract yourself with window lists and *SkyMall* magazine all you want; no matter what you try, the plane will land. Despite the traffic you find worse than you remember, you'll get to Hialeah in time for the burial—finally back, ready to mourn everything.

HOW TO LEAVE "HOW TO LEAVE HIALEAH": A REAL-LIFE EPILOGUE

For a long time, whenever I gave readings, I would immediately eliminate this story—or any part of this story—as a possibility. *It just feels too close*, I told myself. *I don't want people thinking this is me.* I reminded myself, of course, that this was fiction; I'd made this story up, and only the feelings inside it were true. Still, my initial resistance to reading it in public indicated something about what the story had become; yes, this was fiction, but it *felt* so true—the feelings and reactions of the narrator had been, at one point, my feelings—that reading it out loud made me feel exposed.

Despite my efforts to avoid this story, after the book came out, and when I gave readings, something odd kept happening: I would read from some other story, and when the time came for questions, there would always be a woman in the audience—sometimes she was Latina, sometimes she was from Miami, but all of them, I'd soon find out, were some of the first people in their families to go to college—and she would always ask the same question: Is the book's last story about *you*?

While I was thrilled that someone—someone I wasn't even related to!—had bought my book and read it and had come out for a reading, I was scared of this question, of the reasons why the women asked it. *She knows*, I thought. *She knows because it's her in this story, too.* I could talk all I wanted about fiction and emotional truth versus factual truth, but these women saw themselves in the story, could recognize the slight differences between it and whatever they'd gone through. And that meant it *had* to be me—how else could I have written about it?

In one of the greatest compliments I've ever received, a professor who once introduced me at a reading—a fellow Latina in the humanities—said in her opening remarks that when she read that last story, she felt she was reading her own history. She said it felt like I'd read her journals, even read her mind. She said the story made her feel exposed. That's when I realized what I really did when I wrote this story. We've all felt so alone and guilty—about the choices (good ones, right?) that we've made and the consequences (good and bad, right?) we were now living out—that we were desperately searching for each other without even knowing it, and this story was, for many of these women, equivalent to me throwing open my arms for a hug and yelling, *I know! Come here, I know!*

This story came from a place of loneliness and anger and confusion, a place in which a lot of us have had to live because we decided, of all things, to go to college. And this story tells us we aren't alone, and we will be okay—we are strong enough to take this hit for our daughters' sakes, strong enough to have said to the families that made us, *We gotta go. There's some things we want to do.* We can tell them, our voices stronger thanks to the growing chorus of women who see through the fiction and find themselves in it.

Only Daughter

SANDRA CISNEROS

Once, several years ago, when I was just starting out my writing career, I was asked to write my own contributor's note for a literary anthology. I wrote: "I am the only daughter in a family of six sons. *That* explains everything."

Well, I've thought about that ever since, and yes, it explains a lot to me, but for the reader's sake I should have written: "I am the only daughter in a Mexican family of six sons." Or even: "I am the only daughter of a Mexican father and a Mexican American mother." Or: "I am the only daughter of a working-class family of nine." All of these had everything to do with who I am today.

I was/am the only daughter and *only* a daughter. Being an only daughter in a family of six sons forced me by circumstance to spend a lot of time by myself because my brothers felt it beneath them to play with a *girl* in public. But that aloneness, that loneliness, was good for a would-be writer—it allowed me time to think and think, to imagine, to read and prepare myself for my writer's profession.

Being only a daughter for my father meant my destiny would lead me to become someone's wife. That's what he believed. But when I was in the fifth grade and shared my plans for college with him, I was sure he understood. I remember my father saying, "*Qué bueno, mi'ja*"—that's good. That meant a lot to me, especially since my brothers thought the idea hilarious. What I didn't realize was that my father thought college was good for girls—good for finding a husband. After four years of college and two more in graduate school, and still no husband, my father shakes his head even now and says I wasted all that education.

In retrospect, I'm lucky my father believed daughters were meant for husbands. It meant it didn't matter if I majored in something silly like English. After all, I'd find a nice professional eventually, right? This allowed me the liberty to putter about embroidering my little poems and stories without my father interrupting with so much as a "What's that you're writing?"

But the truth is I *wanted* him to interrupt. I wanted my father to understand what it was I was scribbling, to introduce me as "My only daughter, the writer." Not as "This is my only daughter. She teaches." "*Es maestra*" were his exact words. Not even "*profesora.*"

In a sense, everything I have ever written has been for him, to win his approval even though I know my father can't read English words, even though my father's only reading includes the brown-ink *Esto* sports magazines from Mexico City and the bloody *¡Alarma!* magazines that feature yet another sighting of La Virgen de Guadalupe on a tortilla, or a wife's revenge on her philandering husband by bashing his skull in with a *molcajete* (a kitchen mortar made of volcanic rock). Or the *fotonovelas*, the little picture paperbacks with tragedy and trauma erupting from the characters' mouths in bubbles.

My father represents, then, the public majority. A public who is disinterested in reading, and yet one whom I am writing about and for, and privately trying to woo.

When we were growing up in Chicago, we moved a lot because of my father. He suffered bouts of nostalgia. Then we'd have to let go our flat, store the furniture with mother's relatives, load the station wagon with baggage and bologna sandwiches, and head south. To Mexico City.

We came back, of course. To yet another Chicago flat, another Chicago neighborhood, another Catholic school. Each time, my father would seek out the parish priest in order to get a tuition break, and complain or boast, "I have seven sons." He meant *siete hijos*, seven children, but he translated it as "sons." "I have seven sons," he would say to anyone who would listen. The Sears Roebuck employee who sold us the washing machine. The short-order cook where my father ate his ham-and-eggs breakfasts. "I have seven sons." As if he deserved a medal from the state.

My papa. He didn't mean anything by that mistranslation, I'm sure.

But somehow I could feel myself being erased. I'd tug my father's sleeve and whisper, "Not seven sons. Six! And one daughter."

When my oldest brother graduated from medical school, he fulfilled my father's dream that we study hard and use this, our head, instead of these, our hands. Even now my father's hands are thick and yellow, stubbed by a history of hammer and nails and twine and coils and springs. "Use this," my father said, tapping his head, "and not this," showing us those hands. He always looked tired when he said it.

Wasn't college an investment? And hadn't I spent all those years in college? And if I didn't marry, what was it all for? Why would anyone go to college and then choose to be poor?

Last year, after ten years of writing professionally, the financial rewards started to trickle in—my second National Endowment for the Arts fellowship, a guest professorship at the University of California, Berkeley, my book sold to a major New York publishing house.

At Christmas, I flew home to Chicago. The house was throbbing, same as always; hot tamales and sweet tamales hissing in my mother's pressure cooker, and everybody—my mother, six brothers, wives, babies, aunts, cousins—talking too loud and at the same time, like in a Fellini film, because that's just how we are.

I went upstairs to my father's room. One of my stories had just been translated and published in Spanish, and I wanted to show it to him. Ever since he recovered from a stroke two years ago, my father likes to spend his leisure hours horizontally. And that's how I found him, watching a Pedro Infante movie on Galavisión and eating rice pudding.

There was a glass filmed with milk on the bedside table. There were several vials of pills and balled Kleenex. And on the floor, one black sock and a plastic urinal that I didn't want to look at, but looked at anyway. Pedro Infante was about to burst into song, and my father was laughing.

I'm not sure if it was because my story was translated into Spanish, or because it was published in Mexico, or perhaps because the story dealt with Tepeyac, the *colonia* my father was raised in and the house he grew up in, but at any rate, my father punched the mute button on his remote control and read my story.

I sat on the bed next to my father and waited. He read it very slowly. As if he were reading each line over and over. He laughed at all the right places and read lines he liked out loud.

He pointed and asked questions, "Is this so-and-so?"

"Yes," I said. He kept reading.

When he was finally finished, after what seemed like hours, my father looked up and asked, "Where can we get more copies of this for the relatives?"

Of all of the wonderful things that happened to me last year, that was the most wonderful.

Contributors

CHANTEL ACEVEDO's first novel, *Love and Ghost Letters*, won the Latino International Book Award and was a finalist for the Connecticut Book of the Year. *Song of the Red Cloak*, a historical novel for young adults, was published in 2011. Her most recent novel, *A Falling Star*, won the Doris Bakwin Prize in 2013 and is forthcoming from Carolina Wren Press. Her fiction and poetry have appeared or are forthcoming in *Prairie Schooner, American Poetry Review, North American Review*, and *Chattahoochee Review*, among others. She was named a Literature Fellow by the Alabama State Council on the Arts in 2013. She is currently an associate professor of English and Alumni Writer-in-Residence at Auburn University, where she founded the Auburn Writers Conference and edits the *Southern Humanities Review*.

LI YUN ALVARADO is a Puerto Rican poet, writer, and educator. Her work has appeared in several journals, including *Cura: A Literary Magazine of Art and Action, Acentos Review, PALABRA: A Magazine of Chicano and Latino Literary Art*, and PMS *poemmemoirstory*. In 2012 her poetry manuscript was selected as an honorable mention for the Andrés Montoya Poetry Prize. She is currently a doctoral candidate in English at Fordham University and holds a bachelor's degree from Yale University, where she double-majored in Spanish and sociology. She is also a fellow of the American Association of University Women and proudly serves as a member of the board of the American Civil Liberties Union. She has had the pleasure of teaching literature, composition, and creative writing in English and in Spanish to middle school, high school, and college students in New Haven, Boston, New York City, and the Dominican Republic. She is a native New Yorker living in Long Beach, California, with her husband, Michael A. Core. They both take frequent trips to Salinas, Puerto Rico, to visit *la familia*. Visit her website at www.liyunalvarado.com.

JULIA ALVAREZ has bridged the Americas many times. Born in New York and raised in the Dominican Republic, she is a poet, fiction writer, and essayist, author of world-renowned books in each of the genres, including *How the García Girls Lost Their Accents*, *In the Time of the Butterflies*, *Something to Declare*, and most recently *A Wedding in Haiti: The Story of a Friendship*. With her husband, Bill Eichner, she founded Alta Gracia, a sustainable coffee farm and literacy center in the Dominican Republic. She is currently a writer in residence at Middlebury College, Vermont. Visit her website to find out more about her writing: www .juliaalvarez.com.

RUTH BEHAR was born in Havana, Cuba, and grew up in New York. She is the author of acclaimed books that bridge memoir and ethnography, including *Translated Woman: Crossing the Border with Esperanza's Story*, *The Vulnerable Observer: Anthropology That Breaks Your Heart*, *An Island Called Home: Returning to Jewish Cuba*, and *Traveling Heavy: A Memoir In Between Journeys*. She is also the editor of *Bridges to Cuba* and coeditor of *Women Writing Culture* and *The Portable Island: Cubans at Home in the World*. She teaches at the University of Michigan, where she is the Victor Haim Perera Collegiate Professor of Anthropology. She is the recipient of many awards, including a MacArthur "Genius" Fellowship.

NORMA ELIA CANTÚ, a daughter of the U.S.-Mexico borderlands, received her degrees against all odds. The oldest of eleven children born to a working-class typical border family, she grew up and attended public schools in Laredo, Texas. The border is at the center of her work as a folklorist, a professor, a writer, and a poet. She has coedited a number of books, including *Chicana Traditions: Continuity and Change* and *Telling to Live: Latina Feminist Testimonios*, and most recently edited books on Chicana/o art: *Moctezuma's Table: Rolando Briseño's Chicano and Mexicano Tablescapes* and *Ofrenda: Liliana Wilson's Art of Dissidence and Dreams*. Her award-winning novel *Canícula: Snapshots of a Girlhood en la Frontera* received the Premio Aztlán; she edits the book series Rio Grande/Rio Bravo for Texas A&M University Press. She is professor emerita at the University of Texas at San Antonio and teaches Latina/o studies at the University of Missouri in Kansas City.

JOY CASTRO is the author of the memoir *The Truth Book* and a collection of essays, *Island of Bones*, which won a 2013 International Latino Book Award in Nonfiction. She is the editor of *Family Trouble: Memoirists on the Hazards and Rewards of Revealing Family*, and her work has appeared in *Fourth Genre, North American Review, New York Times Magazine*, and other journals. She is the author of two literary thrillers, *Hell or High Water* and *Nearer Home*, both from St. Martin's. Named a 2009 Best New Latino Author, she is an associate professor at the University of Nebraska–Lincoln, where she teaches creative writing, literature, and Latino studies.

SANDRA CISNEROS is the founder of the Alfredo Cisneros del Moral Foundation, the Elvira Cisneros Award, and the Macondo Foundation, all of which work on behalf of creative writers. She is the recipient of numerous awards, including a MacArthur. Her writings include novels: *The House on Mango Street* and *Caramelo*; short stories: *Woman Hollering Creek*; poetry collections: *My Wicked Wicked Ways* and *Loose Woman*; and a children's book: *Hairs*. She is currently at work on several writing projects, including *Borrowed Houses*, a book of essays; *Writing in My Pajamas*, writing tips; *How to Be a Chingona*, life tips; *Infinito*, stories; and *Cantos y Llantos*, poems. Her most recent books are a children's book, *Bravo, Bruno*, with artist Leslie Greene, published in Italy, and *Have You Seen Marie?*, an illustrated book for adults with artist Ester Hernández, published in the United States in October 2012.

INGRID ROJAS CONTRERAS is a Colombian writer living and working in San Francisco. Her work is forthcoming or has been published in *CultureStrike, American Odysseys: Writings for New Americans, F Magazine*, and *Make: A Chicago Literary Magazine*, among others. Her forthcoming novel, *Niebla*, was a semifinalist in the Amazon/Penguin Breakthrough Novel Award. She writes book reviews for KQED. Currently, she is working on a nonfiction novel about her grandfather, a medicine man who could move clouds. She is the recipient of awards and residencies from NALAC, Djerassi Residents Artists Program, the Macondo Foundation, and the Bread Loaf Writers' Conference.

JENNINE CAPÓ CRUCET is the author of *How to Leave Hialeah*, which won the Iowa Short Fiction Award; she is the first Latina to win this prize in its forty-year history. The book also received the John Gardner Book Prize and the Devil's Kitchen Reading Award in Prose and was a finalist for the Chicano/Latino Literary Award, and it went on to be named a best book of the year by the *Miami Herald*, the *New Times*, and the Latinidad List. A winner of an O. Henry Prize and a Bread Loaf Fellow, she served as the fiction editor for the most recent edition of the PEN Center USA's *Handbook for Writers*, which is used in their Emerging Voices and Writers in the Schools programs. Her work has appeared in the *Virginia Quarterly Review, Guernica, Ploughshares, Epoch, Southern Review, Gulf Coast,* and other magazines. Born in Miami to Cuban parents, she worked for several years as a counselor to first-generation college students from South Central and Downtown LA before joining the creative writing faculty at Florida State University, where she teaches fiction and Latino literature.

JENNIFER DE LEON is the winner of the Fourth Genre Michael Steinberg Essay Prize. Her stories and essays have appeared in *Ploughshares, Brevity, Ms., Briar Cliff Review, Poets & Writers, Guernica, Best Women's Travel Writing,* and elsewhere. She has published author interviews in *Granta* and *Agni,* and she has been awarded scholarships and residencies from the Bread Loaf Writers' Conference, Hedgebrook, Virginia Center for the Creative Arts, Vermont Studio Center, and the Macondo Writers' Workshop. She was born in Boston to Guatemalan parents. After graduating from Connecticut College, she moved to San Jose, California, where she taught elementary school as part of the Teach for America program and earned a master's in teaching from the University of San Francisco's Center for Teaching Excellence and Social Justice. After moving back to Boston, she designed college access programs and mentored first-generation college students and then earned an MFA in fiction from the University of Massachusetts–Boston. Currently she teaches at Grub Street, at UMASS Boston, and for Boston Public Schools. She is working on a memoir and a novel.

GAIL M. DOTTIN is a decent Scrabble player and a New Yorker who was a Dean's Nonfiction Fellow at Columbia University, where she earned her MFA in creative nonfiction in 2002. As a 2008–9 Fulbright scholar in Panama, she was the first to receive the grant for creative writing in that country in the previous forty-five years. While there she met many cousins she didn't know she had and learned lots of Spanish that wasn't in any textbook while researching her first book, currently nearing completion. *Where There Is Pride in Belonging* is a memoir and collection of family stories woven around her discovery of facets of her family's Panamanian lives: her grandfather's work on the construction of the Panama Canal in the early 1900s, her father's childhood on the Canal Zone in the 1930s and his migration to New York during the time of the civil rights movement, and her great-uncle, the true "Tailor of Panama," the country's oldest tailor at age ninety-four. You can see photos of her family and Fulbright life in Panama, as well as read pieces about her experience there, on her website: https://sites.google.com/site/gaildottin/. Her work has been published in *Quarto*, TESOL *Panama*, and the anthology *Lesbian Friendships: For Ourselves and Each Other*, edited by Jacqueline S. Weinstock and Esther D. Rothblum. Her piece "Apology Accepted" was recently published in *Dismantle*, an anthology of work by the writers of color from the Voices of Our Nations (VONA) writing workshop.

YALITZA FERRERAS was born in Brooklyn, New York, and raised in New York and the Dominican Republic. She has spent the last twelve years working as a graphic designer in New York and San Francisco. She recently completed her MFA in the creative writing program at the University of Michigan, Ann Arbor, and is currently working on her first novel and a collection of short stories.

IRIS GOMEZ is an award-winning writer and nationally respected immigration rights attorney and law school lecturer. She is the author of *Try to Remember* (Grand Central, 2010), which garnered praise from prominent national magazines such as *O, The Oprah Magazine* and *Latina*, among others, and was listed by the Association of American Publishers among its Recommended Latino Books of 2010, in addition to appearing on the *Boston Globe* bestseller list and winning a 2011

International Latino Book Award in the popular fiction category. She is also the author of two books of poetry, *Housicwhissick Blue* (Edwin Mellen Press, 2003) and *When Comets Rained* (CustomWords, 2004), and her work has been published in dozens of literary magazines as well as professional and mainstream periodicals. She won the 2001 Chicano/Latino Literary Prize, second prize in poetry, from the University of California at Irvine and received the Las Primeras Award for Latina trailblazers from the Massachusetts Association of Hispanic Attorneys, among other awards. Born in Cartagena, Colombia, she now lives in Massachusetts.

STEPHANIE ELIZONDO GRIEST has mingled with the Russian Mafia, polished Chinese propaganda, and danced with Cuban rumba queens. These adventures inspired her award-winning memoirs *Around the Bloc: My Life in Moscow, Beijing, and Havana; Mexican Enough: My Life between the Borderlines;* and the best-selling guidebook *100 Places Every Woman Should Go.* She has also written for the *New York Times, Washington Post, Texas Monthly,* and the *Believer,* and edited *Best Women's Travel Writing 2010.* As a national correspondent for the *Odyssey,* she once drove forty-five thousand miles across America in a Honda hatchback named Bertha. She has been a Henry Luce Scholar in Asia, a Hodder Fellow at Princeton University, and the winner of a Richard Margolis Award for Social Justice Reporting, and she currently teaches creative nonfiction at UC–Chapel Hill. Visit her website at www.mexicanenough.com.

DAISY HERNÁNDEZ is the coeditor of *Colonize This! Young Women on Today's Feminism* (Seal Press), and her memoir is forthcoming with Beacon Press. Her essays have appeared in *Fourth Genre, Bellingham Review,* and *Hunger Mountain,* and her commentaries have been featured on NPR's *All Things Considered.* She is the former editor of *ColorLines,* a newsmagazine on race and politics. To read more of her writing, go to www.daisyhernandez.com.

LORRAINE M. LÓPEZ is an associate professor of English teaching in the MFA program in creative writing at Vanderbilt University. An associate editor for the *Afro-Hispanic Review,* she is the author of five books of fiction and editor or coeditor of two essay collections. Her short story collection *Soy la Avon Lady and Other Stories* (Curbstone Press, 2002) won the inaugural Miguel Marmól Prize for Fiction. Her second book, *Call Me Henri*, was awarded the Paterson Prize for Young Adult Literature in 2007, and her novel *The Gifted Gabaldón Sisters* was a Borders/Las Comadres Selection for the month of November in 2008. Her short story collection *Homicide Survivors Picnic and Other Stories* was a finalist for the PEN/Faulkner Prize in Fiction in 2010 and winner of the Texas League of Writers Award for Outstanding Book of Fiction. She has also edited a collection of essays titled *An Angle of Vision: Women Writers on Their Poor or Working-Class Roots* (University of Michigan Press, 2009). Her recent publications include a novel, *The Realm of Hungry Spirits* (Grand Central Press, 2011), and a collection of essays, *The Other Latin@: Writing against a Singular Identity* (University of Arizona Press, 2011), coedited with Blas Falconer. She has also coedited, with Margaret Crumpton Winter, a collection of critical essays titled *Rituals of Movement in the Writing of Judith Ortiz Cofer* (Caribbean Studies Press, 2012).

ERIKA MARTÍNEZ, recipient of a Fulbright Fellowship to the Dominican Republic (2008) and a Hedgebrook Writing Residency (2008), holds an MFA in English and creative writing from Mills College in Oakland, California. As a founding member of Teatro Luna, Chicago's all-Latina theater ensemble, her work was adapted for the stage and presented at INTAR and PSNBC's Here Theater in New York City. Her writing has been featured in *ColorLines*, *Womanist*, the Seal Press anthology *Homelands: Women's Journeys through Race, Place and Time*, and *Revista Ping Pong*. In addition she participated in the *Terror?* exhibit at the Intersection for the Arts in San Francisco with a poem selected to promote the event on KPFA's Full Circle. Today she works as a full-time author and editor, dividing her days between her childhood memoir titled *One Day My Hands Will Touch the Ceiling* and *Daring to Write: Contemporary Narratives by Dominican Women*.

CELESTE GUZMAN MENDOZA is a published poet. Her work has appeared in *5 a.m.*, *Poet Lore*, *Borderlands*, and *Salamander*, and has been anthologized in *¡Floricanto Sí: A Collection of Latina Poetry* (Penguin). Her chapbook, *Cande, te estoy llamando*, won the Poesia Tejana Prize from Wings Press. She is a longtime member of the Macondo Writers'

Workshop and a founding member and codirector of CantoMundo, a workshop for Latina/o poets. Her first full-length collection of poetry, *Beneath the Halo*, was published in 2013 by Wings Press. She is working on her second collection, *Coming in Waves*. She also is a professional actor and singer. She resides in Austin, Texas, with her husband and three cats, and works at the Teresa Lozano Long Institute of Latin American Studies at the University of Texas at Austin.

CECILIA RODRÍGUEZ MILANÉS is an associate professor of English at the University of Central Florida, where she teaches Latino/a literature, women's studies, and writing. She has published essays on teaching, race, class, and feminism in various collections and is the author of a book of short fiction, *Marielitos, Balseros and Other Exiles* (2009), and *Everyday Chica* (2010), a chapbook of poems. Her story "Muchacha" was included in *The Norton Anthology of Latino Literature* (2010).

TONI MARGARITA PLUMMER grew up in South El Monte, California, a working-class suburb of Los Angeles. She graduated from the University of Notre Dame with a BA in philosophy and went on to earn a master's in professional writing from the University of Southern California. Her short story collection, *The Bolero of Andi Rowe*, won the Miguel Mármol Prize and was a Mariposa Award finalist. She is a member of the Macondo Foundation and a board member of *Kweli Journal*, and she has served on the board of the Hispanic Alumni of Notre Dame. She is an editor at Thomas Dunne Books/St. Martin's Press in New York City.

BEATRIZ TERRAZAS is a writer, photographer, and visual storyteller whose credits include *More, Skirt!, Cure*, the *Washington Post*, the *Dallas Morning News*, and the anthology *Literary El Paso*. Her work has won first place from the American Society of Sunday and Feature Editors, the Society of American Travel Writers Lowell Thomas Awards, the National Association of Hispanic Journalists, and others. She was part of a *Dallas Morning News* team to win the Pulitzer Prize in 1994. She is a reader for *Carve* magazine and a coach and consultant with its literary services. She is a Harvard University Nieman Fellow, class of 1999, and a member of the Macondo Writing Workshop.

BLANCA TORRES is Mexicana from Washington State. She grew up on the dry, eastern side of the state in Pasco, one of three Tri-Cities. She left home to attend Vanderbilt University, where she earned a BA in English and Latin American studies. She has worked as a reporter for several newspapers throughout the country, including the *Tri-City Herald, Detroit News, Kansas City Star, Contra Costa Times, Fort Worth Star-Telegram, Seattle Times, Baltimore Sun,* and *San Francisco Business Times,* where she writes about commercial real estate and development. She earned an MFA in fiction from Mills College in Oakland and was the 2009 winner of the Marion Hood Boess Haworth Prize for Fiction for Children & Young Adults. She participated in a writing residency with Ana Castillo as part of the Voices of Our Nations conference. She is a founding member of the Sunday Stories Writers Group, which brings Bay Area writers together and organizes literary readings such as Brown People Don't Read, a yearly event for San Francisco LitCrawl. She lives in San Francisco, where she is working on a collection of short stories and a memoir about her mother's childhood in Mexico.